THINKING
AGAINST
THE GRAIN

"America's circus of worldviews presents a monumental challenge to Christian integrity. Most Christians are watching this circus of ideas as uninformed spectators, and this spells disaster for the church. This generation must develop biblical discernment and authentic Christian thinking—and fast. Allan Moseley is a gifted Christian teacher, pastor, and thinker. He has given us a faithful guide in developing a Christian worldview in *Thinking Against the Grain*. Read this book, and think like a Christian."

—R. Albert Mohler, Jr., President
The Southern Baptist Theological Seminary

"Thinking against the grain is like swimming against the stream: it requires motivation, intentionality, and a moral compass guided by a transcendent source of truth. Allan Moseley is a pastor-theologian with firsthand knowledge of the things he writes about, and he has given us a compelling account of what it means to be a faithful follower of Jesus Christ in a culture of disarray. Highly recommended!"

—Timothy George, Dean
Beeson Divinity School of Samford University

"The title is right on! Christians who think biblically think against the grain of the modern American mind. 'You have heard it said by modern culture . . . But the Bible says . . .' is Moseley's major motif. In this book you will not only learn the Christian worldview but see it stand out from its many current alternatives such as secularism, naturalism, relativism, hedonism, and postmodernism. But the book is more than theoretical. It works out in detail the Christian worldview's major implications for action. An excellent book for intense study by individuals and groups who want to love God with all the strength of their minds."

—James W. Sire
Author of *The Universe Next Door* and
Naming the Elephant: Worldview as a Concept

"Dr. Moseley has touched the pulse of the crisis facing Christians in contemporary culture. The singularity of the Gospel in a pluralistic society stands against the stream of tolerance that believers encounter. The issues addressed in this insightful book provide practical biblical answers for the church. I highly recommend *Thinking Against the Grain* as a reference for the believer seeking a solid foundation of faith."

—Dr. Tommy Green
Senior Pastor of First Baptist Church, Brandon, Florida
President of the Florida Baptist Convention

THINKING AGAINST THE GRAIN

Developing a
Biblical Worldview in a
Culture of Myths

N. Allan Moseley

Kregel
Publications

Thinking Against the Grain: Developing a Biblical Worldview in a Culture of Myths

© 2003 by N. Allan Moseley

Published by Kregel Publications, a division of Kregel, Inc., P.O. Box 2607, Grand Rapids, MI 49501.

Index by Melody Englund, Songbird Indexing Services

Library of Congress Cataloging-in-Publication Data
Moseley, N. Allan.
Thinking against the grain: developing a biblical worldview in a culture of myths / by N. Allan Moseley.
    p. cm.
Includes bibliographical references and index.
    1. Christian life—Biblical teaching. I. Title.
BS680.C47M67   2003
261'.0973—dc21   2003012166

ISBN 0-8254-3343-6

Printed in the United States of America

03 04 05 06 07 / 5 4 3 2 1

For Sharon,
you bring
אוֹרָה וְשִׂמְחָה וְשָׂשֹׂן וִיקָר
("light and gladness and joy and honor")
—Esther 8:16

Contents

Preface

As I was finishing this book, the words from Miguel de Cervantes's prologue to *Don Quixote* came to mind:

> Idling reader, you may believe me when I tell you that I should have liked this book, which is the child of my brain, to be the fairest, the sprightliest, and the cleverest that could be imagined; but I have not been able to contravene the law of nature which would have it that like begets like.

Indeed, this book suffers from the same limitation as *Don Quixote*—it is the child of my brain. It is also afflicted with the handicap that its author is no Cervantes.

As I lamented the infirmities of this book, it occurred to me that Don Quixote's mission may be an apt analogy for what I have written. Intrepid but demented knight that he was, Don Quixote went out to slay mythical enemies that existed only in the books in his library. I am on an errand to slay cultural myths that inhabit the books of this modern/postmodern age. The analogy breaks down, however. The people of Don Quixote's culture saw things as they really are. Only Don Quixote lived a fantasy. In our day, those armed with a biblical worldview see things as they really are. The ideas that contradict the Christian worldview are mythical, and those who live by those myths waste their lives tilting at windmills.

The concept of *fighting* is also analogous to the effort of developing a biblical worldview. Wrestling with the ideas in this book engages us in spiritual warfare. The spiritual battle waged against "the spiritual forces of wickedness" (Eph. 6:12) is actually a war of ideas. This is precisely how the apostle Paul portrays the reality of spiritual warfare. "We are destroying speculations and every lofty thing raised up against the knowledge of God, and we are taking every thought captive to the obedience of Christ" (2 Cor. 10:5).

"Speculations . . . every thought." Here is the arena of spiritual warfare. No small number of teachers in the modern church speak of spiritual warfare as if it consisted of chasing and reciting formulaic chants over ubiquitous demons. To the contrary, spiritual warfare is training ourselves to think God's thoughts, destroying the unholy trinity of the world, the flesh, and the Devil that would cause us to think thoughts other than God's. And we know that we are victorious when "we have the mind of Christ" (1 Cor. 2:16). The central difference between living for God and living for the world, the flesh, and the Devil is that those who live for God think biblically and act accordingly.

Since I often use such words as *worldview, philosophy,* and *mindset,* some may conclude that I'm merely proposing an intellectual exercise—academic theory divorced from practical reality. Nothing could be further from the truth. The emphasis on contemporary ethical issues in this volume dispels the notion that the work of framing a biblical worldview is merely an interesting pastime for those who have the inclination and leisure to dabble in the philosophy of religion. To the contrary, the subject of these pages affects every decision every day we live. In building a Christian mind, or worldview, philosophical issues and moral issues are bound together inextricably. Who could argue that thought is unrelated to decision-making? Good thinking leads to good living, and good living is the best (or only) reliable indicator of good thinking.

I am particularly concerned about life in the church. In the young twenty-first century, will we embrace biblical truth or the enchantment of cultural myths? I make no claims for originality as I propose that we embrace truth. As I call the church to faithful thinking, I realize that my own thoughts have been shaped as the faithful church has taught me. I cite some sources that have most influenced my life, but many others who have taught me must go nameless. So I take this opportunity to thank pastors, teachers, writers, and friends who taught me how to think biblically. If I am able to help readers do the same, I will be grateful both to those who helped me, and to God.

Certain individuals deserve special thanks for their help in the preparation of this book. Cindy Stevens and John Tarwater assisted with the early stages of the manuscript. Jennifer Vest, Beth Coley, and Christina Todd gathered resources. Kay Milioni somehow was able to give helpful materials and advice as she endured a particularly difficult time in her son's illness. Jim Weaver at Kregel Publications supported this project from the beginning and provided outstanding editorial direction. I am most grateful for my family—Jonathan and Laura Leigh, David, Anna, and my wife, Sharon, to whom this volume is affectionately dedicated. They are the greatest human sources of joy in my life and the best arbiters of whether the author of this book thinks and lives as a Christian.

Introduction

We are no longer to be children, tossed here and there by waves and carried about by every wind of doctrine; . . . we are to grow up in all aspects into Him, who is the head, even Christ.

—Ephesians 4:14–15

What underlies the atheistic commitment to novel sexual and marital and political patterns is a stultification of Biblical conscience, an irreligious redefinition of the good, a profane willset. . . . The Christian world-life view and the secular world-life view engage as never before in rival conflict for the mind, the conscience, the will, the spirit, the very selfhood of contemporary man. Not since the apostolic age has the Christian vanguard faced so formidable a foe in its claims for the created rationality and morality of mankind.[1]

—Carl F. H. Henry

As my wife and I waited in the drive-through lane of a fast food restaurant, we watched a car pass that had two symbols on the bumper. One was the sign of the fish, representing Christianity. The other was a sticker promoting "gay pride." Assuming that the presence of one or the other of those symbols was not the result of vandalism, an interfaith marriage, or schizophrenia, that car bumper symbolizes the philosophical and moral chaos of our time. The owner of the car seemed to celebrate two worldviews that have always been understood to be in mutual opposition. This book is for the owner of that car.

As our pastor's wife waited with her children in a hospital lounge, her daughter began reading *Nickelodeon* magazine. Since *Nickelodeon* is aimed at a pre-adolescent target audience, this seemed a safe choice of reading material. Then her daughter showed her an article. The adult writer was recounting her experience at a nudist colony when she was eight years old. The author's portrayal of public nudity was entirely positive. She suggested that everyone should be more open to displaying their bodies, and more people ought to give public nudity a try. The article even cited the Bible in support of this philosophy, alluding to the original nudity of Adam and Eve in the Garden of Eden. Our pastor's daughter has been homeschooled to think biblically, so she was not convinced by this shameless effort to promote "the repeal of reticence" among the young.[2] This book is for the many children who read such literature without having developed a biblical worldview.

Many Christian young people have held certain beliefs as "givens"— assumptions about God, self, society, and what is right and wrong. These assumptions may be Bible-based, but they are also second-hand. They were handed down from parents or church and accepted uncritically. The theological assumptions of these young people are just that—the result of someone else's study and thought that they *assumed* to be true. However, if those beliefs have not already been challenged, they soon will be. Our culture is calling into question every absolute and replacing eternal truth with popular opinion. What's a Christian to do? Unfortunately, many compromise with the culture, buying into the myth that much of what the Bible says is a vestige of a more superstitious era. We should grow out of its teachings as we grew past belief in Santa Claus and the Tooth Fairy. Other Christians who are challenged by the culture will irrationally cling to their beliefs, although they have no idea why those beliefs are superior to the "isms" of our age. This book is written to provide a third option—the development of an intellectually coherent and biblically faithful worldview.

A friend told me that his mother describes herself as a Christian, but, he added, "it's obvious that she doesn't know what that means."

He sorrowfully described his mother as thoroughly secular. Her opinions about everything are shaped by the culture and not by the Bible. In fact, he said, "She couldn't tell you the first thing about the Christian worldview." This book is also for my friend's mother and others like her. In their senior adult years, they still do not realize how the truths of the Bible intersect with the influential ideas of our time. They do not expose themselves regularly to the ideas of the Bible, so the ideas of the culture win by default. Perhaps some of them will pick up this book and rethink the issues raised.

This book is also written with pastors and other spiritual leaders in mind, to help them articulate the relevance of Scripture to the people they serve. They will have to look elsewhere for a more extensive discussion of philosophical issues, such as modernism and postmodernism. This book is intended as an overview of contemporary ideologies and their implications, and I have attempted to compensate for its brevity on complex issues by suggesting further reading resources in the endnotes.

So, this book has several purposes, but two of these are primary. First, we would motivate and enable people to think biblically. What does it mean to think as a Christian, and how does that thought process differ from other common ways of thinking? Second, we would demonstrate the contours of a consistently biblical worldview. What are distinguishing benchmarks of a Christian worldview? What are some practical, or ethical, implications of thinking that is faithful to the Bible?

Books have been written on either of these two subjects. However, because philosophy and ethics—thinking and deciding—go together in life, it is appropriate that they are viewed together in one discussion of Christian thinking. As James W. Sire has put it, "In the Christian worldview, how we know is intimately related to how we ought to act. That is, knowledge is so tied to ethics that on the most important issues of life, knowing the good and doing the good are one and the same."[3]

My hope is that bringing philosophy and ethics together in one book will be helpful to readers.

While I try to be temperate in language, I feel passionately about the subject of this book. I serve and speak before local congregations. As I observe members and leaders of the contemporary church, I do not believe it is an exaggeration to say that the theological integrity and future direction of the church of Jesus Christ are in question. Jesus said, "I will build My church" (Matt. 16:18b), and for those who believe that promise, the future *existence* of the true church is not in question. But what will the future visible church look like? Will its theology remain consistent with historic Christian orthodoxy? Will its teachings parallel the ideas prevalent in contemporary culture?

Such questions trouble those who love the church and know the culture. Modern secularists possess the hubris necessary to believe the church should adopt their values, but those values are connected to a history of consequences. Twentieth century value systems contributed to two world wars, the Soviet gulags, the human incinerators of Auschwitz, the killing fields of Cambodia, the ethnic cleansing of Bosnia, the tribal barbarities of Rwanda, the proliferation of abortion as a method of contraception, the normalizing of same-gender sexuality, and the celebration of mass murder by jihad terrorists. We are hardly justified in trusting current moral "values." In current Western society, the concept of goodness is associated with a homemaking guru's statement, "It's a good thing," in reference to her advice on living in gracious style, even as she was implicated in an "insider-trading" stock scandal.

The idea that the church of Jesus Christ, which has always been defined by the New Testament and not by the culture, could adopt such depraved standards is almost unthinkable. Yet in many corners of the church, New Testament standards have all but disappeared. Consider, for example, the case of Bill Phipps, moderator of the United Church of Canada. Phipps said in a newspaper interview that he does not believe Jesus Christ is God, or that Christ was bodily resurrected, or that He is the only way to God. When faced with the inevitable public relations problem his remarks had stirred, Phipps apologized for any pain felt by church members, but he reiterated his unbelief. Such apostasy from "the faith which was once for all delivered to the saints" (Jude 3) is indeed tragic. It causes people to wonder how someone so devoid of Christian belief rose to a position of leadership within a significant segment of the church.

The answer to how this could happen was not long in coming. After Phipps's remarks hit the media, the seventy-member general council of lay and clergy members of the United Church of Canada met to consider their response to the uproar. Should they remove from his position of spiritual leadership one who was not "holding fast the faithful word which is in accordance with the teaching" (Titus 1:9)? Should they take steps to ensure that such a situation would never arise again? They voted unanimously to support him and said his comments fall "well within the spectrum of the United Church."[4] A denomination that could pass such a resolution has more in common with the pluralism and relativism of this age than with historic Christianity.

We will cite other examples of the unprecedented level of compromise with the world. Such capitulation to a corrupt culture indicates an organized religious structure that has little capacity to think biblically. For this reason, I believe that the greatest threat to the church's integrity is not methodological. It is not difficult to identify "new-wave" churches that have abandoned long-practiced methods of worship and instruction. Consider, for example, the "Christian raves" or dance parties of Philadelphia's "Club Worship." D. J. Frank Horvath (also known as Frankie Vibe) said, "We're ministers on turntables. I can't make you believe, but I can make you dance yourself closer to God."[5] Dancing as a spiritual discipline has doubtful claims as worship that honors and glorifies God as He is revealed in Scripture. But I do not believe that these worship ravers pose the greatest threat to the health of the church. Their idea is merely one symptom of the root problem: sloppy biblical thinking. The church will survive such experiments. However, if the church does not recover a biblical way of thinking, it will continue its drift toward assimilation with a corrupt culture. An assimilated church will become more and more difficult to differentiate from the world. A church that thinks like the world will act like the world. Worldly thinking already is rampant in the church.

So how do we develop a kind of thinking that deserves the name "Christian"? We have to spend some effort understanding that common notion of philosophy called a "worldview." We often hear of this term, but what is a worldview? In another book I have likened a worldview to a pair of sunglasses, the tint of which colors the way we look at everything.[6] Although the sunglasses analogy makes that point, perhaps eyeglasses would be a more appropriate analogy. Sunglasses soften reality for the convenience of the wearer, so they might be compared to worldviews that are not based in truth. However, the biblical worldview brings reality into perfect focus, as do prescription eyeglasses. The biblical worldview helps us to see things as they really are.

Perhaps some additional definitions will help clarify:

> [A worldview is] a more or less coherent frame of reference for all thought and action. . . . A worldview is a set of presuppositions (assumptions which may be true, partially true, or entirely false) which we hold (consciously or subconsciously, consistently or inconsistently) about the basic make-up of our world.[7]

> We all have values. We all have some viewpoint about what life is all about. We all have some perspective on the world we live in. We are not all philosophers but we all have a philosophy. Perhaps we haven't thought much about that philosophy, but one thing is certain—we live it out. . . . The theories we live are the ones we really believe.[8]

> A worldview is a set of beliefs about the most important issues in life. The philosophical systems of great thinkers such as Plato and Aristotle were worldviews. Every mature rational human being . . . has his or her own worldview just as surely as Plato did. . . . Achieving awareness of our worldview is one of the most important things we can do. . . . A worldview . . . is a conceptual scheme by which we consciously or unconsciously place or fit everything we believe and by which we interpret and judge reality.[9]

James Davison Hunter, in his provocative book *Culture Wars,* concluded that the culture conflicts in the United States are a result of the interaction of incompatible worldviews. Hunter named the two cultural polarities "orthodox" and "progressive." By "orthodox," Hunter refers primarily to Judaism, Catholicism, and Protestantism. He concludes:

> What is common to all three approaches to orthodoxy . . . is the commitment on the part of adherents to an external, definable, and transcendent authority. Within cultural progressivism, by contrast, moral authority tends to be defined by the spirit of the modern age, a spirit of rationalism and subjectivism. What all *progressivist* worldviews share in common is *the tendency to resymbolize historic faiths according to the prevailing assumptions of contemporary life.*
>
> Each side operates from within its own constellation of values, interests, and assumptions. At the center of each are two distinct conceptions of moral authority—two different ways of apprehending reality, of ordering experience, of making moral judgments.[10]

Hunter's research shows that *both* orthodox and progressive polarities now exist inside the organized church. The fact that persons or groups are in the church does not necessarily mean that they can be described as *orthodox.* Indeed, they may be *progressive,* and thus, according to Hunter's definition, have "the tendency to resymbolize historic faiths according to the prevailing assumptions of contemporary life" and "the tendency to translate the moral ideals of a religious tradition so that they conform to and legitimize the contemporary *zeitgeist*" ("spirit of the times").[11] The debacle within the United Church of Canada demonstrates that progressives may not only be *in* the visible church; they may be *leading* it.

In such a context, it is long past the time when Christians should be encouraged to think biblically. A host of Christians have avoided serious thought about the implications of their faith and the differences between biblical belief and the *zeitgeist.* Some of these Christians know what they believe, but they do not know why they believe it. Their faith comes across as hopelessly naive in public conversation. This is because they have never done the work of developing a Christian mind. This book is intended to help them in that great work.

Those who aspire to possess a Christian worldview must make a commitment . . .

1. to think in a manner that is consistent with the propositional truth of the Bible;
2. to learn *why* the truth of the Bible is both reliable and rational;
3. to understand the ways in which a biblical worldview differs from other worldviews;
4. to *live* in accord with the truth of the Bible;
5. to develop the ability to *communicate* to others coherently and compellingly the basis and implications of a biblical worldview.

I will sketch the philosophical issues involved in the worldview debate, but I am particularly interested in considering the *ethical product* of the worldview clash, the ways in which philosophy affects behavior at the individual and societal levels. As John Henry Newman put it, "Good thoughts are only good so far as they are taken as means to an exact obedience, or at least this is the chief part of their goodness."[12] This is where theory meets practice for most Christians, and I am writing for Christians and Christian students, not for academicians. I want to show Christians how differences in systems of morality arise from different worldviews. I want to demonstrate that the Christian worldview and its inherent system of morality make sense.

Carl F. H. Henry, quoted above, wrote of a "willset" as well as a mindset. The latter leads inevitably to the former. The pages that follow will show that an unprecedented level of immorality is being accepted and practiced within the church because Christians have not developed a Christian view of the moral issues of our time. They are not thinking biblically. This book is written with the prayer that *all* the church will yet practice biblical thinking and living, and will influence the culture to do the same.

Loving God with Your Mind

*And one of the scribes came and heard them arguing,
and recognizing that He had answered them well, asked
Him, "What commandment is the foremost of all?" Jesus
answered, "The foremost is, 'Hear, O Israel! The Lord
our God is one Lord; and you shall love the Lord your
God with all your heart, and with all your soul, and
with all your mind, and with all your strength.'"*
—*Mark 12:28–30*

Stephen Brown, a well-known preacher and writer, often concludes his sermons by saying, "You think about that. Amen." Evidently he believes that Christians should think as a part of worship and spirituality. I agree. Unfortunately, careful thought regarding biblical ideas and their relation to philosophical currents is rare among churchgoers.

Most Christians know that they are to *listen* to Christian teaching and preaching, and that is good. Listening exposes them to biblical truth to direct their lives. Many believers also want to *feel* something when they go to church. At the movie theater, they like to laugh and cry, and they tend to expect the same thing from their experiences at church. We *ought* to feel deeply about our faith. Most Christians also accept the fact that much of their religious experience is designed to lead them to decision. They understand that such decisions affect the way they *act*, which is an expression of our love for God with all our strength. We also comprehend that we should desire a spiritual encounter with Christ to express our love for Him with all our souls.

23

However, Christ also said that the greatest commandment involves loving God with all of our minds. *What does it mean to love God with our minds? It means to become more mentally equipped to live the Christian life, more committed to the propositional truth of the Word of God, and more dedicated to use our minds for the glory of God.* Further, it means that everything we do with our minds should in some way express our love for God. Jesus was all-inclusive when He said, "Love the Lord your God with . . . *all* your mind." Moreover, since Jesus commanded us to use all of our minds as an expression of our love for God, Christians ought to be thinking and studying people—all for the glory of God. First, we ought to know the content of the Bible and how to interpret it. Second, we ought to be fully conversant with the substance and proscriptions of historic Christian orthodoxy. In other words, we should know what we believe and why we believe it. In so doing, we will follow Augustine's sound principle of *fides quaerens intellectum*—faith seeking understanding.

A Description of the Problem

Many modern Christians thoughtlessly adopt the ideologies of the culture and relegate their faith to the realm of sentiment. This is not a new problem. In 1913, J. Gresham Machen wrote, "The chief obstacle to the Christian religion to-day lies in the sphere of the intellect. The Church is perishing to-day through the lack of thinking, not through an excess of it."[1] The "lack of thinking" about which he wrote has endured and intensified over the past ninety years. The culture of modern America exalts feeling and preference over thinking and truth more than does any other Western culture in history. Generally speaking, American Christians succumb to this cultural disposition more commonly than they obey the command of their Lord to love God with all of their minds.

Fast forward from 1913 to 1963 when Harry Blamires wrote an often-quoted book, *The Christian Mind*, in which he states,

Except over a very narrow field of thinking, chiefly touching questions of strictly personal conduct, we Christians in the modern world accept, for the purpose of mental activity, a frame of reference constructed by the secular mind and a set of criteria reflecting secular evaluations. *There is no Christian mind.* . . . One must admit that there is no packed contemporary field of discourse in which writers are reflecting christianly on the modern world and modern man.[2]

Thirty years after Blamires's words were written, Mark A. Noll noted that the situation had not changed. In *The Scandal of the Evangelical Mind,* Noll writes, "The scandal of the evangelical mind is that *there is not much of an evangelical mind.* . . . Notwithstanding all their other virtues, however, American evangelicals are not exemplary for their thinking, and they have not been so for several generations."[3]

Others echo this message about today's church. Alister McGrath has written,

> Evangelicalism has generally not fostered any serious attempt to engage with the life of the mind, by encouraging believers to think within a specifically Christian framework across the entire spectrum of modern learning and culture. This clearly signals the need for evangelicalism to engage with the leading worldviews of our day, with a view to laying the foundations for the emergence of what Mark Noll has termed "the evangelical mind."[4]

Philosopher William Lane Craig is another Christian leader who is troubled by the dearth of Christian thinking. He comments,

> Our churches are filled with Christians who are idling in intellectual neutral. As Christians, their minds are going to waste. One result of this is an immature, superficial faith. . . . They know little of the riches of deep understanding of Christian truth, of the confidence inspired by the discovery that one's faith is logical and fits the facts of experience, of the stability brought to one's life by the conviction that one's faith is objectively true. . . . But the results of being in intellectual

neutral extend far beyond oneself. If Christian laymen don't become intellectually engaged, then we are in serious danger of losing our children. . . . For the sake of our youth, we desperately need informed parents who are equipped to wrestle with the issues at an intellectual level.[5]

An illustration will help demonstrate the lack of clear thought on the part of the culture. A television show about the life and death of Elvis Presley, called "The Elvis File," presented "evidence" for the possibility that Elvis is still alive. Some people believe that they had seen "the King," and handwriting experts declare that they have seen notes written by Presley after his demise. A background of spooky music accompanied all of the testimonies. Near the end of the show, host Bill Bixby asked people in the studio audience and those viewing on television to cast their votes as to whether they believed Elvis was still alive. After tabulating the votes, they announced that 79 percent of the audience believed Elvis to be alive. (No, I didn't vote.)

The results of that survey offer only one of many examples of the credulity of Western people. I may be going out on a limb, but I believe the evidence to be conclusive that Elvis really is dead. If that offends some true believers reading this book, let me state it this way: Even if Elvis *is* still alive, the evidence presented on that program was extremely weak. Weak or not, it convinced 79 percent of those who, like me, were wasting their time watching a show about Elvis being alive.

That television program illustrates that we are weak in our ability to reason. It also offers a paradigm of the way in which many people in the general populace make up their minds. They hear a televised news report or talk show interview with an "expert." The expert supplies a few supporting "facts," so the proposition must be true. In light of the philosophical presuppositions of most of Western culture, it is impossible for Christians to adopt such a method and still expect God to be glorified and loved in the mind. If a Christian mindset, or worldview, is to develop, Christians must master the truths of the Bible and weigh the ideas encountered in the culture against those truths.

This is certainly true with reference to the messages communicated by the media, but it is also true in the educational culture. It is no exaggeration to say that few educators in mainstream American higher education know that there is such a thing as a "Christian mind." If "Christian scholarship" was explained to them, they have no frame of reference for understanding it. When George Marsden wrote *The Soul of the American University: From Protestant Establishment to Established Nonbelief*, he "explored how and why American university culture, which was constructed largely by Protestants, has come to provide so little encouragement for academically rigorous perspectives explicitly shaped by Christian or other religious faith."[6]

Marsden's view of the appropriateness of merging faith and scholarship was criticized, largely by those who evidently believe that "Christian scholarship" is an oxymoron. In Marsden's words, "Many people find this idea strange unless it refers only to theology or to study *about* religious topics. Outside of that, they have no idea what it might mean."[7] In order to respond to such critics and to clarify the ancient endeavor of relating faith and learning, Marsden wrote *The Outrageous Idea of Christian Scholarship*.

Indeed, the idea of Christian scholarship, or a Christian mind, is unknown and does sound outrageous in most academic circles. Therefore, if Christian students are to love God and glorify Him in the way they think, they cannot accept uncritically the philosophical conclusions proposed by textbooks or teachers. In fact, they must do their academic work from the presupposition that their textbook authors and professors probably are not aware of the existence of an academically credible Christian worldview, much less its parameters. In addition, the views of these Christian students about everything must be evaluated with reference to what God has said in His Word.

The Church's Response

Sadly, the situation in the church seems bleak. Christians have an appalling lack of knowledge of, and commitment to, the Bible. They understand little of theology. The Barna Research Group cites the following survey results regarding Christian beliefs:

- Fifty-two percent of those who describe themselves as "born again Christians" rejected the existence of the Holy Spirit (2001).
- Thirty-five percent of those who identify themselves as "born again" say that Jesus Christ was crucified but not physically raised to life on the third day (1997).
- Forty-five percent of those who call themselves "born again" deny Satan's existence (2001).
- Thirty-two percent of those who identify themselves as "born again" state that they believe in moral absolutes (2001).
- Twenty-six percent of "born again" adults stated that they make their choices on the basis of principles taught in the Bible. Twenty-four percent said that they make choices on the basis of "whatever feels right or comfortable in the situation" (2001).[8]

If those who identify themselves as Christians either do not know basic biblical concepts or are not committed to those concepts, it would be optimistic in the extreme to expect them to have constructed a biblical view of life and to be able to respond cogently to philosophical challenges to that worldview.

How did we arrive at this point? Os Guinness traced some of the roots of the problem in *Fit Bodies, Fat Minds: Why Evangelicals Don't Think and What to Do About It.*[9] Guinness charges that several factors are contributing to the creation of an anti-intellectual movement within evangelicalism. An obsession with "heart religion" fosters a false dichotomy between heart and mind. The preference for the simple and primitive disparages anything that is complex or institutional. A religious populism distrusts formal education. The pragmatism of American evangelicalism emphasizes prosperity over theological accuracy. Christians have adopted the mind of an "idiot culture" and its vacuous television entertainment, commercials, and tabloid information collecting. Perhaps because I live in an academic subculture, I think Guinness' assessment is too negative. Some evangelicals *do* think! Nevertheless, if one trusts the statistics cited above, supported by the testimonies of numerous leaders, the paucity of biblical thinking in the modern church seems indisputable.

The problem is not limited to laypeople. As a pastor, one of my responsibilities was to interview potential members of our ministerial staff. Such interviews always included a multitude of issues, but a main purpose of the interviews was to evaluate the candidates' theological breadth and depth. I asked a general, open-ended question that allowed the individual to choose a personal way to express theological perspectives. The responses were less than encouraging, and in many cases dismally deficient. Answers often were only one or two sentences. When pressed, candidates would identify themselves with reference to a group known to be of a certain theological persuasion, or they talked about their personality, saying, for example, "I'm not a dogmatic person." Several times I wanted to interrupt them to say that I had not asked them about their ecclesiastical politics or their personality, but about their theology. I became convinced that many of these seminary graduates did not even possess the theological vocabulary necessary to describe what they believe and why they believe it. That is disturbing. Our churches, to say nothing of our Christian colleges and seminaries, ought to be training people to think biblically and to express biblical faith intelligently in relation to the neo-pagan culture in which we live.

David Wells, in *No Place for Truth,* argues that theology is disappearing among the clergy.[10] His case is convincing that, among Christian ministers, theology has been replaced by sensitivity about professionalism and marketing. Greater importance is placed upon the minister as manager of a corporation, agent of growth, counselor of the codependent, and motivator of volunteers, than on theological preparation to lead people to know God and to shun false ideologies. Wells states that the point in the modern church seems to be to respond to the felt needs of people, giving them what they want, rather than to respond to the truth of the Bible, giving them what they need. J. P. Moreland makes a similar point:

Since the 1960s, we have experienced an evolution in what we expect a local church pastor to be. Forty years ago he was expected to be a resident authority on theology and biblical teaching. Slowly this gave way to a model of the pastor as the CEO of the church, the administrative and organizational leader. Today the ministers we want are Christianized pop therapists who are entertaining to listen to."[11]

To break this popular mold, writes John Seel, is to be subject to the criticism of having "an inward product-orientation rather than an outward market-orientation."[12] Of course, this is not to say that the needs of people, felt or otherwise, are not important. They are. However, when an orientation toward felt needs is combined with a lack of biblical understanding, the result is the disappearance, or forfeit, of evangelical theology.

This anti-intellectual bias has matured just as the need for a coherent and convincing biblical worldview is urgent and its issues are pressing. For example, how are Christians to respond to the ideological wake of the sexual revolution, to the proliferation of homosexuality, and to "safe sex" ideology? How are Christians to relate themselves to possessions in a culture that is defined by greed? What should Christians think and do about the genocidal slaughter of the innocent unborn? How can we express our personal faith meaningfully in an atmosphere of anti-Christian bigotry? What does the Bible have to say about our relationship to the environment? These questions cry out for answers. However, many Christians are unprepared to answer them from the perspective of a biblical worldview.

The Importance of a Christian Worldview: A Biblical Case

In 1 Corinthians 2:16, the apostle Paul makes the bold statement that "we have the mind of Christ." In Philippians 2:5, he urges the Christians in Philippi to "have this mind in you, which was also in Christ Jesus." These verses assert the real possibility of thinking in the same way Jesus thought. As Johannes Kepler described his scientific work in prayer, the Christian mind involves "thinking thy thoughts after thee."[13] Because I believe the Bible expresses reality, I embrace the assertions in 2 Corinthians and Philippians. In fact, the Bible supplies at least six reasons why it is important to develop a Christian, or biblical, worldview.

First, as we have already seen, *a biblical worldview is a requirement for obedience to the greatest commandment, which is to love God with all of our being.*

Jesus said that loving God is the *greatest* commandment. That He assigned top priority to this command should give us pause. Christians ought to be willing to evaluate their lives on the basis of Christ's priorities. Based on Jesus' statement, we can say with confidence that making money is not the most important thing we will ever do. Nor is it to gain the prestige of position, nor even to serve other people. The most important thing that anyone in the human race will ever do is to love God. Everything else is secondary to this and flows from it.

Further, Jesus made it plain that this love for God should be emotional, spiritual, physical, *and* intellectual. How tragic, therefore, that some Christians have compartmentalized their love for God. They feel it emotionally, but the feeling has little effect on what they do with their bodies. Or they seek a spiritual experience in which they can express a mystical love for Christ, but their spirituality has little contact with their intellectual life. Some Christians express their love for God by doing good works, but they never feel any passion for God, and they seem uninterested in enlarging their spirits. But Jesus made it clear that, if we are to obey the greatest commandment, it will involve loving God with every part of our being, including our minds.

A second reason it is important to develop a distinctively biblical worldview is that *our mindset is a reliable indication of the essence of our identity.* Proverbs 23:7 states, "As he thinks within himself, so he is." Our thoughts reveal the kind of persons we are—our essence. We are not what we appear to be; we are what we think about. The images projected in the theater of our minds express who we are, and they have the power to set the direction of our lives. What goes on in our minds expresses our essence. If, therefore, we don't love God in our minds, we just don't love God.

Third, *how can we possibly claim that Jesus is the Lord, or Master, of our lives if He is not the Lord and Master of our minds?* Obviously, if He is truly Lord, then He will be Lord of the thought life. In 2 Corinthians 10, Paul writes about spiritual warfare. The primary battlefield of this war is the mind. There is a spiritual being named Satan who wants to influence the way we think. Our sinful flesh is disposed to deny the lordship of Christ in the mind. Each of us naturally wants to be a "free thinker." But give careful attention to what Paul says about the struggle for control, or lordship, of our minds: "We are destroying specula-tions and every lofty thing raised up against the knowledge of God, and we are taking every thought captive to the obedience of Christ" (2 Cor. 10:5). The message is clear: We are waging warfare in the mind. That war must be won *thought by thought* as Jesus takes charge of our thinking, and we relinquish control.

The clear teaching of 2 Corinthians 10:5, as well as other passages, is that Jesus is to be Lord of what happens in our minds. A great num-ber of Christians have picked up ideas about the use of their minds that contradict this teaching, and they have never realized it. For ex-ample, it is common for Christians to assume that they are to do their best to have their own ideas and opinions about issues. Some even speak of being "free thinkers," or having "a mind of my own." They have not come to grips with the biblical truth that Christ is to invade their thinking and establish His rule there. But if His rule is resisted in their minds He will never be the Lord of their lives. They have lost the spiritual battle for the mind by default.

A fourth reason that it is necessary to develop a Christian mindset is that *the renewing of the mind is God's method of transforming us into the image of Jesus.* God's plan for Christians is that they will be "conformed to the image of His Son" (Rom. 8:29). Disciples of Jesus are not to remain the same. We are to "grow in the grace and knowledge of our Lord and Savior Jesus Christ" (2 Peter 3:18). How does that happen? How are we transformed from a corrupt and small self-orientation, to the obedience and purity of spirit that is Christlikeness? That is the great question of discipleship. One part of the answer is clear: If we are to be transformed, something must happen in our minds. Romans 12:2 states, "Do not be conformed to this world, but be transformed *by the renewing of your mind*" (emphasis mine).

The goal is our transformation—from conformity to the world to conformity to the image of Jesus. According to Romans 12:2, in order for that transformation to occur, our minds must be renewed. As Donald Whitney has put it, "Growth in Godliness involves a mental renewal that cannot happen without learning. And the alternative to transformation via learning is conformity to the world."[14] Do not make the mistake of imagining that the goal of Christian thinking is to achieve some religious form of intellectualism. The goal is Christlikeness, and the means is a mind that has been renewed so that its chief characteristic is love for God. Os Guinness has stated this well:

> Our passion is not for academic respectability, but for faithfulness to the commands of Jesus. Our lament is not for the destruction of the elite culture of Western civilization but for the deficiencies in our everyday discipleship as Christians. Our mission is not the recovery of some lost golden age of purportedly better Christian thinking but the renewal of a church today that has integrity, faithfulness, and effectiveness in its thinking. . . . Thinking Christianly is first and foremost a matter of love—of minds in love with God and the truth of his world.[15]

A fifth biblical exhortation necessitates the development of a Christian worldview—*Christians are to be able to refute theological errors in the church.* In the first century church, some were teaching errors to Christians. They were advocating "philosophy and empty deception, according to the tradition of men" (Col. 2:8). John writes of "those who are trying to deceive you" (1 John 2:26). Jude says that "certain persons have crept in unnoticed" who were teaching false doctrine in the church (Jude 4, 12–13). What was, and is, the antidote to such false teaching in the church? Paul counseled the Christians in Colossae to realize Christ's sufficiency so that they would not covet ideas that were "according to the tradition of men." John exhorted his children in the faith to identify false prophets and to resist their influence (1 John 4:1). He emphasized that Christians should "know the spirit of truth and the spirit of error" (v. 6). Jude commends knowledge of the Bible when he writes that Christians "ought to remember the words that were spoken beforehand by the apostles of our Lord Jesus Christ" (Jude 17).

Realize Christ's sufficiency. Identify and resist preachers of falsehood. Remember the words of Scripture in order to recognize and refute theological error. These are just a few of the biblical prescriptions for responding to false doctrine in the church. The important point here is that it is impossible to do any of this without developing a Christian, or biblical, way of thinking. Theological error continues to abound in the modern church. Indeed, heresy has assailed the truth in every generation. In order to be equipped to obey God's command to refute such heresy, we must know the Bible and understand its philosophical implications and practical applications. Which is to say, we must have a worldview that is thoroughly Christian.

The sixth biblical reason for developing a Christian worldview is that *we are to be ready to defend our faith.* Not only must we contend with false ideas in the church, but also we must be ready to encounter false ideas in the culture at large. Will we be able to interpret the meaning and relevance of faith in Christ to those who hold such ideas? First Peter 3:15 says that we sanctify Christ as Lord as we are "always being ready to make a defense to everyone who asks you to give an account for the hope that is in you." In other words, Christians are always to be ready to give an account, or defense, of their faith. It does not suffice to say, "I just feel good when I go to church." A lot of people feel good when they *don't* go to church. Nor is it enough to say, "Well, I may not know much about theology or the Bible, and I may not be able to answer your questions, but I know I believe in Jesus." Really? Are you saying that you believe even though you don't know why you believe and even though you cannot give a reasonable answer to those who challenge the truth of your faith? Have you separated the spiritual from the rational? Do you realize how many people are turned off by Christians who cannot rationally explain why it makes sense to be a

Christian? The Bible says that we are to be ready to defend the faith. If we are going to be able to do that, something must happen upstairs.

Introduction to a Solution

A Christian mindset does exist, and in forming a worldview the Christian mind defers to what God has said in His Word. But how do we cultivate this mindset? How do we develop a worldview that addresses modern philosophical and ethical issues in a way that is consistent with historic Christian orthodoxy?

Reading the Bible

Perhaps the most familiar statement in the Bible *about* the Bible is found in 2 Timothy 3:16–17: "All Scripture is inspired by God and profitable for teaching, for reproof, for correction, for training in righteousness; so that the man of God may be adequate, equipped for every good work." A worldview that deserves the name "Christian" begins with the question, "What does God have to say about this issue?" And 2 Timothy 3:16 states that what the Bible says, God says. Furthermore, verse 17 states that a knowledge of the Bible will make us "adequate, equipped for *every* good work" (emphasis mine).

How are we to gain access to the intended positive benefits of the Bible? How do we become "adequate" and "equipped"? Second Timothy 2:15 states, "Be diligent to present yourself approved to God as a workman who does not need to be ashamed, handling accurately the word of truth." If we are to know, understand, and accurately handle the word of truth, we must "be diligent" to read, study, and meditate upon the Bible. Further, we must tap into the vast reservoir of Christian literature that aids us in understanding and applying the biblical message. I know of no shortcuts; we must be lifelong students of the Scriptures.

Christians at the beginning of the twenty-first century must move beyond the idea that "merely" knowing the Bible is somehow simplistic and not sufficiently sophisticated to prepare them to engage the complex but errant ideas of our culture. Even some cultural observers who do not write from a Christian perspective see the importance of studying the Bible to obtain real wisdom for living. Allan Bloom, professor at the University of Chicago, wrote a critique of the state of American education in his influential book, *The Closing of the American Mind*. He noted that

> A highly trained computer specialist need not have had any more learning about morals, politics or religion than the most ignorant of persons. All to the contrary, his narrow education, with the prejudices and the pride accompanying it, and its literature which comes to be and passes away in a day and uncritically accepts the premises of current wisdom, can cut him off from the liberal learning that simpler folk used to absorb from a variety of traditional sources. . . .
>
> My grandparents were ignorant people by our standards, and my grandfather held only lowly jobs. But their home was spiritually rich because all the things done in it, not only what was specifically ritual, found their origin in the Bible's commandments, and their explanation in the Bible's stories and the commentaries on them. . . .
>
> I do not believe that my generation, my cousins who have been educated in the American way, all of whom are M.D.s or Ph.D.s, have any comparable learning. . . .
>
> I am not saying anything so trite as that life is fuller when people have myths to live by. I mean rather that a life based on the Book is closer to the truth, that it provides the material for deeper research in and access to the real nature of things.[16]

The sad fact is that many in the contemporary church would be more impressed with Bloom's M.D. and Ph.D. cousins than with his grandparents. That reality underscores just how much the church has become like the world. It is time for the church to recognize that her members simply are not educated and do not possess a Christian way of viewing the world if they are not mature students of the Bible.

How does one go about studying the Bible? Many books are available to help interpret the Bible, but there is no substitute for reading the Bible for oneself, not sporadically, but consistently and systematically. Stephen Douglass and Lee Roddy have provided some practical guidelines for Bible study in *Making the Most of Your Mind*. They include the following steps:

1. Learn to like to study the Scriptures. You can do this by asking God to give you the motivation to study His Word. Other helps in motivation are meditating on the great benefits of studying the Bible and studying with someone you like.
2. Pray for enlightenment. Ask God to reveal truth to you.
3. Learn how to dig into the Scriptures. Douglass and Roddy recommend Howard Hendricks's four-part method: (1) *Observe*. Note the theme, context, key terms, geographical and biographical features; (2) *Interpret*. Define the meanings of key terms, note features of the passage such as action, repetition, and questions, and try to paraphrase the passage; (3) *Apply*. What implications does the passage have for your thought and actions? and (4) *Correlate*. How does the message of this passage relate to other passages of Scripture?
4. Have a plan. Develop a definite plan for reading, memorizing, applying, and sharing the Bible.
5. Spend the time. It takes time to become proficient at anything. Pick a regular time when you are alert.[17]

Also, one's perspective in reading the Bible is all-important. Knowledge of the words of the Bible does not ensure that an individual has a biblical worldview. Many students of the ancient text read it in Hebrew and Greek only out of academic interest, but they cannot discover truth because they do not believe they are reading words of God. It is also possible for a Christian to read the Bible while remaining so committed to a personal agenda that they do not submit to God's truth. Such people are directed by their own opinions and experiences, rather than by the Word of God. Their theme song is, "God gave you a mind and He expects you to use it!" That statement is used to defend any opinion that makes sense to the one who holds it. Of course, that statement is not in the Bible, but Proverbs 3:5 is: "Trust in the Lord with all your heart, and do not lean on your own understanding." We are to trust God, not our own minds. Yes, we are to *use* our minds in the service of God, but we are not to "lean on" our own understanding.

If we approach the Bible with that perspective, we will find help in developing a biblical worldview. If not, it is inevitable that we will view the world through glasses of our own making, twisting the meaning of the Bible's text to fit our notions.

Reading the Culture

One who has a biblical worldview also is willing and able to read the culture critically. Most Christians do not have the capacity to do so. The extent of their interaction with the culture is to watch and complain. Christians need greater facility in understanding and interpreting culture. This involves two commitments. First, we must commit to *read* the culture. In order to communicate the gospel to a foreign culture, cross-cultural missionaries are trained in the idiosyncrasies of that culture. In the same way, Western Christians must be trained to know their culture if they expect to profess their faith in a way that makes sense to the foreign culture around them.

Several years ago a teacher in the public school system invited me to speak to a class of fourth graders. Before coming to the class I was to read the book that they were reading in order to help them interpret it. The book was about dying and death. I saw this opportunity as a perfect moment to share what the Bible says about the subject. Fully aware that I was in a public school, I chose to supply the students with nonreligious information about the grieving process before I shared Christian beliefs. I was unprepared for their questions. When I asked them if they knew what "terminal" meant, one of the children asked, "You mean like the 'Terminator'?" When I spoke about my Christian beliefs concerning the afterlife, another child gave a brief review of Bill and Ted's "excellent adventure" to the underworld and then asked if that was realistic. My seminary education didn't prepare me to answer theological questions about Bill and Ted. In fact, my academic training was in Old Testament and Hebrew. I could have answered a question about ancient Ugarit, but they were interested in modern Hollywood.

In order for a biblical worldview to be relevant, it must be seen alongside contrasting worldviews. It must critique the culture that proffers those worldviews, even if it's in the form of an otherwise vacuous motion picture. As Terry Mattingly has written, "Our popular culture has baptized the churched and unchurched alike in its media messages to the point where we can no longer even attempt to state a case for faith without some knowledge of the marketplace."[18] As I present the implications of Christian thinking in this volume, I interact with popular cultural ideas that run contrary to a Christian worldview.

A second commitment involved in reading the culture critically is the commitment to *critique*. When we walk into a movie theater, turn on the TV, read the newspaper, or even engage in conversation, we cannot check our worldview at the door. That would be harmful for us and for those around us. For one thing, we cannot assume that we will be unaffected if we passively soak up the media's images and ideas. In subtle and brazen ways, our culture undermines and replaces the biblical worldview. We are moved by what enters our minds, so if we listen to our culture's communication, we must sanitize it by filtering it through a belief system that is thoroughly biblical. Also, we must critique the culture conspicuously for the sake of our families, friends, and coworkers. Often we will need to fill the role of cultural contrarian in order to influence them toward godliness. If we fail to interact openly and candidly with wrong messages, our spiritual and mental lethargy can be interpreted as agreement. We are called to influence those around us for the sake of the kingdom of God (Matt. 5:13–16; 28:19–20), and we must not let them down by failing to supply them with the truth.

Making a Commitment to Grow

Every new Christian is, spiritually speaking, a child. The problem is that some Christians began the Christian life when they were physical children and have stayed in childhood spiritually. Their capacity to think and their knowledge of the culture has matured, but their biblical understanding has remained at the level of a child. No wonder Christian faith seems to be naive and inadequate for the challenges of sophisticated living in the twenty-first century. First Peter 2:2 has the solution: "Like newborn babies, long for the pure milk of the word, so that by it you may grow." *When we commit to study the Bible diligently and to read the culture critically with a mind that is devoted to discovering truth, the natural result is growth.* And if our minds are immersed in the truth, a biblical worldview will begin to form. We will cultivate "the mind of Christ." As spiritual adults we can face the complex issues of our time with a worldview that is both faithful to the Word of God and intelligible to those who need that Word.

CHAPTER 2

The Dorothy Syndrome: Where Are We?

Do not be conformed to this world, but be transformed by the renewing of your mind, that you may prove what the will of God is, that which is good and acceptable and perfect.

—*Romans 12:2*

The history of much of the twentieth century, with its struggles against communism and fascism and national socialism and so on, will be best written as the record of a war for the command of men's minds.[1]

—*Gilbert Highet*

One of the best-known lines from the movie *The Wizard of Oz* comes as Dorothy takes her first look around at Munchkinland. With an awed and fearful voice, she says to her dog, "I don't think we're in Kansas anymore, Toto." She had been transported via tornado to the Land of Oz, and the Land of Oz looked nothing like Kansas. At the end of her sojourn in that foreign land, she clicked her heels together, went back to Kansas, and found out that it had been just a dream.

In the fourteen delightful children's books on which the movie was loosely based, Dorothy actually returned to Oz. Author L. Frank Baum sent Dorothy and her family on many adventures in the land called Oz. What is especially interesting and germane to our subject is that some people perceive the changes in our world to be just as drastic as the changes Dorothy experienced. Maybe you have seen the bumper sticker with the message, "We're not in Kansas anymore, Toto." Indeed, we are not.

Any adult can attest that, since about 1960, Western culture has undergone a radical transformation. Ideas about God and humanity, rooted in radical academic circles, began to be accepted in the popular culture in the 1960s. Hence, the "God is dead" movement was spawned, as was the sexual revolution, the drug culture, and the idea that the church is antiquarian and has an irrelevant message. Those phenomena and others have had such a profound effect on the culture that when Christians exit a worship service, it is as if they are leaving Kansas and entering Oz.

Where Are We?

If this is not Kansas anymore, where are we? What philosophical forces have combined to create this culture that is so alien to the one in which Christianity flourished? This question is enormously important for the church to answer at the beginning of the twenty-first century. As Francis Schaeffer wrote, "If we are to communicate the Christian faith effectively, therefore, we must know and understand the thought-forms of our own generation."[2] In postmodern, post-Christian America, evangelical Christians live in a culture that is foreign territory. Learning the philosophical contours of the culture is a mandatory part of our worldview curriculum if we are to communicate the gospel effectively.

To locate us on the philosophical map, I will briefly sketch a few of the philosophies that are exerting the greatest influence on our culture. This sketch should show how far Western culture has drifted from a biblical worldview and demonstrate why there has been a resulting shift in behavior. Once we comprehend the philosophical currents that are dominating the *thinking* of people, we should easily understand the significant shift in *ethics*. People act according to their beliefs. Morality follows philosophy. People may talk about their system of beliefs, but it is their actions that reveal what they *really* believe. Later we will consider the beliefs that underlay some of the most contested ethical battlegrounds. It is essential that the community of faith learn how to think about those issues not as members of the culture but as members of the church. In order for Christians to draw a bold line between cultural and biblical standards, they must apprehend the vast differences separating these standards. That is the purpose of chapters two and three.

The Confluence of Two Rivers

For ten months, I preached in a church located about two hours' driving time from where I live. The pastor had retired, and those dear people were in the process of prayerfully searching for their next pastor. In the meantime, they asked me to preach. Five years later, after their next pastor left, I returned to serve there again for several months. During both stints, they arranged for me to stay in a local motel on Saturday nights. The motel was situated at the confluence of the Neuse and Trent rivers. I could look out my motel room window and see where the two rivers come together and empty into Pamlico Sound. The Neuse River flows just a few miles from my home, 125 miles away from its confluence with the Trent River.

A similar phenomenon is at work in Western culture. The watershed streams of the Enlightenment have fed two great philosophical rivers that now take parallel courses toward the sea. Modernistic rationalism is the river whose course is better known and extensively traveled. Ideas central to modernism continue to exert significant influence on Western culture. The second and later river, postmodernism, has been fed from the same sources but has moved in a divergent course. Postmodernism is now an independent philosophical system with its own distinct characteristics, and in some areas of thought it holds almost exclusive sway. These two rivers combine to form the philosophical and cultural mix that is Western culture. Either river has its own characteristics, and their combination, or confluence, results in an unprecedented blend of philosophical currents. We ought to be interested in these rivers, for both flow by our homes.

Modernism

The term *modernism* is used here philosophically, not chrono-
logically. That is, modernism is a way of thinking that can be distinguished from pre-modern and postmodern thought. In the
pre-modern period of Western civilization, people generally believed
in the supernatural. Though the identity of the gods differed from
culture to culture, each culture *did* worship. Socrates was executed
for "corrupting youth and interfering with the religion of Athens"—
not because he did not believe in a deity or the supernatural, but
because he did not believe in the official Athenian gods of Olympus.
The Greeks and Romans believed in the divine and were searching
for God. This situation provided fertile soil for the missionary activity of the early church.

When the Roman Empire converted to Christianity, the people were
influenced by the worldview found in the Bible. They already believed
in a reality that transcends the physical world. Christianity defined
that reality as the one true God of Israel, who had revealed Himself in
Jesus Christ. Though it is not proper to associate Christianity exclusively with pre-modern ideas, it is true that for about fifteen hundred
years Christianity was generally believed to reflect the true nature of
things; so Christians enjoyed a privileged status in the West.

In the 1700s, however, the supremacy of Christianity, or more properly supernaturalism, was displaced by the belief that unaided human
reason, independent from God, could discover truth. Human reason,
human autonomy, and scientific discovery became the foci of Western thought. The ascendancy of this new way of thinking is usually
dated to the Enlightenment. Some have specifically dated the emer-
gence of modernism to the fall of the Bastille in 1789 and the ensuing
French Revolution, though such a precise date has more heuristic than
historical value.

Some leading philosophical developments of the modern mindset
can help us understand the currents of modernism in the river of
Western culture.

Naturalism

Enlightenment thinkers emphasized the ability of humans to discover truth on their own, without the aid of divine revelation. A sharp division was made between spiritual knowledge and physical knowledge. The division between these two kinds of knowledge widened until spiritual knowledge came to be regarded as unreal or unknowable, while physical knowledge was considered real and discoverable by human reason using the scientific method. Francis Schaeffer called the two kinds of knowledge, or reality, "upper storey" and "lower storey."[3] When knowledge that was accessible by faith was separated from knowledge that was accessible by rationality, it was only one short step to the conclusion that faith is not rational. When Enlightenment philosophers and scientists reached this point, the reaction of some people of faith, notably Søren Kierkegaard, was to propose that, in order to believe anything in the upper storey, a "leap of faith" was necessary. And if Enlightenment categories of thought were accepted, the leap of faith was of necessity a leap from the rational to the irrational.[4]

The sharp division between upper-storey knowledge and lower-storey knowledge is the starting point of *naturalism*. Naturalism operates from the presumption that the physical world (lower storey) is real and the spiritual world (upper storey) is unreal, or at least unknowable by human reason, which is the only kind of rational knowledge. S. D. Gaede has defined naturalism in this way:

The naturalistic world view rests upon the belief that the material universe is the sum total of reality. . . . The supernatural, in any form, does not exist. . . . The naturalistic world view assumes that the matter or stuff which makes up the universe has never been created but has always existed. . . . Naturalism normally assumes that always-existing matter has developed into the ordered universe which we see by a blind, timeless process of chance.[5]

In other words, only nature exists (no God), nature has always existed (no creation), nature is uniform (no miracles), and nature is deterministic (no free will). Phillip Johnson has provided another helpful definition:

> According to naturalism, what is ultimately real is nature, which consists of the fundamental particles that make up what we call matter and energy, together with the natural laws that govern how those particles behave. Nature itself is ultimately all there is. . . . To put it another way, nature is a permanently closed system of material causes and effects that can never be influenced by anything outside of itself—by God, for example. To speak of something as "supernatural" is therefore to imply that it is imaginary.[6]

Atheism is not a logically necessary component of naturalism. That is, a deity could theoretically exist in a naturalistic system, but in the words of naturalist physicist, Stephen Hawking, there would be "nothing for a Creator to do."[7] In other words, nature is eternal and the cause of nature is, well, nature, not God. Nature is a closed system, not open to the intervention of outside forces, such as God. Carl Sagan went further than this, as most naturalists do, leaving no room even for the existence of God. He believed that, not only is nature eternal, but it is the *only* thing that is eternal. His oft-quoted line in *Cosmos* is, "The Cosmos is all that is or ever was or ever will be."[8] Obviously, this leaves no room for God.

Naturalism's relationship to the divine is further illustrated by scientist Francis Crick's question, "If the members of a church really believe in a life after death, why do they not conduct sound experiments to establish it?"[9] Another popular illustration is the reported statement by one of the first Soviet cosmonauts who returned from circling Earth and said that he had not seen God out in space. This cosmonaut did not see Him as an observable phenomenon in nature, so He must not exist. Such a statement proves nothing, of course, unless one begins with naturalistic presuppositions. No believer in the

God of Scripture ever claimed that God lives just on the other side of the exosphere. Nor do any believe that if we could just get there we might drop in for a visit and maybe get an autograph. But a consistent naturalist believes that one must be able to spot God somewhere, because the observable phenomena of nature are all that exist.

Naturalism is not an extremist philosophy found only on the fringes of society. Anyone who believes it is has been desensitized to the presence of naturalism by constant exposure. Far from being on the periphery of culture, naturalism pervades the dominant cultural systems of Europe and North America. It is the foundation of the scientific community, education, the judicial system, and the news media. Johnson writes of the current cultural domination that "the most influential intellectuals in America and around the world are mostly *naturalists,* who assume that God exists only as an idea in the minds of religious believers."[10] Ronald Nash has called naturalism "the major competition to the Christian worldview in the part of the world normally thought of as Christendom."[11]

Benjamin Wiker has provided an excellent historical description of naturalism, although he prefers the term *materialism.* He states:

> The public square . . . is guarded by those who are trained to believe that there are only the two stark alternatives: materialist science (which defines the very meaning of rationality) or immaterialist irrationalism. That there are rational arguments for the existence of an intelligent cause is simply ruled out by declaring that if the argument is not materialist, then it must be irrational (or, more kindly, "theological").[12]

The influence of naturalism is seen in the way the natural sciences have replaced theology as "queen of the sciences." Theologians no longer occupy teaching chairs in public universities; the emphasis is now on the study of the history and practice of religion as a sociological/psychological/historical phenomenon. This has led David Wells to make the comment that if one is a theologian and wants to teach at a public university, he must disguise himself as something else.[13] Public sentiment seems to be that anyone can have ideas about God, but the superior contributions are made by those who study the natural world—biologists, chemists, astronomers, physicists, and even the psychologists who study the natural operations of the human mind. The average man or woman on the street tends to regard hard data or empirically verifiable evidence with much more respect than the truths of the Bible. This is the case because of a philosophical predisposition toward naturalism and away from supernaturalism. Although they may not be thoroughgoing naturalists and may not even be able to define naturalism, they are strongly influenced by it.

The inevitable result of the domination of naturalism has been the marginalization of Christianity, with its belief in God and the supernatural. According to naturalism, God is an invention of humankind, so knowledge of God is a product of our imaginations. Belief in God, then, is by definition irrational. Furthermore, naturalists believe it is impossible for theists (believers in God) to disprove naturalism. It is impossible to construct a rational argument based on an irrational premise—the existence of God. Science is based on reason; religion is based on blind faith.

Consider three areas of thought in which naturalism is exerting an influence. As each is described, contrasts with central doctrines of Christianity should be immediately clear. These will be explored in detail in chapter 3.

The Origin of Life

According to naturalists, the world is the result of an initial chance combination of atoms and innumerable genetic changes that took place over billions of years. This scenario is the only option if one begins with the presupposition that belief in God is irrational. The universe must have originated from natural forces, since nature is all that exists. Providing a case against evolution is beyond my purpose here.[14] I simply want to state that evidence for development within species, called *microevolution*, does not contradict Scripture and has never been an issue between Christians and science. Evidence for microevolutionary processes can be found in the fossil record. However, the fossil record does not give such support for *macroevolution*, the naturalistic theory that life and species originated and changed by chance over time. The idea that one kind of life developed from other kinds of life is far from proven, but its tenets are treated as established, unassailable facts in our culture. It is the "culturally dominant creation story."[15]

The significance of the cultural acceptance of a naturalistic explanation of the origin of life cannot be overestimated. How do we answer the question, "Who are we?" or "What are we?" People have always answered that question in part by answering the question, "Where did we come from?" Ancient cultures possessed their own origin stories that helped them understand who they were in relation to the world, the gods, and one another. The Bible asserts that we are the special creations of the one, true, personal God. That helps define who we are and how we are to relate to the world, God, and others. If we arrived on earth by natural forces interacting randomly, ultimately there is no meaning. How could meaning or purpose result from a purposeless process of development? Modernist naturalism inevitably leads to a dead end of meaninglessness.

The Human Mind

How does the naturalist theory of origins relate to human thought? If all that exists is the physical, humans have no soul or spirit. In fact, we have no intelligence, as intelligence is popularly defined. Instead, the work of our minds is nothing more than a series of chemical processes. Crick, co-discoverer of the structure of DNA, expressed the view that "your joys and your sorrows, your memories and your ambitions, your sense of personal identity and free will, are in fact no more than the behavior of a vast assembly of nerve cells and their associated molecules."[16]

Once we understand the implications of naturalism, we see why scientists would seek a purely chemical/neurological explanation for what happens in the mind. The only alternative to a scientific explanation is some religious notion of a "soul," which Crick referred to as "the superstitions of our ancestors."[17] Of course, Crick and other naturalists have no basis to complain about such religious explanations. According to Crick's theory of the mind, those who think from a Christian worldview are doing so only because of certain chemical reactions in their brains. Likewise, naturalists believe as they do merely because of "the behavior of a vast assembly of nerve cells and their associated molecules." Therefore, we can hardly argue about the rightness or wrongness of someone else's ideas; they really have no choice but to think as they do. This leads to a third way in which naturalism is especially relevant to those who are interested in developing a Christian worldview.

Morality

The moral system that has been standard in Western culture is based upon the commands of the Bible. Since Christianity has been the predominant religion of the West, and the Bible is the authoritative book for Christians, it is not surprising that the superstructure of Western laws was derived from the moral prescriptions of the Bible. The Bible, of course, says that its commands are from God. Never does the Bible state that its system of moral principles is one option among many, or merely the opinion of one group of people in distinction to the opinions of other cultures. To the contrary, these moral standards are the very words of the One who created mankind.

Naturalism, however, starts with the presupposition that matter, or nature, is all that exists. God, therefore, has been created by the human mind. If that is the case, then the moral principles believed to have been given by God necessarily originated with people. In the case of the laws found in the Bible, naturalists would say that they were written by Jewish priests to bring order to the life of their communities. Further, these laws were written for herdsmen and farmers who lived in a prescientific age. Now that humankind has progressed (evolved), it is about time we realized that many of the commands of the Bible no longer suit modern society. Because the commands originated with human thought, human thought can revise them. We need look to no higher authority than ourselves, for there *is* no higher authority.

This modernist approach to moral law allows no transcendent principles. All that is left is human opinion. Since everyone's opinion is different, the inevitable result of the loss of transcendence is the loss of absolute moral standards. In the modern age, people have realized this for a long time, but for pragmatic reasons society has been willing to cling to at least vestiges of Judeo-Christian ethics. Completely jettisoning our ethical system would lead to cultural chaos. However, in the shift from modernism to postmodernism, the implications of the loss of transcendence in morality are beginning to be applied by the populace, and the result is nothing short of moral anarchy. If there are no transcendent moral principles, but only moral opinions, anyone who asserts that a particular moral system (e.g., the one found in the Bible) should be applied universally is hopelessly out of date, ignorant as to the existence of other systems, or pathologically dogmatic. Many Christians do not yet fully see this inescapable application because they have been educated in schools monopolized by the worldview of naturalism and entertained through media monopolized by modernist presuppositions. Most Western Christians have been so saturated with these assumptions about reality that they know this worldview better than they know the Bible. They need a new pair of glasses.

Secularism, as naturalism, rejects the existence of the eternal. The exclusive focus is on the "here and now"—the present rather than the eternal. Because there is no eternity, there are no eternal principles—no absolutes. Secularism draws a bold line between this world and the spiritual world, and all that matters is what is on this side of the line. In fact, there may be nothing at all on the other side of the line. Even if there is, such a reality makes no practical difference if the only thing that counts is what happens here and now in the visible (secular) world. *Secular* is often used as a modifier of *humanism,* emphasizing humanism's focus on human endeavor devoid of eternal or spiritual values.

Secularism is also similar to naturalism in that it exerts great influence in Western society. R. C. Sproul called it "the dominant ism of American culture."[18] The emphasis of our culture is on getting everything *now*, and focusing on the material to the exclusion of the spiritual. Contrast that with the exhortation of Jesus to "lay up for yourselves treasures in heaven" (Matt. 6:20). The secular world is important; it's where we live. But there is more to life than the secular. The Bible also affirms that there is an eternity waiting for us on the other side of this life. If secularism were true, then we would have to omit all that Jesus said about heaven and hell. Indeed, some have tried to do just that.

Hedonism

Hedonism as a philosophy, or worldview, measures the rightness or wrongness of a particular course of action by whether it is pleasurable. "If it feels good, do it; do it if it's what you feel" is the contemporary proverb that expresses the philosophy of hedonism. Of course, everyone seeks pleasure. It could be argued that it is human nature to seek that which is pleasurable instead of that which is painful (see Eph. 5:28–29, for example). However, hedonism formulates this natural tendency into a philosophy of life, an *ism*.

Hedonism is not new. The pleasure principle influenced various ancient religions. The goal of many religions was to secure personal and corporate blessing from the gods—fertility of the land, fertility of the womb, wealth, and ease of life. Some ancient religions even included physical pleasures in the religious rites themselves. This was part of the reason for cult prostitution in the Near East and the drunken orgies of the Dionysian cult in Greek culture. In this hedonistic approach, religious people did not serve the gods; it was the other way around. These religions aimed at serving the worshipers, not the gods. The point was to bring blessing, or pleasure, to humans, not glory to the gods. Indeed, mythic stories describing the behavior of these gods illustrate why they deserved no glory.

Epicurus, a Greek philosopher of the fourth and third centuries B.C., taught that "the chief aim of human life is pleasure."[19] In fact, according to Epicurus, the pleasure principle is the standard dividing right from wrong. If an action is pleasurable, it is good; if it is painful, it is bad. Epicurus set out to determine which kinds of pleasure were most valuable to individuals.

Especially interesting is the connection between naturalism and hedonism in Epicurus's writings. The goal was to avoid that which disturbs or troubles. And the two realities that are most troubling are the divine and the afterlife. If gods exist, we must worry over whether we are offending them. As divine creatures, they may place restrictions on our lives, and that would disturb what we want to do. The afterlife is also disturbing, because if it exists we must dread the possibility of facing the wrath of the gods. Such anxiety mitigates against the state of contentment that should be our goal. The Epicurean remedy for discontent was the study of nature. The purpose of studying nature was not the advancement of knowledge *per se* but the maintenance of a state of mind unperturbed by thoughts of the gods and the afterlife. Therefore, Epicurus's approach to natural science excluded any possibility of divine influence on nature. Epicurus was quite explicit about this approach and commended it to all his adherents. For example, he wrote, "the totality [of things] has always been just like it is now and always will be."[20]

This is remarkably similar to Sagan's statement about the eternality of the cosmos, which was written twenty-three hundred years later. Indeed, the philosophies of naturalism and hedonism are connected in two ways. First, hedonism is the result of a naturalistic view of nature. Once God is excluded from nature, as in naturalism, we need answer to no one except the self. Second, naturalism is the result of hedonism. When one establishes self-pleasure as the highest good, as Epicurus did, one's view of nature inevitably will exclude the divine, since thoughts of the divine may hinder one's pursuit of pleasure.[21] Thus, the connection between naturalism and hedonism runs both ways.

Stoicism, also a Greek philosophy initiated in the fourth century B.C., was similar to hedonism in promoting happiness as the goal of life. Unlike the Epicureans, the Stoics sought happiness through their own brand of wisdom. They would control what they could, and accept with dignified resignation those things that they could not control.

Hedonism as a formal philosophy has survived into the modern era. Modernism is particularly fertile soil for hedonism. If God and His laws are disregarded, and if there are no limits to what man's reason can achieve, then humanity is free to explore the way to achieve the pleasure that is most reasonable. John Stuart Mill is an example of a modern hedonist. In the nineteenth century he wrote that "actions are right in proportion as they tend to promote happiness, wrong as they tend to produce the reverse of happiness. By happiness is intended pleasure, and the absence of pain; by unhappiness, pain, and the privation of pleasure."[22]

Mill also invoked the name of God to lend support to his philosophy, writing that "God desires above all things the happiness of His creatures."[23] I have heard words like that spoken by Christians to justify patterns of behavior that were clearly prohibited by the Bible. "But I know that God wants me to be happy." These Christians would have denied that they were hedonists, but they were more hedonist than Christian.

Hedonism also has survived in informal, popular, ways. The term *epicurean* describes people who have good taste in things like gourmet food, and who enjoy the "finer" things of life in their pursuit of a sophisticated level of pleasure. Those who maintain dignity and serenity in the midst of difficulty are said to take life "stoically."

But hedonism has survived in more ways than the use of terminology. Hugh Hefner and other pornographers have made a fortune from articulating this philosophy and urging others to live by seeking sexual pleasure. Entire segments of our society and economy are based on hedonistic pursuits. Where would the pornography industry be if men did not think they should seek personal pleasure, even at the expense of degrading women as objects? The pursuit of pleasure creates the demand for cigarettes, alcohol, and other drugs.

The structure and stability of the institution of the family has been profoundly affected by hedonism. Husbands and wives pursue extramarital affairs for the sake of personal pleasure, usually with the result of divorce. Other couples file for divorce simply because marriage no longer seems as pleasurable an alternative as singleness. Abortions are performed because the pain of childbirth and the work of child rearing would not be pleasant.

Hedonism has also infected the church. People who profess Christ have participated in all of the aforementioned activities in pursuit of "self-fulfillment" and happiness. Even attendance at gatherings of the church can have a hedonistic motivation. People are visiting churches on Sunday mornings to investigate how religion, or church attendance, can "help *me.*" People want to be more successful in their jobs, finances, families, and in their inner dispositions. They go to church, therefore, looking for how the church is going to help them reach their personal goals. A diminishing number of people are walking into church thinking, "I want to find the truth and live the way God intends for me to live. Show me how." In fact, according to a *USA Today* survey, of the 56 percent of Americans who attend church, 45 percent do so because "it's good for you." Christians look for a church to "meet my needs," never thinking that perhaps they should look for a church where they can meet someone else's needs. Pastors and other ministers are rarely evaluated solely on the basis of their Christlikeness and spiritual leadership (knowledge of the Bible, inclination to teach and exhort scripturally). Rather they often are judged on the basis of their pleasing personality and ability to entertain while speaking.

Hedonism is molding the church into the image of the surrounding self-indulgent culture. It is time for the church to realize that living according to hedonistic principles does not arise from the New Testament but from a culture steeped in a naturalistic view of the universe in which nothing is left to worship except oneself. Given that naturalism, and usually hedonism, begin with the assertion that God, heaven, and the soul do not exist, why doesn't the church reject such worldviews instead of enjoying the self-centeredness that results from them?

Christians by definition do not believe that here and now is all there is. Yet some live as if it was their philosophy, to "Eat, drink, and be merry, for tomorrow we die," and to "Go for the gusto."

Hedonism is a dead-end road, a "broken cistern" (Jer. 2:13). The paradox within hedonism is that this philosophy contains the seeds of pain, not pleasure. In fact, this contradiction is recognized by unbelieving philosophers as "the hedonistic paradox."[24] The paradox is this: If a hedonist does not reach the level of pleasure he desires, he experiences frustration, and frustration is painful. It is common for people to fail to achieve the pleasure they seek and so to find disappointment and pain in their lives, not pleasure. On the other hand, if a hedonist obtains all the pleasure he desires, he becomes bored with that level of pleasure, or he becomes addicted to the source of pleasure—like alcohol, drugs, or sex. Boredom and addiction are also painful. So if we don't get the pleasure we seek, we experience pain, and if we *do* get what we seek, we experience pain. Either way, hedonists lose. The outcome of hedonism is the opposite of its goal; its only consequence is pain.

Postmodernism

The inherent diversity, cynicism, and volatility of postmodernism make it difficult to define. David Harvey calls postmodernism "a minefield of conflicting notions" and "a battleground of conflicting opinions and political forces."[25] Though the fruits of postmodernism are heterogeneous, perhaps its roots are easier to identify. In Harvey's words, it arose from "anti-modern" sentiments that eventually formed a "vast wave of rebelliousness."[26] Alister McGrath has provided an excellent general definition of the Enlightenment way of thinking that modernism inherited and applied:

The primary feature of the movement may be seen as its assertion of the omnicompetence of human reason. Reason, it was argued, was capable of telling us everything we needed to know about God and morality. The idea of some kind of supernatural revelation was dismissed as an irrelevance. Jesus Christ was just one of many religious teachers, who told us things that anyone with a degree of common sense could have told us anyway. Reason reigned supreme.[27]

The river of postmodernism began to branch off modernism when those in the academy began to lose confidence in the supremacy of reason. Since the beginning of recorded history, philosophers have tried to comprehend reality and arrange it into a coherent system. The Enlightenment promised that mankind would soon be able to understand all of reality by using human reason with the aid of science. Philosophers proposed theories they believed to be comprehensive and accurate, but then other philosophers followed them with equally comprehensive, but contradictory, theories of their own. Philosopher followed philosopher, each with a similar promise, but the only result was a string of contradictory theories about the nature of things.

The situation within science was similar. Science stretched our understanding of the natural world. However, the ambitious hope of discovering a verifiable explanation of the origin of the universe, bolstered by the doctrines of Darwinism and quantum physics, has proved unsuccessful. As hope of a grand unified metaphysical theory was deferred decade after decade, finally some began to believe that human reason would never discover the elusive, unified "theory of everything." This pessimism about the possibility of any ultimate truth is one of the hallmarks of the postmodern mood. In effect, postmodernism is built on the rubble of the failed experiment of the Enlightenment.

This pessimism about modernism's optimism is expressed well in an oft-quoted statement by neo-Marxist Terry Eagleton:

> We are now in the process of awakening from the nightmare of modernity, with its manipulative reason and fetish of the totality, into the laid-back pluralism of the post-modern, that heterogeneous range of life-styles and language games which has renounced the nostalgic urge to totalize and legitimate itself. . . . Science and philosophy must jettison their grandiose metaphysical claims and view themselves more modestly as just another set of narratives.[28]

Eagleton leaves no doubt about the postmodern rejection of modernism; he personifies modernism as a defensive, manipulative tyrant

with a messiah complex. For all of its faults, modernism at least contributed to significant scientific progress, but Eagleton, far from acknowledging this, considers modernism a "nightmare." Reason, the
Enlightenment ideal, he says, is "manipulative," and the hope of a unified theory of everything is a "fetish." Even science is dismissed as "just
another set of narratives."

Contrasts between modernism and postmodernism abound. Ihab
Hassan gives these examples:

- Modernism emphasizes purpose and design; postmodernism
  emphasizes play and chance.
- Modernism seeks a hierarchy; postmodernism cultivates anarchy.
- Modernists value the type; postmodernists value the mutant.
- Modernism pursues the underlying meaning of the universe expressed in language; postmodernism rejects both a discoverable
  meaning of the universe and "meaning" in language.[29]

Millard Erickson also summarized the features of modernism and
postmodernism. Contrasts between the two are evident when his lists
are placed side by side. In the chart below, additional aspects of
postmodernism have been added to better illustrate the contrasts. Such
a chart is helpful, but it has inherent limitations. It is virtually impossible
to depict complex dialectics and developments as simple polarities.

Modernism	Postmodernism
1. *Naturalism.*	1. *New Relativism.*[30] We know nothing of upper-storey "truth." "Knowledge" of nature is also suspect because it is socially conditioned.
2. *Humanism.* The human is the end of reality rather than the means to serve a higher being.	2. *Pluralism.* There are many ways to define what is "human," and each is culturally constructed.

3. *The scientific method.* Knowledge is good and can be attained by humans; the best method for attaining it is the scientific method.

4. *Reductionism.* The scientific method, with its objectivity and passivity, came to be regarded as the only method of knowing.

5. *Progress.* Humans are attaining knowledge and overcoming problems.

6. *Nature.* It is dynamic and developing through the processes of evolution.

7. *Certainty.* Since knowledge is objective, we can be confident that we can attain it by objective means.

8. *Determinism.* What happens in the universe—physical phenomena and human behavior—are effects that result from fixed causes.

9. *Individualism.* Individuals can discover truth by freeing themselves from "the conditioning particularities of their own time and place."

10. *Antiauthoritarianism.* The individual is the final arbiter of truth; externally imposed authority must be subjected to scrutiny.

3. *Intuition.* The scientific method is called into question; truth can be discovered through other means. The goodness of knowledge is also questioned.

4. *Subjectivism.* Knowledge is not objective, and the knower is active, not passive, engaged, not detached, in the knowing process.

5. *Despair.* The knowledge explosion has not resulted in progressing beyond human problems, as was shown by the twentieth century.

6. *Advocacy Scholarship.* Scientific "truth" is a language game that advances a particular ideological agenda.

7. *Uncertainty.* Foundationalism, or belief in first principles, has been abandoned.

8. *Denial of unified field.* All-inclusive systems of explanation are impossible and should be abandoned.

9. *Community-based knowledge.* Truth is determined by and for the community.

10. *Antifoundationalism.* Systems, or "authorities" are suspect insofar as they manipulate language to create "totalizing discourses."

Literary Deconstruction

The term *postmodernism* can be found as early as the 1930s, and it was used about thirty years later to refer to new forms in art and architecture. Hence, Charles Jencks could date the symbolic end of modernism and the transition to postmodernism to 3:32 P.M. on July 15, 1972, when the Pruitt-Igoe housing development in St. Louis (a prize-winning example of modern architecture) was imploded by demolition workers.[31] Certainly, postmodernism is reflected in architecture and other cultural artifacts. However, this mood-become-movement began to pick up cultural steam under the influence of the literary theory of deconstruction. Deconstruction arose as an extension of the literary theory called *structuralism*. Structuralists maintain that the structure, or form, of a literary composition reflects the structure of the society in which the composition was produced. The methods of verbal communication are determined by the societies in which those methods are constructed. The structures of societies are reflected in their literary products. In addition to the structure, the meaning of the text is determined culturally. A particular culture has a way of understanding reality, and that way is reflected in the structures of language. Meaning, therefore, is determined culturally. Structuralists also "contend that all societies and cultures possess a common, invariant structure."[32]

Poststructuralism agrees with each of these theses except the last. Instead of structures of meaning being culturally standard, or "invariant," poststructuralists emphasize that meanings, or structures, may be determined by cultures *or* by individuals. Therefore, "there are as many meanings of the text as there are readers. For that matter, there are as many meanings as there are readings, as there may be more than one meaning for the same reader at different readings of the same text."[33]

Although meaning is determined by individuals (which leads to the method of interpretation called "reader-response"), postmodernists emphasize that individuals cannot be separated from their cultural communities. Therefore, in some sense, meaning is community-derived, or culture defined. Postmodernists contend that language is a cultural creation and that language has no inherent meaning beyond what is socially constructed, and so, socially or politically determined. There is no objective absolute interpretation if individual readers and their cultures assign meaning. Language, therefore, does not *reveal* meaning as much as it *constructs* meaning.

With this foundational argument, *deconstructionism* follows the reasoning of both *structuralism* and *poststructuralism*. Deconstructionists assume that language and meaning are social constructs without a single objective interpretation. The structure of society is reflected in the structure of language. Deconstructionists, however, go on to assert that the status quo in each society expresses its power as it assigns meaning to language, and these societal power structures are inherently oppressive. Language is a tool of power and oppression. The goal of deconstruction is to undermine this power by taking apart the process of meaning-making. By *deconstructing* texts, one can disrupt this abusive power base. Deconstructionists approach a text not to find out what it objectively means, but to unveil the ideas that are being covered up and divest the text of any power to oppress.

Postmodern deconstructionists view literary creations, as well as nonverbal cultural artifacts, as constructions of society. Just as language constructs meaning, so do other aspects of culture—fashion, means of transportation, architectural styles, and art forms of all sorts. All aspects of culture can and should be deconstructed. This includes products of the historical and scientific disciplines. "Facts" are merely narratives or stories to be deconstructed. Claims of objective truth are dismissed as oppressive structures of control. In fact, all "truth" is merely a construction of language. For example, figures from history who have been set apart as heroic, can be remade into villains. A classic example in North America in recent years was the reinterpretation of the life of explorer Christopher Columbus. Postmodernists believe that Columbus only became a hero in the first place because the white male establishment manipulated language to give him a heroic persona. This interpretation served their purposes in controlling society. Similarly, screen adaptations of historical events may engage in revisionist history without being regarded as pure fiction. The "real" history was only a narrative constructed by those in power anyway. A new historical reality can be framed for a new society with a different set of values.

In the same way, scientific facts can also be reconstructed to take away the advantage of those who have in the past played a linguistic power game. "Scientists who formulate 'laws' are attempting to impose human political power on the natural order. . . . The so-called scientific objectivity and all of Western science's technological achievements are 'texts' that mask the male desire to subjugate, exploit, and sexually abuse 'Mother Nature.'"[34]

Since science is a text that can be deconstructed as just one more agent of an oppressive scientific guild, postmodernists feel free to reconstruct their own science "narrative" to fit their own ideology. This is why university curricula have come to include such courses as "Feminist Botany" and "Feminist Approaches to History."[35] If every aspect of society is merely a language construction to promote the ideology of the establishment, postmodernists believe that they can construct a language structure to advocate their own ideology. "Scholarship" is reduced to rhetorical manipulation.

Deconstructing Reality

Just as postmodernists deconstruct the "narratives" of history and science, they also reject the possibility that a "metanarrative" can exist. *Metanarrative* is a term coined by postmodernists to refer to a grand narrative, or interpretation that has universal application. Synonyms sometimes used for metanarratives are *totalizing discourses* or *worldviews*. The grand story of the Bible as regarded by historical Christianity is an example of a metanarrative. Such metanarratives serve as explanations of reality—of God, man, and the world. They are the philosophical foundations upon which we base our lives—our worldview. However, postmodernism rejects the very notion of such totalizing foundations. There is no universal foundation, only local foundations defined by the community in which we participate. Patricia Waugh expressed it this way:

Counter-Enlightenment, of course, is as old as Enlightenment itself, but whereas in the past (in Romantic thought, for example), the critique of reason was accompanied by an alternative foundationalism (of the Imagination), Postmodernism tends to claim an abandonment of all metanarratives which could legitimate foundations of truth. And more than this, it claims that we neither need them, nor are they any longer desirable.[36]

During the age of modernism, a worldview might be shown to be inadequate and was replaced by another worldview. However, postmodernism dismisses the very idea of a worldview that makes any claim to represent the true nature of things. Postmodernism is a worldview that rejects the possibility of a worldview. In fact, McGrath believes that this "deliberate and systematic abandonment of centralizing narratives" is postmodernism's "leading general feature."[37] This is radical relativism, the central characteristic of postmodernism that underlies every other facet.

The mood of postmodernism—generally pessimistic, communal, and diverse—is a fascinating study. However, our discussion will be limited to *relativism* and *pluralism* as the two pervasive themes that have significant implications for both Christians and the culture at large. Later we will consider the effects of postmodern deconstructionism on biblical interpretation (see pp. 70–73).

Relativism

At the outset, we must be certain to distinguish *relativism* from Albert Einstein's theory of *relativity*, a scientific theory that seeks to prove that all motion is relative to a reference point. It is entirely different to say that *everything* is relative, which is the premise of *relativism*. According to relativism, there are no absolute truths. We may have values, but no one ultimate, absolute value. According to this worldview, each person follows a personal values system that works for the individual. Each person's system is equally "right," so none can be used to contradict another person's system. Christianity is great if it works for the Christian, and Islam is just as valid if one chooses to be Muslim. Obviously, this sets up a conflict between the relativist and the Bible's affirmation that only one true God exists, and He has given laws that are immutable and universally applicable.

Modernism contains a current of relativism, but relativism pervades postmodernism. Stanley Grenz identifies "the central dictum of postmodern philosophy: 'All is difference.' This view sweeps away the 'uni' of the 'universe' sought by the Enlightenment project. It abandons the quest for a unified grasp of objective reality. It asserts that the world has no center, only differing viewpoints and perspectives. . . . In the end, the postmodern world is merely an arena of 'dueling texts.'"[38]

For the postmodernist, objective truth does not exist, so all that is left is deconstructive interpretation of texts. Further, whereas modernism defined interpretation as the work of an individual, postmodernism is more communal. "Truth" becomes "our truth," the truth of the community with which one identifies. The result is feminist truth, African-American truth, Eurocentric truth, Native American truth, and California surfer truth. This is the ideological basis for advocacy science and revisionist history. The possibility of finding what Francis Schaeffer called "true truth" has been abandoned. All that is left is community truth: One can only say, "This is what I believe is true as a Southern-U.S., Caucasian, babyboomer, heterosexual, Christian, married male." "My truth" is necessarily different from "your truth" if you belong to another group. With "my truth" in tow, each group promotes its own community agenda. Of course, the deconstructionist view is that "truth" is never really the issue when it comes to promoting the community agenda. The issue is power. The goal is for my marginalized group to be empowered by our "truth." The empowering truth was not discovered by amassing objective evidence. It developed through cultural pressure. It is not promoted by rational argument but by the rhetoric of power. This is relativism with an attitude. Gene Edward Veith Jr. observes, "The traditional academic world operated by reason, study, and research; postmodernist academia is governed by ideological agendas, political correctness, and power struggles."[39]

Is relativism common in our culture? Remember the Barna Research Group survey finding that only 32 percent of those who described themselves as born again Christians were willing to state that they believe in moral absolutes. In another survey of the general population, only 22 percent of adults disagreed with the statement that truth is always relative to the person and their situation. Among American teens, the picture is worse—only 6 percent said moral truth is absolute, and 83 percent said that moral truth depends upon the circumstances.[40]

Postmodern relativism, then, is not just a conclusion reached by academics who are infatuated with a particular brand of literary criticism. It is influencing the way the general populace thinks about everything. What is causing this wholesale adoption of relativism? Surely there are many contributing factors, including the numbing effect of a public education system that formally eschews any absolute values (except for the absolute that there are no absolutes), the ascendancy of a newly defined "tolerance" that celebrates even the most harmful and vacuous notion as "okay," the influence of liberal and neo-orthodox theology in many churches where no absolutes are ever preached or taught, and the commercial promotion of an entitlement mentality that encourages consumers to make self desires the center of their lives instead of the external authority of God and His Word.

The primary cultural vehicle for conveying relativism to the general populace is television. Televisions are ubiquitous, and satellite and cable technology advances multiply the influence in at least two ways. First, as Neil Postman documented, *television is a medium of entertainment, not truth.* The whole point of television is to entertain, not to inform. Therefore, even information-based programs must be entertaining, or the public will conclude that the content communicated just doesn't matter. Television has helped to create an insatiable appetite for entertainment and a corresponding lack of hunger for truth. Postman contends that in a television-saturated, entertainment-obsessed culture, the distinction between truth and myth does not matter unless it is entertaining.[41] And if the distinction between truth and myth does not matter, the result is relativism.

Second, television contributes to the atmosphere of relativism by blurring the line between truth and fiction. Consider a typical evening of television programming:

> The news broadcast is followed by a plethora of prime-time programs that seek to attract and hold an audience by focusing on action, scandal, violence, and sex. The evening's sitcoms and dramas seem to be invested with the same weight as the earlier news stories. In this manner, television blurs the line between truth and fiction, between the truly earth-shattering and the trivial. And as though a single channel's programming did not supply the viewer with enough discordant images, contemporary television offers the viewer dozens—soon to be hundreds—of different channels.[42]

Television does not differentiate between truth and fiction. In fact, it has the effect of presenting them as identical—news is made to be entertaining and fiction is made to be realistic. This, too, fosters the philosophy of relativism.

Relativism also poses a new set of problems for the legal system, and these problems are being encountered every day in the courtrooms of our country. In order to enact and enforce laws that restrain undesirable behavior, it must be believed that some actions are right and others are wrong. But once the consensus of absolutism has been lost, how can we pass and enforce laws? Every law or rule has some sort of moral principle behind it. If every idea of morality is equal, whose morality do we use? We must resort to what Francis Schaeffer called "arbitrary absolutes,"[43] which for a Christian is a contradiction in terms.

Allan Bloom has called attention to the pervasive presence of relativism in today's universities in *The Closing of the American Mind*. Bloom contends that the one absolute truth that every college student in America confronts is that there are no absolutes.[44] In this environment, evangelism becomes the ultimate sin because it suggests that another person's values are less adequate, or less true, than those of the evangelist. The presupposition of evangelism is that one way to God is right while all other ways to view reality are wrong. This is unacceptable to a relativist.

Pluralism

Pluralism is variously defined. D. A. Carson, for example, in *The Gagging of God*, refers to three kinds of pluralism:

1. *empirical pluralism*, which simply acknowledges the fact of plurality, or diversity.
2. *cherished pluralism*, which refers to the opinion that the diversity is a good thing. Carson suggests that God Himself likes racial and cultural diversity, which is why He made us all so different.
3. *philosophical* or *hermeneutical pluralism*. In one way of defining these terms, the first two sorts of pluralism may be properly called "plurality." In contrast, philosophical pluralism is the idea that "any notion that a particular ideological or religious claim is intrinsically superior to another is *necessarily* wrong. . . . No religion has the right to pronounce itself right or true, and the others false, or even . . . relatively inferior."[45]

Philosophical pluralism is the inevitable result of postmodern relativism. As cultural analyst Os Guinness has written,

There is no truth, only truths. There is no grand reason, only reasons. There is no privileged civilization (or culture, beliefs, norms, and styles), only a multiplicity of cultures, beliefs, periods, and styles. There is no universal justice, only interests and the competition of interest groups. There is no grand narrative of human progress, only countless stories of where people and their cultures are now.[46]

Truth unites individuals and groups. Relativism and community-defined "truth" divide people. Even when people disagree about the truth, they still share common philosophical ground if they at least can agree that truth *exists*. When the quest for truth is abandoned, every viewpoint, however spurious, is legitimized, so there is no reason to search for consensus under the banner of *the truth*. The result is a plurality of communities, grouped together according to the "truth" of each sub-culture.

Plurality is a fact of life in a mosaic culture of ideologies and religions. What makes *plurality* into *pluralism* is the cultural doctrine that each community's ideology or religion is equally legitimate, or "true." This doctrine is possible in a climate of relativism. When all connections to absolutism are severed, no abiding principles transcend our experience or opinion. Therefore, no idea or system of morality can lay claim to a higher authority. All philosophies are on equal ground, so they should all be given equal validity. Thus the reality of *plurality* becomes the doctrine of *pluralism*. No unifying principle exists, so no unity is possible. In terms United States citizens can relate to, the Latin national motto, *E pluribus unum* ("Out of many, one") has become *E pluribus plurus* ("out of many, many").

This has led Grenz to describe the postmodern ethos as "centerlessness."

> The architects of modernity sought to design the one perfect human society in which peace, justice, and love would reign— utopia. Postmoderns no longer dream of utopia. In its place they can offer only the incommensurable diversity of the postmodern heterotopia, the "multiverse" that has replaced the universe of the modern quest.[47]

Canadian, U.K., and U.S. societies always have been diverse. But postmodernism is willing to take the step from empirical and cherished pluralism to philosophical pluralism. No longer does *plurality* merely describe our social and racial diversity, with many groups bound together and seeking unity. Instead, *pluralism* is the inevitable expression of the fact that each community creates its own reality, each "reality" being equally legitimate.

While this equal legitimacy is a logical corollary of relativistic pluralism, one religion is not allowed equal status—Christianity. As chapter 4 will show, those who profess Christ are the only acceptable targets of strident religious polemic by those in the mainstream culture. For example, Tom DeLay of Texas, a member of the United States House of Representatives, was criticized for making the following statement at the First Baptist Church of Pearland, Texas:

> Christianity offers the only viable, reasonable, definitive answer to the questions of "Where did I come from?" "Why am I here?" "Where am I going?" "Does life have any meaningful purpose?" Only Christianity offers a comprehensive worldview that covers all areas of life and thought, every aspect of creation.[48]

One might think that in an atmosphere of postmodern pluralism, such a statement would be perfectly acceptable as a statement of personal faith on the part of an adherent of one particular religion. Others do not have to believe it, but it is certainly legitimate for DeLay to say it if *he* believes it. It is, in postmodern terms, "his truth." Enter Barry Lynn, executive director of Americans United for Separation of Church and State. Lynn charged that Delay's comments indicate that the congressman "lacks appreciation for the religious pluralism" of the United States. Actually, it is Mr. Lynn who lacks *understanding* of the *meaning* of religious pluralism. According to any of the definitions above, pluralism allows for an individual to believe and say what DeLay believes and said. Perhaps Mr. Lynn knows the definition of religious pluralism but has decided to exclude Christianity from having an equal voice in the public square. Unfortunately, the rules of the pluralism game are not fairly applied in Western culture. Since Lynn's quibble with Congressman DeLay stems partly from the fact that DeLay is an elected official, Lynn's comments also reveal a gross misapplication of the idea of separation of church and state, an issue I will address in chapter 5.

Postmodernism and Biblical Studies

In order to understand the ways in which postmodernism intersects with the study of the Bible, one must first appreciate the changes that postmodernism has produced with regard to reading in general. Perhaps these changes are best summarized by Kevin Vanhoozer's statement: "The history of literary criticism is one of successive preoccupation with author, text, and reader, respectively."[49] Obviously, these developments overlap. That is to say, many people, including me, still believe that the author and text are central to discovering a text's acceptable meaning. Nevertheless, describing such successive stages is valid, and is a common way of describing the development of literary criticism *per se*. In the first stage, the task of interpretation seeks to uncover authorial intent—the text means what the author intended it to mean.

With the advent of the "New Criticism," authorial intent began to be eclipsed by the text. The "literary turn," as it is often called, was toward the text itself as the locus of meaning, not the intention or mind of the author. The text was seen as a cultural artifact, and its embedded linguistic structures have "a life of their own," so to speak. The text is a meaning-bearer independent of the author. Someone asked a musician what he meant by the lyrics to a song he had written. He responded by merely repeating the lyrics. The musician was demonstrating his knowledge and acceptance of the idea that meaning resides in the text, not in the author. The text means what it means. An attempted explanation only becomes another "text" that has its own meaning.

The next shift in literary criticism was perhaps inevitable. If the meaning of a text is not determined by authorial intent but is located in the text itself, then every reader becomes competent to determine his or her own meaning. In fact, the author's interpretation of the text is no more or less legitimate than any reader's interpretation. Thus, the final stage in literary criticism is the turn to the reader (or to the "subject," as the reader often is called). A text's meaning is not determined by the author or by the text alone, but by the reader's experience of the text. Granted, the interplay between text and reader is defined variously,[50] but the emphasis here is on the reader as the locus, or creator, of meaning. This broad and diverse method is often called "reader-response criticism." According to one description, reader-response critics "deny that texts make meaning; rather, they affirm that readers make meaning."[51]

With reader-response criticism and deconstruction, one encounters ways of reading that may be properly described as postmodern. When it is recalled that the Bible is a work of literature and that many interpreters view it as *merely* literature, it may be seen that a postmodern reading of the Bible can introduce all sorts of mischief into the process of biblical interpretation. When reading the Bible with a postmodern mindset, "the biblical text is an interpretive battlefield in which power is sought by all and truth is claimed by everyone."[52] An advocate of postmodern biblical interpretation, Fernando F. Segovia describes a postmodern world "in which readers become as important as texts and in which models and reconstructions are regarded as constructions; a world in which there is no master narrative but many narratives in competition and no Jerusalem but many Jerusalems."[53] One begins to see why Grenz identifies postmodernism's motto as "All is difference."

Outside the evangelical subculture of Christianity (and sometimes inside), the mood and mindset of postmodernism profoundly affect the interpretation of the Bible. Perhaps the implications of postmodernism can be seen so clearly in the discipline of biblical criticism because "the way individuals and communities interpret the Bible is arguably the most important barometer of larger intellectual and cultural trends."[54] In order to get a glimpse of the permutations that postmodernism stimulates in the study of the Bible, we need only to superimpose a grid of the primary features of postmodern thought over our approach to the Bible. In other words, how will a postmodern reading influence our conclusions about meaning in a Bible text? Remember that this way of reading is pessimistic about ultimate truth. It assumes that the meaning (or meanings) of a text is determined by the reader, not the author or even the text. It dismisses claims of truth as attempts to control, denying the existence of metanarratives. It rejects the existence of any worldview that claims to represent the true nature of things. Obviously, there are far-reaching consequences to such assumptions, whatever Bible text is in view.

While thinking of the task of interpreting the Bible, consider David Harvey's description of Jacques Derrida's approach to postmodern interpretation:

> Minimizing the authority of the cultural producer [author] creates the opportunity for popular participation and democratic determinations of cultural values. . . . The cultural producer merely creates raw materials (fragments and elements), leaving it open to consumers to recombine those elements in any way they wish. The effect is to break (deconstruct) the power of the author to impose meanings or offer a continuous narrative. Each cited element, says Derrida, "breaks the continuity or linearity of the discourse and leads necessarily to a double reading."[55]

"Double reading" is technically inaccurate here, for a postmodern process inevitably leads to multiple "readings." But what Harvey is getting at is that one meaning is the result of following the continuity of the author's (the cultural producer's) narrative; at least one other meaning results from dismantling the text into its constituent parts and recombining the fragments into whatever form the reader (as "consumer") chooses. The result is a construction of meaning built according to the ideology of the reader, with no resemblance to the intention of the author, who conveniently does not exist in postmodern deconstruction.

An example of such a dismantling and reconstruction of a biblical text is Mieke Bal's interpretation of the story of Samson (Judges 13–16). Bal assigns meanings to the constituent parts of the story that could not have occurred to anyone who lived before the twentieth century. Thus, the riddle that Samson presents to the Philistines symbolizes sexual maturity, the honey in the lion is also a symbol of sex, and its sweetness is related to lust. The cutting of the hair represents castration, which is why middle-age men fear their receding hairlines. The Nazarite vow that forbade the cutting of hair was a formalization of this fear of castration. The pillars of the Philistine temple represent his mother's thighs, and Samson pushes against them to enlarge the birth canal in order to reverse the pain of childbirth.[56] To use Harvey's terms, Bal has taken the raw materials of the story, recombined them in the way she wished, and constructed her own meaning, thus breaking the power of the author to impose meaning.

Such examples of postmodern biblical criticism from various ideological perspectives could be multiplied *ad nauseum*. Suffice it to say that, no, we're not in Kansas anymore.

CHAPTER 3

The Alice Syndrome: Who Are We?

Prepare your minds for action, keep sober in spirit, fix your hope completely on the grace to be brought to you at the revelation of Jesus Christ. As obedient children, do not be conformed to the former lusts which were yours in your ignorance, but like the Holy One who called you, be holy yourselves also in all your behavior.
—*1 Peter 1:13–15*

To ignore the culture is to risk irrelevance; to accept the culture uncritically is to risk syncretism and unfaithfulness. Every age has had its eager-to-please liberal theologians who have tried to reinterpret Christianity according to the latest intellectual and cultural fashion. . . . But orthodox Christians have also lived in every age, confessing their faith in Jesus Christ. . . . They were part of their culture. . . . Yet they also countered their culture, proclaiming God's law and gospel to society's very inadequacies and points of need."[1]
—*Gene Edward Veith Jr.*

The premise of Lewis Carroll's *Alice's Adventures in Wonderland* is similar to that of L. Frank Baum in his stories of Dorothy and her friends in the land of Oz. In Carroll's fantasy story, Alice is accidentally transported to a land of fantasy and wonder. She shrinks to a tiny size, then expands to a very large size, then small, large, and small again. She then encounters a caterpillar that asks her, "Who are you?" Alice answers, "I—I hardly know, sir, just at present—at least I know who I *was* when I got up this morning, but I think I must have been changed several times since then. . . . I can't explain myself, I'm afraid, sir, because I'm not myself, you see."

The fact that we, like Dorothy, are not in Kansas anymore is not our most serious problem. With a little observation, we can locate where we are on the philosophical map. Even if our surroundings are hostile to our beliefs (wicked witch and all), we can thrive. We should remember that the earliest Christians also found themselves in a culture permeated with immorality and idolatry. Their only leverage to change it was the power of the gospel. The greater problem is not that we, like Dorothy, are in a culture in which everything is foreign to us; it is that we, like Alice, forget who we are. When that happens, we Christians begin to feel right at home in a land that is *not* home. We adopt the thinking patterns and lifestyle choices of the people around us, losing touch with our different nature as Christ-followers. We may carry the title *Christian* and observe the formal rituals identified with Christianity, but our faith is eviscerated of its more scandalous tenets and radically new lifestyle.

The influence of the surrounding philosophies may be seen in the lives of individual Christians and the decisions of organized churches. One night I received a call from a Christian friend in another city. She and her husband were wondering whether they should remain in the church where they were members. It had been proven that their pastor had committed adultery with at least two women. The deacons were preparing to sever the church-pastor relationship as compassionately and as quickly as possible. However, the pastor was popular, and many in the church believed that the gracious thing would be to allow him to continue as pastor. In the meeting where this issue was being discussed, someone stood and said he wanted to read the biblical qualifications for pastors found in 1 Timothy 3:1–7, which includes the words "above reproach, the husband of one wife, temperate, prudent, respectable." When he announced that he wanted to read this passage that makes the term "adulterous pastor" an oxymoron, some of the people groaned audibly and shook their heads. They *really* didn't want that passage of Scripture to be read. When my friend asked whether her family should stay in the church, I told her that I am not the Holy Spirit and could not tell her if she should stay as a positive influence or give up and leave. However, I added that it would be exceedingly difficult for me and my family to remain in a church in which any portion of the Word of God was not welcome, and in which the biblical qualifications for spiritual leaders were willfully disregarded. Evidently, some of the people in that church had been more influenced by the relativism of the culture than by the instructions of the Bible. In short, these Christians had forgotten who they are. My prayer is that the amnesia was temporary.

This chapter will look more closely at the way in which a biblical worldview defines who we are in relation to the culture in which we live. On a daily basis we rub shoulders with these philosophies. If we choose to accept the biblical worldview, how will we think and live differently from those around us? If we desire to be transformed by the renewing of our minds (Rom. 12:2), what form will this transformation take? If our intent is to gird our minds for action in order that we may be holy (1 Peter 1:13–16), what sort of action will we take and how will our holiness be expressed? What characteristics will brand us as strangers in this foreign land? I will describe five contrasts between Christians and the culture.

Christians Are Supernaturalists

Before contrasting Christianity with naturalism, we should point out that naturalism is not the same as the study of nature. Neither historic Christianity nor the Bible opposes scientific investigation. In fact, work in the natural sciences is part of the dominion over the earth commanded in Genesis 2. Many Christian scientists have seen their vocation as a divine calling. However, the philosophy of naturalism excludes the possibility, or rationality, of the divine, or of anything spiritual. Conflicts between the biblical worldview and naturalism are abundant and immediately evident.

First, *naturalism denies the existence of spiritual realities.* The biblical assertion that "God is spirit" (John 4:24) contradicts the claims of naturalism in two ways: (1) "God *is.*" He exists. Also, "God is *spirit.*" He is spiritual, not material, in being. The Bible clearly teaches that something other than the material world exists. In fact, a whole spiritual world stands outside of what can be observed or explained by the scientific method. The Bible frequently refers to angels as the messengers of God, and to "the spiritual forces of wickedness in the heavenly places" (Eph. 6:12). Christians are urged to "test the spirits to see whether they are from God" (1 John 4:1). People experience life within the context of nature, but they are not mere flesh and neural responses. Humans are essentially spiritual beings (1 Thess. 5:23).

Second, *naturalism excludes the possibility of the special creation of nature by God.* The Bible teaches that God created all that is. In contrast, the claim of naturalism is that life began by the mechanistic interaction of matter guided only by chance and natural laws. Not usually addressed by a naturalist is the question, "From whence came the natural laws?" Conspicuously missing from naturalistic theories of the origin of the universe is any First Cause, a Designer, or Creator. Those who hold to these theories replace the one, true, personal God with the "god" of macroevolutionary chance.

Third, *naturalism is not rational.* This statement, of course, contradicts naturalism's claim of rationality. However, a question that is being asked regularly today is, "Is it rational to believe in a design without a designer?"[2] Look at this book that you are now reading. Is it reasonable to conclude that it evolved by chance, or was it designed and constructed by trained designers, printers, and binders with a purpose in mind? Consider also the well-known statues on Easter Island. They are standing stones in the shape of human heads. No one is sure how they were made or who put them there. As far as I know, no one has ever proposed that they *evolved* into their present form. Why not? They have a design, and design does not occur randomly, or by chance; it is the result of intelligence and intention. The only logical conclusion is that there was a designer; someone made them.

Such obvious products of endeavor, like this book or the statues on

Easter Island, are the result of human intelligence, but what is the origin of human intelligence? The human brain is perhaps the most complex, intricate structure in the universe. Is it reasonable to believe that this complicated and orderly design came into existence without a designer? It's just as reasonable to believe that a wristwatch is the result of metal particles accidentally coming together. That sort of thing does not happen. Those who believe this world did not "just happen" are necessarily supernaturalists, not naturalists. Behind the design is a Designer who acted supernaturally to create the design. The Bible teaches that this Designer is God. "In the beginning God created the heavens and the earth" (Gen. 1:1). God is other than nature. He acted upon nature, and has existence prior to nature. If God is not part of nature, nature is not all that exists. Nature is not a closed system. And if God necessarily existed before nature in order to act upon its beginning, nature has not always existed. Each biblical assertion about creation opposes naturalism.

Fourth, *no consistent naturalist can believe the Bible and the fundamental truths of Christianity, so any evidence for Christianity is proof against naturalism.* It is outside the scope of this volume to lay out reasons why Christians can be rational as supernaturalists. They are not outside reason when they believe that the Bible truthfully records that at points in human history, God broke in from outside and acted upon the natural order. God caused ten plagues in Egypt, parted the Red Sea, caused an edible food substance to form on the ground, healed the sick, raised the dead, incarnated Himself in Jesus of Nazareth, and rose from the dead after crucifixion. Scripture depicts what really occurred in time-space reality, and according to Scripture, nature is not a closed system; it is open to the intervention of God.

Fifth, *naturalists are not consistent.* They are not true to their principles that nature is all that exists and beliefs must be based only on material evidence. Some scientific hypotheses that are dear to naturalists have never been supported by experimentation, but they cling to them anyway. Certainly the theory of macroevolution still awaits archaeological verification. An example of unverified belief involves the view among some scientists that life exists or once existed on the planet Mars. In

1996, scientists announced that a rock found in Antarctica was a chunk of Mars. Further, it contained microbe fossils that virtually proved the existence of life on Mars. However, about eighteen months later, in January 1998, those who studied the rock concluded that the initial studies had misinterpreted the data. Though some apologized for this mistake, others did not change their hypothesis, even though they now had no evidence on which to base it. One U.S. scientist for the National Aeronautics and Space Administration (NASA) said that none of the evidence "changes our original hypotheses. It doesn't shake our belief one bit."[3] The use of the word "belief" in the context of a frank acknowledgment of a lack of evidence indicates that this opinion is hardly based on the hard data that is supposed to characterize naturalistic science. This is belief *in spite of* the facts, not *because of* them. This is precisely the sort of belief-without-evidence that naturalists accuse supernaturalists of irrationally promoting.

In contrast with inconsistent naturalism, orthodox Christianity has always insisted on the accuracy of its assertions. Christianity, in fact, is a religion that is based upon historical events that are verifiable by conventional methods of substantiation. The events described in the Bible are not mythic; they are historical. The God of the Bible has acted in space and time. Events in the life of Jesus—His life, teaching, death, and resurrection—are replete with documentation. The earliest Christians knew that the truth of their faith rested upon the historical authenticity of such events. Paul writes, "If Christ has not been raised, then our preaching is vain, your faith also is vain" (1 Cor. 15:14). Far from leaving this issue unresolved, however, Paul reminds his readers of the historical evidence for the resurrection. Christ "was raised on the third day according to the Scriptures" (v. 3). Paul appeals to the eyewitness evidence that "He appeared to Cephas, then to the twelve. After that He appeared to more than five hundred brethren at one time, most of whom remain until now" (vv. 5–6). Paul was informing the first century recipients of his letter that if they had doubts about the reality of the resurrection, they need only speak with one of the many eyewitnesses of the resurrected Jesus.

The apostle John, an eyewitness to the life of Jesus who recorded the events of His life in the Gospel of John, also states that Christian faith is no mere speculation or wishful thinking. Instead, "What was from the beginning, what we have heard, what we have seen with our eyes, what we have looked at and touched with our hands . . . we proclaim to you also" (1 John 1:1, 3). John knew the truth he proclaimed was real; he had seen, heard, and touched the Truth. Nothing is harder on myth than a good dose of fact. Naturalists claim their worldview is based on reality. When, however, they cling to theories that conflict with the evidence, they reveal the true nature of their belief. God is real, and His acts in history are verifiable. To believe otherwise is to believe in myth, not fact.

Sixth, it makes sense to be a supernaturalist because *there are many realities naturalism cannot explain.* Scientists cannot put love under a microscope and observe it, yet how irrational it would be to deny the existence of love. About the time we think we have realities such as altruism, worship, compassion, and kindness pinned down in a petri dish, they disappear, yet they keep popping up in the most unexpected places. The very idea of free will—decisions, good and bad—cannot be accounted for fully by natural processes. According to the Christian worldview, human beings have the capacity to make choices that are independent of (though perhaps influenced by) the forces of nature. The first example of free will comes early—the first man and woman chose to eat the forbidden fruit. Reducing such realities to chemical reactions in the brain, as pointed out above (see pp. 49–50), is inadequate, yet it is the only explanation naturalism can muster. This is why consistent naturalists are not very common. Rigid naturalism is unable to explain *why* we should live in one way and not another, and most people have some sense of moral "oughtness"— even naturalists. Though they profess naturalism as truth, they do not live as if it is true. Neither should Christians, because it's *not* true.

Christians Are Servants

Christians are servants of the living God, not hedonists who pursue self-pleasure. Jesus said the greatest commandment is to love God with all our being. In reality, Christians struggle with that. We do not always love God with all that we are. But if we are consistent Christians, the progress of our lives is toward greater love for God and less love for self. However, the opposite is true in Western culture. Emphasis on the self increased exponentially over the second half of the twentieth century. The idea that we are to be self-interested and self-loving is regarded as a fundamental, universal truth. The moral restraint of the self has been abandoned in favor of self-gratification. This outlook of self-satisfaction—what some have called the "psychology of entitlement"—now dominates the way people think. For many, God is not the object of devotion and service, but the means whereby we can get what we want. To the selfish, He is a supernatural, celestial Tool. God is rendered a servant of the self. Even many Christians live by the premise that the church and God exist to "meet my needs," and they would be shocked to find out that it is really the other way around—we exist to glorify God.

One obvious result of the mindset of self-love is the sort of advertisement that tries to convince us to buy a product because "you deserve the best. Sure it costs more, but you're worth it." They tell us that we should pamper ourselves with their product; we should buy it to be good to ourselves no matter what it costs. The only reason advertisers spend millions of dollars on this approach is that it works. When I see that kind of commercial, I think of how my grandmother's generation would have reacted to such a marketing strategy. "Pshaw! If the only reason to pay more for this brand is luxury, I'll get the less expensive kind, or maybe I can do without it altogether." Within two generations we shifted from the values of self-restraint and deferred gratification to self-love and the psychology of entitlement.

When people in a culture begin their worldview with self, not God, it affects the way they think about morality. "What is right to do is right because it makes me happy, or self-fulfilled. It may not make you happy, and if it doesn't it's not right for you." Thus, morality becomes a matter of personal preference, not an objective, absolute standard that we *ought* to follow in order to be right and moral. That is why people can hold widely divergent views on moral issues and still say to one another, "That's okay. What's right for you is different from what's right for me."

But it's not okay. When our starting point is God, not self, we are willing to recognize that God has given us an objective standard to follow in the Bible. To follow it is to be right; to disobey it is to be wrong.

The cultural adjustment of the spotlight from God to self affects the outreach of the church. How are churches to respond to the hedonism of its surrounding culture? How do lovers of God reach lovers of self? Do we go easy on the gospel and the Bible and heavy on encounter groups and self-help classes? Do we emphasize how God is going to help Christians be healthy and wealthy, but play down the sacrifice thing? A lot of churches have opted to play down words like *sin* and *repentance* too, because they are too convicting. The result of that kind of approach is a religion that feels good to its adherents and asks nothing of them. This is not a Christianity that resembles the church described in the New Testament.

Of course, the church *ought* to tell people that following Christ and obeying His Word will help them, because that is true. It will help in this life and in the life to come. God's Word gives us help, insight, and direction for our modern problems. Because of the mindset of our culture, the church is going to have to do a good job of communicating the benefits of God's Word if we are going to reach this generation with the gospel. Paul did that when he "became all things to all men, so that I may by all means save some" (1 Cor. 9:22). However, at some point we have to tell people that we are intended to love God first, not self. We who belong to Christ are not to be conformed to this world. We are to be transformed by the renewing of our minds. One of the ways in which we are to be transformed is through a change in what we love the most—not self, but God.

Christians Are Absolutists

Philosopher Richard Bernstein has written that the conflict between absolutism and relativism is "the central cultural opposition of our time."[4] A good example of the consistent application of relativism is Walter Truett Anderson's book, *Reality Isn't What It Used to Be*. Anderson, a postmodernist, divides people into two camps—objectivists and constructivists. Objectivists claim that objective truth, "true truth," is knowable. One can have a "God's eye view of nonhuman reality." Constructivists such as Anderson, on the other hand, believe that reality, or truth, is "an ever-changing social creation." Reality, according to constructivists, is constructed by cultures, or individuals within those cultures. Some individuals, according to Anderson, become creators, or entrepreneurs, of reality. These people write the "stories" of their own reality. If they don't like the plot of someone else's reality, they can try their hand at creating another and see if anyone wants to become a consumer of their version. All of us become consumers of reality, choosing which narrative of history, science, religion, or politics we prefer.[5] "Which one is true?" is not the correct question, for none of them is true in the absolute sense. All of them are "true" to the extent that they work for a segment of society. So goes the postmodern brand of relativism (see pp. 63–67).

This view of truth is impossible to reconcile with biblical Christianity. There is no way that Christians can be consistent in their thinking and remain relativists. Christians are absolutists. We believe that what God has revealed in the Scriptures is truth that is absolutely true. It is not true for some but false for others. It is not true for the moment. It is true permanently. Its truth is not malleable. It is unalterable. Dan McCartney and Charles Clayton called the postmodern biblical criticism sketched in chapter 2 (see pp. 70–73) "an exaltation of subjectivity": "The whole idea of the constant undermining of meaning also runs completely counter to the acceptance of God speaking in a Word. . . . The rejection of the idea of metaphysical truth cuts straight across biblical assumptions, which ground truth not in man, but in an absolute God."[6]

As Isaiah put it, "The grass withers, the flower fades, but the word of our God stands forever" (Isa. 40:8). Near the end of His earthly ministry, Jesus prayed for His disciples, "Sanctify them in the truth; Thy word is truth" (John 17:17). Jesus also said, "If you continue in

My word, then you are truly disciples of Mine; and you will know the truth, and the truth will make you free" (8:31–32). Furthermore, Jesus said of Himself, "I am the way, and the truth, and the life" (14:6a). The use of the definite article (*the* truth) indicates that Christ did not come to be *one* truth among many. Nor can it be claimed that Jesus as the truth and God's Word as the truth were socially constructed. Indeed, Jesus was countercultural. Christianity is the religion of the One who said He is the truth; to abdicate truth is to abdicate Christianity.

"No problem," says the postmodernist, "Jesus and his word are truth for the Christian subculture, but not for everyone." This is precisely where the rub has come throughout the history of Christianity. Early Christians were not burned at the stake because they were followers of Jesus. They were executed because they would worship nothing and no one else, and they proclaimed Jesus as the *only* way to be right with God—absolute truth. Postmodernists regularly inveigh against "the Enlightenment project." While we should appreciate the enormous impact of the Enlightenment, we must also remind ourselves that the concept of absolute truth did not take its maiden voyage in the seventeenth and eighteenth centuries. Postmodernists must answer to all of the history of human thought before the Enlightenment as well.

The result of the relativistic climate is that tolerance has been exalted over truth. Tolerance, of course, has value, as long as it is defined as the ability to coexist with and love those who are different from us. In fact, Christians could use a heavy dose of that kind of tolerance. But that is not the way tolerance is being defined today.

The popular definition of tolerance is to be open-minded enough to accept any idea or philosophy as correct as long as someone wants to believe it. The converse is also true: *To believe in any absolute truth or to state disagreement with any idea or practice is to be intolerant.* Such a definition of tolerance flourishes in an environment of relativism.

Our culture lives according to the fantasy that tolerance and relativism lead to freedom, and absolute truth leads to narrow parochialism and religious bondage. Real life shows just the opposite. To be independent from God and His truth is to be in slavery to the world, the flesh, and the Devil. Jesus had in mind this slavery dynamic when he said, "Everyone who commits sin is the slave of sin" (John 8:34). The freedom that is outside of Christ is cheap and artificial. It is freedom from Christ's love and rule but it also is bondage to other malevolent masters. Better to choose one's master wisely, as Jesus explained, "So if the Son makes you free, you will be free indeed" (v. 36). Followers of Jesus know this freedom. They also know that freedom is based on truth, not someone's fantasy passed off as truth.

Postmodern relativism is indeed fantasy, and it will not survive in the real world, which is where most people (except professional philosophers and show business performers) have to live. Consider one example. D. A. Carson was teaching a class on hermeneutics in which he was making the point that truth is objective and knowable, and absolute truth is possible. One student was unconvinced, and stated as much in class. Then, in Carson's words,

> I joyfully exclaimed, "Ah, now I think I see what you are saying. You are using delicious irony to affirm the objectivity of truth." The lady was not amused. "That is exactly what I am *not* saying," she protested with some heat, and she laid out her position again. I clasped my hands in enthusiasm and told her how delighted I was to find someone using irony so cleverly in order to affirm the possibility of objective knowledge. Her answer was more heated, but along the same lines as her first reply. I believe she also accused me of twisting what she was saying. . . .
>
> When she finally cooled down, I said, rather quietly, "But this is how I am reading you. . . . You are a deconstructionist," I told her, "but you expect me to interpret *your* words aright. More precisely, you are upset because I seem to be divorcing the meaning I claim to see in your words from your intent. Thus, implicitly you affirm the link between text and authorial intent. I have never read a deconstructionist who would be pleased if a reviewer misinterpreted his or her work: thus *in practice* deconstructionists implicitly link their own texts with their own intentions. I simply want the same courtesy extended to Paul."[7]

As Carson demonstrated, postmodern relativism simply cannot apply its pretense of the deconstruction of truth consistently. Imagining that true truth does not exist but is merely a socially constructed power play just doesn't work in the real world. Sometimes it doesn't even work in a classroom.

The fact is that absolute precision, or correctness, is not only possible, it is expected all the time. In countless contexts, only absolute truth will suffice and relativism is insufficient. Alister McGrath illustrated that giving tolerance and openness greater weight than truth "is, quite simply, a mark of intellectual shallowness and moral irresponsibility":

> If I were to insist that the American Declaration of Independence took place in 1789, despite all the evidence which unequivocally points to the year 1776, I could expect no commendations for maintaining my intellectual freedom or personal integrity; nor could I expect to receive tolerance from my fellow historians. The much-vaunted virtue of academic "openness" would be rendered ridiculous were it to allow me to be taken seriously. . . . An obedient response to truth is a mark of intellectual integrity.[8]

McGrath's illustration has to do with history, and Carson's has to do with language, or texts. Similar illustrations could be given from fields as diverse as chemistry and cooking, mathematics and auto mechanics. In short, relativism does not work because it is unsound intellectually, and it is not in accord with reality.

Relativists are habitually guilty of logical inconsistency in ethics. Their claim that absolute truth does not exist should lead them to moral indifference. That is, if every socially constructed "truth" is equally valid, relativists should oppose no one's values. Oppression would be as valid as freedom. When greeting someone, murder would be as acceptable as a handshake. However, relativists find it impossible to live out this position consistently. David Harvey recited this problem cogently:

If, as the postmodernists insist, we cannot aspire to any unified representation of the world . . . then how can we possibly aspire to act coherently with respect to the world? The simple postmodernist answer is that since coherent representation and action are either repressive or illusionary . . . we should not even try to engage in some global project. Pragmatism . . . then becomes the only possible philosophy of action. . . . Action can be conceived of and decided only within the confines of some local determinism, some interpretative community, and its purported meanings and anticipated effects are bound to break down when taken out of these isolated domains.[9]

Harvey questions postmodern philosopher Jean-François Lyotard for referring to justice as a universal value. If all values are merely assertions of power or language games, then there are no universals, or absolutes. Harvey charged that the effort by postmodernists to establish universals is "defeatism."[10]

Francis Schaeffer pointed out Jean-Paul Sartre's similar inconsistency in signing the Algerian Manifesto. Sartre was an ethical nihilist, for whom morals have no meaning. There is no right or wrong. The Algerian Manifesto was a protest against the continuing French occupation of Algeria. As a signatory, Sartre took a deliberate moral position. He could not live with the conclusions of his relativistic philosophical system.[11]

Relativists inevitably live by some code of conduct, for it is the only way to survive and lead a productive life in society. This should tell them something. Living according to moral truth is in accord with the structure of reality. In fact, in the writings of relativists one may detect a longing for a unified answer to the whole of reality. Christians have found this answer in Christ.

Christians Are Particularists

The New Testament states that Jesus died on a cross for the sins of humanity. The Qur'an states that He did not. The New Testament and the Qur'an cannot both be correct. One is correct and the other is incorrect, unless the law of noncontradiction is now extinct and A = not A. Pluralism simply has not dealt adequately with this fact.

Pluralism is the doctrine that multiple belief systems or ways of knowing can be simultaneously "true" (see pp. 67–69). Somehow this sounds possible with reference to metaphysical "theories." However, pluralism has not reckoned with such historical incompatibilities as Jesus' death on a cross and Muhammad's ascension from the Temple mount. Which is true—Christianity or Islam? They cannot both be true.

Pluralism has two agenda items with reference to religions—*standardization* and *homogenization*. Standardization claims that the different religions are just different ways of getting to the same destination. Each religion points beyond itself to another Reality. This Reality is the same for all religions. It merely goes by different names. What is needed, therefore, is a Copernican revolution in religion.[12] Each religion should stop seeing its central doctrines as unique and instead discover that the different religions are merely following different orbits around the same God. "We're all headed to the same place; we're just on different roads" is the popular way to express this standardization of religions. This kind of pluralism asks people to accept and even celebrate other religions' contributions. A character in P. D. James' novel *Original Sin* expresses the inevitable result of such an approach:

> There were a dozen different religions among the children at Ancroft Comprehensive. We seemed always to be celebrating some kind of feast or ceremony. Usually it required making a noise and dressing up. The official line was that all religions were equally important. I must say that the result was to leave me with the conviction that they were equally unimportant.[13]

Orthodox Christianity has always claimed that Jesus is the *only* way to be right with God, not one way among many other legitimate ways. When the apostle Paul preached to the philosophers of Athens, surrounded by the idols on Mars Hill, he did not present Christ as one god among many. Instead he proclaimed that there is one "God who made the world and all things in it, since He is Lord of heaven and earth" (Acts 17:24). Paul went on to proclaim the resurrection of Jesus from the dead (v. 31). If Paul's monotheism did not make it clear that Christianity contrasts with the polytheism of Athens, his belief in the Resurrection certainly did. The philosophers who did not believe in a resurrection "began to sneer" (v. 32). Paul did not present similarities between Christianity and Greek religions. He made it clear that the two were different, and he boldly presented Jesus as the only Lord. This reference to a *particular* Savior is particularism, in contrast to pluralism. Paul certainly did not preach pluralism—Christ as one way to God among many ways. Christianity is wonderfully *inclusive* in that Christ came for all, and anyone who wants to receive Him and follow Him as Lord may do so. Nevertheless, Christianity is *exclusive* in that a person can come to God only through Christ.

When Christian sociologist Tony Campolo spoke at Wake Forest University in January of 1998 as part of that school's "Year of Religion," he was asked about other ways to God. He responded, "I hope they're as wonderful as mine. I want them all to work."[14] One must wonder what Campolo meant by this. By saying that he hopes other religions are wonderful, does he sincerely believe they could be? If they are not true, then how could they be wonderful? And what could Campolo have meant by saying that he wants other ways to God "to work"? Does he believe they *can* work? Though Campolo, a popular speaker at Christian gatherings, may believe that one may know God only through Christ, when he had an opportunity to acknowledge that belief, he uttered only politically correct doublespeak, leaving Christians bewildered as to whether he believes Jesus is the only Savior. Christians who look to Campolo as a leader were left wondering whether they, or anybody, should confess Christ as the only Lord and Savior.

The church has always believed the words of Jesus that "No one comes to the Father, but through Me" (John 14:6). In the face of pluralistic challenges, the church has responded by proclaiming the one true God in love, not by hoping that other ways to God might be true.

In fact, the church has proclaimed Jesus Christ as the only Savior in the face of enormous and sundry pressures. Postmodernism, with its flattening of all truth claims into parity, is only the latest philosophical challenge. Campolo capitulated to the pressures of postmodern pluralism, abandoned the scandalous exclusivism of Christianity, and therefore failed to confess Christ.

Religious homogenization is similar to standardization in that it is an effort to make all religions say the same thing. However, unlike standardization, it does not give adequate respect to the diversity of different religions. It goes beyond saying, "We're going to the same place on different roads," to suggest that "The roads are really not that different after all." McGrath has written at some length about this effort, for example:

> Discussions about religious pluralism have been seriously hindered by a well-meaning but ultimately spurious mind-set which is locked into the "we're all saying the same thing really" worldview, which suppresses or evades the differences between faiths in order to construct some artificial theory which accounts for commonalities.[15]

At this point, pluralists seem to be attempting to construct some middle ground on which all religions of the world can stand. Ironically, this brings them close to the absolutism that they want so desperately to avoid. If they were to succeed in inventing some kind of "lowest common denominator" religion, they would no longer be pluralists. They would be particularists, promoting their own composite religion and claiming that it is suitable for everyone.

The religion of the one true, living God has encountered pluralism before. In the Old Testament period, Israel existed alongside other people groups, each with its own deities and rituals. God's people were tempted to worship other gods to ensure fertility and health. Yet faithful worshipers obeyed the first of the Ten Commandments: "You shall have no other gods before Me" (Exod. 20:3). They acknowledged the nonexistence of the other gods and mocked their mythical attributes (e.g., Isaiah 44). Worship of the Lord was also constantly in danger of being synthesized with the other religions. People sympathetic with Baal worship sought to incorporate aspects of that religion into the worship of the Lord. Their efforts were frequently successful, and Yahweh's prophets had to speak out against syncretism. However, through the centuries, pure faith in the one true God endured. Sometimes this was because of heroic efforts, as when Elijah stood against the syncretistic campaign of Jezebel and her prophets of Baal (1 Kings 18).

Some in the church today seem to be falling short of this biblical heritage of heroic particularism. For example, Alan Culpepper, in an address to Christian educators, referred to the fact that students from many religious backgrounds attend schools that have a Christian heritage. He cited the postmodern emphasis on "the importance of the perspective of the interpreter. . . . The objective now is not to ignore our diverse and distinctive perspectives but to do our work as scholars self-consciously and critically from our individual perspectives."[16]

Instead of seeing this situation as an opportunity to forthrightly assert the truth and exclusivity of Christianity, Culpepper was satisfied to say, "In this post-modern world, the Christian perspective is at least as legitimate and important as any other."[17] One can only imagine the course of Christian history had Paul stood on Mars Hill and proclaimed to the Athenian polytheistic philosophers that faith in Jesus is "at least as legitimate and important as any other." What if Peter had said the same to the Sanhedrin, or Elijah to the prophets of Baal concerning the religion of the one true God?

Culpepper suggested that the church in a pluralistic age should be satisfied merely to be heard, or to exist alongside other religions. For all its appeal to urbane postmodern ears, this position represents compliance with pluralism and therefore abandonment of the historic Christian posture of proclaiming the truth of Christ as the only truth. It hardly measures up to the practice of the heroes of the Bible and of Christian history "to exhort in sound doctrine and to refute those who contradict" (Titus 1:9b). Through the centuries, particularism, not pluralism, has been the very nature of biblical religion. Peter said flatly to the Sanhedrin, "There is salvation in no one else; for there is no other name under heaven that has been given among men, by which we must be saved" (Acts 4:12).

God help the believing church to follow Peter's example.

Christians' Source of Values Is God

The biblical worldview begins with God, not humanity. For orthodox Christians, finding, believing, and following His truth as revealed in the Scriptures is a greater virtue than tolerance of anyone else's "truth." Therefore, in determining values, the Christian looks to an external, rather than an internal, source. The biblical worldview presupposes that the only source of authority is God. Historic Christian orthodoxy has always confessed that God reveals Himself and His will for humankind in the canonical Scriptures. This is the source of Christian values—the propositional truth of the Word of God, not the suppositions of mankind.

More and more our culture treats the Bible as the words of men, not God. What is most lamentable is that some in the church have capitulated to this kind of thinking. For example, several years ago the National Council of Churches produced a lectionary that portrayed God as male and female. In doing so they also elicited no small controversy. In response to the firestorm of criticism, Burton Throckmorton, chairman of the committee that wrote the document, said, "The Bible is the church's book. The church can do whatever it wants to with its book."[18] Actually, the Bible is God's book, which He has given to humanity through human instrumentality. What the church is called to do with His book is submit to it and share its truth. Adopting this perspective does not negate the question of interpretation; Christians will seek a clearer understanding of the meaning of various texts until the end of the age. However, in terms of one's approach to the Bible, only two options exist. The Bible clearly purports to be the Word of God. If it is not the Word of God, then it is a fraud and should be discarded with the morning trash. If it *is* the Word of God, then we have a message from our Creator, and we should listen to it and obey it.

Many religious leaders today would side with Throckmorton. For example, at a 1992 conference at Trinity Episcopal School of Ministry in Ambridge, Pennsylvania, orthodox Episcopalians from that school met with the liberal wing of the denomination to discuss several issues. Not only was there disagreement, but the sides could not even find a point of contact. They could only agree to the date of the meeting and that they all use the same prayer book in worship. One observer of the event wrote, "Whether both parties had a common Lord was questionable—that they had distinctly different faiths was beyond doubt. Trinity students came away from the conference convinced there are two religions in their denomination and that everything Episcopal is not necessarily Christian." One student said, "They worship a different God than we do; that was clear."[19]

Why is there such wide and unprecedented diversity in the organized church? Somewhere along the way we lost the importance of building our shared commitments upon a biblical worldview. Rather than loving God with all of their minds, some have used their minds to exclude the supernatural, relativize absolutes, compromise with other religions, exalt tolerance over truth, and choose personal preference over the Bible. The result is that the visible church becomes merely an insipid, liturgical version of the culture, not the bold, countercultural church of the New Testament.

Both Alice and Dorothy woke up from their dreams and found themselves at home. But our fantasyland is no dream; it's reality. And we are called to make up our minds about how we will live in this world where fantasy is passed off as truth. We will have to keep making this decision until one day we wake up in heaven in God's presence. When we stand before Him, we will be judged according to what we thought of Him and His Word.

CHAPTER 4

When Jesus Is Not P.C.

> *Where is the wise man? Where is the scribe? Where is*
> *the debater of this age? Has not God made foolish the*
> *wisdom of the world? For since in the wisdom of God*
> *the world through its wisdom did not come to know*
> *God, God was well-pleased through the foolishness of*
> *the message preached to save those who believe.*
> *—1 Corinthians 1:20–21*

Kyu Shu had been in the United States less than six months when I visited him in his apartment. He was from China and had moved to the United States to work toward a graduate degree in chemistry at Duke University. He had attended worship at our church, partly out of cultural curiosity and partly out of gratitude for the help one of our members had provided for him. I dropped by to see him in order to get better acquainted and talk to him about faith in Christ. During our conversation, Kyu Shu told me that he worked as a chemist for the Chinese government, where any kind of religious commitment was discouraged. In fact, he said, persons who professed to be Christians would not be promoted. He did not believe they would be fired, but they would remain in low-level positions. In his home society, it simply is not popular, or even acceptable, to be a follower of Jesus. Commitment to Christianity is countercultural.

I had heard a similar report from Christians living in the Soviet Union before its collapse. It was rare to find Christians with high levels of education, they said, because believers found it difficult to advance in that society. As I listened to Kyu Shu speak of the situation in China, two other cultures came to mind. One was the Roman Empire in the first century A. D. Being a Christian was countercultural then, too. The religion of Mithras flourished among Roman soldiers. Speculation about the gods continued to be popular with the philosophers of Athens. Fertility religions thrived in such cities as Corinth where a thousand prostitutes served devotees at the temple of Aphrodite. Members of professional guilds gave homage to their patron deities. Many Roman citizens burned incense to the emperor as divine, whether they believed he was actually a god or not. In Palestine, the social and political structures were inextricably intertwined with Jewish religion. Christians, on the other hand, had no foothold in the structures of society and no forum from which to propagate their convictions. They were a disenfranchised minority. In the beginning, most of them were Jews, so they spoke about Christ in the synagogues. However, it wasn't long before they were kicked out and began to meet primarily in private homes. As the numbers of Christians grew, persecution intensified, and many were executed. Imagine what it must have been like to receive Christ as your Savior and Lord, knowing that your faith would lead to a loss of social acceptance, political leverage, and financial prosperity. There are striking similarities to the realities of Christian life in China and many other societies.

The other culture that came to mind as I visited with Kyu Shu was the United States of America in the first years of the twenty-first century. This sounds odd, given that, outwardly at least, Christianity was an integral part of the culture as recently as forty years ago, especially in those areas of the Southern, Western, and Midwestern United States known as the "Bible Belt." Things have changed. The Roman Empire in the first century was *pre-Christian*; twenty-first-century America is *post-Christian*. This is not to say that there are few Christians, for there are many believers in the Christ of the Bible in the United States. The significant number of churches and Christian organizations testifies to the continuing influence of Christianity as a social force. However, in the culture at large, and even the culture of many of those churches, the biblical worldview is marginalized or nonexistent. It is no longer politically correct to be a Christian with a thoroughgoing Christian worldview.

Although the popular phrase "politically correct" (hereafter referred to as P.C.) implies a connection to politics, it usually has come to refer to a way of thinking, one that pervades Western culture, including the church. In its best expressions, P.C. ideology means to eradicate racism, sexism, provincialism, and other forms of condescension from vocabulary and behavior. The point is to identify with and be sensitive to those groups that have been abused in the past because they were in the minority or had no power. Who would argue that this is not a worthy goal? The establishment of racial and gender equality should be pursued by every just society. Language that denigrates a certain class of people is unacceptable. Those who seek to eradicate that language should be applauded. So far so good.

However, in their effort to give special protection to those deemed to be oppressed, political correctness looks with disdain on those who are not considered to be oppressed—especially males of European descent and Christians. Take, for example, William Shakespeare who was not of an oppressed race and was a man. Too bad. Or at least that's the conclusion of the P.C. movement. His plays have been dropped from the curricula of many universities. In fact, Arizona State University denied tenure to one professor, Jared Sakren, because he taught Shakespeare and other classics, which his colleagues declared to be "sexist" and "offensive to feminists."[1]

In another example, the English department of the University of Texas is reported to have redesigned its remedial writing course for freshmen around the theme of white male racism. The textbook for this "writing course" identifies forty-six kinds of white male privilege. There is a place for objectively studying how society has offered special privileges to white males, but is a remedial writing program the appropriate place to study it? Will the students be able to write any better as a result? Possibly not, since only four of the eighty professors in that English department "believe that a central mission of their department is to teach people how to write."[2] Apparently, in this case, the goal of indoctrination overshadowed the goal of teaching composition and grammar skills.

The redefinition of subject matter by P.C. ideology is not limited to English. Asa Hilliard III of Georgia State University called the sciences the "citadel of white supremacy."[3] A professor at Duke taught a seminar in "Feminist Botany." One wonders exactly how this subject is different from "Botany."

I have not written this chapter because I am a white male trying to defend myself and my kind. Nor is my purpose to make a political statement, correct or incorrect. I do wish to reveal and respond to one aspect of the P.C. movement that is especially relevant to all Christians. Though the movement is supposed to be about sensitivity to all groups, it is characteristically insensitive, and even intolerant, toward those who openly express devotion to Jesus Christ and His Word. Christianity, as the dominant religion of Western civilization, is blamed for society's shortcomings. Christians are regularly censored, opposed, or just ignored, not because they have nothing of value to contribute, but *because they are Christians.*

Allow me to supply a few examples.

A Christian friend worked in a supervisory role in a dormitory on the campus of Duke University for six years. Each year, those who work with the students in a residential position are required to attend an orientation seminar. The purpose of the seminar is to prepare workers to handle such issues as discipline, morale, personal crises, and other issues that arise in a residential setting. Orientation included a "values clarification seminar," designed to help deal with those who have different values. This seminar provides a forum for the D.G.L.A. (Duke Gay and Lesbian Association) to help the "straights" deal appropriately with homosexuals. A prominent theme is an insistence on "tolerance."

It became strikingly evident to my friend that "tolerance" meant something more than simply treating others with dignity and worth as human beings. Rather, one should not believe that any moral choices relating to the gay-lesbian lifestyle are wrong. That, according to the seminar leaders, would be intolerance. The word *homophobic* was thrown around a lot, as if disagreeing with the homosexual lifestyle or movement means that one is afraid of, or hateful toward, those who are involved in either. It is assumed that one who thinks homosexuality is morally wrong is not qualified to counsel those who practice it. All of this, my friend says, is "very much a putdown" of Christians as second-class students who don't fit into the relativist (and therefore amoral) culture of Duke. It's Kyu Shu's China all over again.

In 2002, Stanford University was looking for a new head football coach. Ron Brown, assistant coach at the University of Nebraska, was seriously considered and seemed on a track to be hired. Suddenly, however, he was dropped from consideration. Why? The Stanford administration freely admitted it was because Brown is a Christian and believes homosexuality is a sin. Brown said, "They had no problem telling me it was because of my Christian beliefs."[4] One can only think of the enormous energy and money being spent to ensure that no one is denied a job because he or she is a homosexual. This same concern for "tolerance" is not extended to Christians.

College student Sarah Trafford chronicled her experiences in women's studies classes, where "There is so much bias, so many slurs against Christians, that it's a real gamble whether I will even pass the classes while wearing my crucifix necklace." Not that the professors are necessarily against "spirituality," as long as it's "feminist spirituality." In one class, students were given the assignment to come to class with a unique feminist spell, ritual, or prayer to a goddess.[5]

Three students at three different middle and high schools in Davenport, Iowa, were denied permission to give their fellow students Bibles and flyers advertising a Christian event during noninstruction time. The United States Constitution does not bar religious expression on personal time, even if on public property. Furthermore, students give one another material expressing their personal beliefs all the time. Imagine what would happen if a school prohibited one student giving another student a flyer advertising a heavy metal band that lauded Satan, or one student giving another an invitation to a gathering of her Wicca coven. Hence, the students rightfully brought suit against the school board for this institutional discrimination.[6] Meanwhile, the Byron Union School District near Oakland, California, intentionally incorporated into classroom time a curriculum that encouraged public school students to "intone Islamic prayers, take Islamic names, and use a dice game to simulate a jihad."[7]

Perhaps even more disturbing is what is being said about Jesus. Belief in Jesus as God in the flesh, the second Person of the Trinity, and the only way by which we may be reconciled to God, precludes belief in the ultimate truth of other religions. That's a problem for the P.C. movement, because it's not politically correct to tell anyone that their way of living and believing is inadequate. Jesus said things like, "I am *the* way, and *the* truth, and *the* life; no one comes to the Father, but through Me" (John 14:6). And the disciples of Jesus said things about Him like, "There is no other name under heaven that has been given among men, by which we must be saved" (Acts 4:12). Obviously, Jesus and His disciples were not enlightened by the P.C. police.

Therefore, Jesus is politically incorrect. This, of course, is nothing new. During His life on earth He was so politically incorrect that they conspired to have Him executed. To the Jews, His crime was religious— blasphemy. While He was found not guilty in Pilate's Roman court, ostensibly the Romans killed Him for a political crime—treason. He was doubly "incorrect."

Ever since, people have continued to malign Jesus. They have denied that Jesus is God or accepted His divinity but rejected His humanity. They have denied the Virgin Birth and Resurrection. But now heresy has taken a different turn; it has a sleaze factor. Take, for example, the "art" exhibit that displayed the piece entitled "Piss Christ," a Christ figure upside down on a cross submerged in urine. An exhibit at the Brooklyn Museum of Art included a photograph portraying Jesus attending the Last Supper as a naked woman. The same "artist," in another work, depicted Christ on the cross castrated and dressed as a nun with naked women kneeling before her in prayer. Two years before the Last Supper desecration, the Brooklyn Museum of Art presented a painting of Mary decorated with elephant dung.[8]

Then there are the spate of movies that portray Jesus as an ordinary man who committed adultery and was confused about His place in the world.

The Last Temptation of Christ and *Christ of Toronto* are two of the more publicized examples. In the past, heretics went to great lengths to "prove" that their arguments were rational, that they had a basis in historical fact and found support in the biblical text. Not so with sleaze heresy. "Never mind the truth or historical fact; let's just pretend that Jesus was immoral and present Him as such to the public without even a pretense of evidence." If that were done to a living human, the producers could be convicted of libel, but they tell slanderous lies about Jesus with impunity. To movie producers we could add political power brokers, commerce barons, and media gatekeepers. The Western cultural hegemony has had some success in vilifying, or at least marginalizing, Christianity.

Certainly Christians should harbor no personal animosity toward any of these people who persecute them. The church is to confess Christ and follow Him whether or not it is popular or even legal to do so. Nevertheless, if ultimate truth resides in Jesus as God incarnate and in the Bible as the Word of God, those who oppose the church are wrong, and their antagonism is misplaced. This raises the practical question of how Christians should respond when Jesus and the church are maligned as politically incorrect.

The Nonresponse

One option is to do nothing. We can conclude that, if the claims of P.C. ideology do not interfere with personal devotion to Christ, why bother with them? "It does not touch my life, so I see no reason to respond in any way."

We would be hard-pressed to make a case for such strict individualism using the Bible. Numerous passages show that Christians are to influence their culture. For example, Jesus said that we are to be salt in a bland and decaying society, and He said that we are to be lights in a dark world (Matt. 5:13–16; see also Phil. 2:15–16). Further, He commissioned us to "make disciples of all the nations" (Matt. 28:19–20; see also John 20:21; Acts 1:8). Living cloistered from the world and its evil is not an option for one who is obedient to Jesus. The Lord's plan for His followers is not to remain isolated from society, or insulated from it by our Christian friends, but to infiltrate and influence. We are not to be on the defensive, but on the offensive.

The choice to do nothing was made by most German Christians when Adolf Hitler controlled Nazi Germany. The comparison of individualistic Christians in post-Christian America with silent Christians in Nazi Germany may be unpleasant or even repugnant. Still, there are similarities. The two reasons most Christian leaders gave for their lack of opposition to Hitler's human incinerators and death camps were ignorance of the atrocities, and the desire to remain out of politics. Christians who spoke out against the Third Reich were accused by other Christians of politicizing the church. Many Christians even joined the military under the naive belief that they were fighting for the Fatherland, not for Hitler. Although about a third of the Protestant pastors put up some resistance, more pastors died fighting for Hitler than fighting against him.[9]

Of course, the comparison between Nazi Christians and American Christians breaks down. There are no human incinerators or imperialistic invasions for American Christians to oppose. The manifestations of current P.C. thought seem much more sterile and benign. However, the number of abortions has reached infanticide proportions, fetuses are being harvested for organs, and "mercy" killing of the elderly is becoming common. One wonders if the analogy is more appropriate than we would like to admit. The church must not lose the battle for the souls of twenty-first-century Westerners simply because we decline to publicly address the issues. Too much is at stake to respond by merely reading the news, sighing "Oh well," and returning to our golf game or knitting.

The Militant Response

Another response to the marginalization of the Christian worldview is the opposite of noninvolvement. As a result of the lack of status of Christian convictions, some have resorted to violence. Some Christians support the killing of doctors who perform abortions, and others have actually done so. A pastor in Pensacola, Florida, formed a group called

Defensive Action. This group publishes position papers justifying the killing of abortionists. On another front of the culture war, the National Gay and Lesbian Task Force reported that in 2000 there were 1229 "incidents of hate crimes based on sexual orientation reported to the F.B.I."[10] The violence also flows in the other direction. One proabortion group's literature called for "mass militant action" against pro-life organizations. When pro-life people picketed an abortion clinic in Minneapolis, opponents blocked church entrances on Sunday morning, staged a "queer kiss-in," and vandalized vehicles. Local authorities charged pro-life and proabortion activists with "stalking" one another.[11]

The Litigation Response

Other groups and individuals have avoided the streets, but take the war to the courts. As a result of what my Duke friend called the "put-down" of Christians and their beliefs, some cry "unfair" and "unconstitutional." The Rutherford Institute, the American Center for Law and Justice, the Christian Legal Society, the Home School Legal Defense Association, the Christian Law Association, the Western Center for Law and Religious Freedom, and the legal department of the American Family Association are major players in this arena.

Two things should be said in passing about such organizations. First, they are necessary in order to preserve the legal rights of Christians in a post-Christian culture. As John Whitehead of the Rutherford Institute put it, "Our agenda is not to have a Christian nation, but to enable religious people to survive."[12]

Second, the very existence of such organizations and the pressing need for them underscores the extent to which the United States has strayed from its roots as a refuge of free worship for persecuted Christians.

Four Alternative Responses

How should Christians respond when Jesus and the church are not politically correct? The above responses of noninvolvement, violence, and litigation are difficult or impossible to justify on biblical grounds.

I would like to suggest four responses that seem to be healthier and more in keeping with the teachings of Scripture.

First, *Christians should welcome the emphasis on sensitivity to other people and their beliefs.* Christians ought to join the politically correct chorus in denouncing racism, gender inequality, and other forms of injustice. No one should be judged or discriminated against because of skin color, gender, cultural background, or economic status. Christians, of all people, ought to know that under God we are equal. Some Christian analysis of the P.C. movement leaves out this positive note, which is regrettable. We ought to be speaking in defense of the oppressed. The Bible tells us to "honor all people" (1 Peter 2:17, NKJV).

The Bible also promises that Christians will suffer for their association with Jesus (2 Tim. 3:12). We should not be ashamed of such rejection and persecution. On the other hand, we must make sure that we are not suffering for doing what is wrong. It is important to hear 1 Peter 4:12–16 in this regard:

> Beloved, do not be surprised at the fiery ordeal among you, which comes upon you for your testing, as though some strange thing were happening to you; but to the degree that you share the sufferings of Christ, keep on rejoicing; so that also at the revelation of His glory you may rejoice with exultation. If you are reviled for the name of Christ, you are blessed, because the Spirit of glory and of God rests on you. Make sure none of you suffers as a murderer, or thief, or evildoer, or a troublesome meddler; but if anyone suffers as a Christian, he is not to be ashamed, but is to glorify God in this name.

So, let no Christian be guilty of racial slurs or jokes. Let us all be innocent of valuing someone less merely because of gender. May we never be guilty of earning persecution by looking down on someone because of his or her cultural heritage or nationality. "What credit is there if, when you *sin* and are harshly treated, you endure it with patience?" (1 Peter 2:20, emphasis added). Obviously, there is no credit for that. Christians are to be people of love, and we are to love *every* person, not just those who are like us. To the extent that the P.C. movement promotes love, we can agree with it.

Second, *Christians also should remember that our sensitivity is informed by God's revealed truth, not popular opinion.* The concern to be *correct* in the politically correct movement carries the apparent assumption, unrealized though it may be, that there is such a thing as right and wrong, or correct and incorrect. This is a step in the right direction. Unfortunately, however, what is deemed correct is determined by human preference, or opinion, and the shifting tides of politics. Therefore, right and wrong are not based on eternal truth but are pulled out of thin air.

For Christians, "Theologically Correct" thinking (T.C.), takes precedence over P.C. In order to be T.C., we must adhere to unchanging standards found in God's Word. Those standards of right and wrong for which God holds us accountable are eternal and unerring, unlike today's preferences of the political, educational, and media establishments. In order for us to follow God's standards, we should immerse ourselves in God's truth on a daily basis so that our thinking will be biblical thinking and our worldview will be a Christian worldview. Only then will we recognize falsehood for what it is. We are to be people of love, but according to 1 Corinthians 13:6, love "does not rejoice in unrighteousness, but rejoices with the truth." The truth of God's Word guides our sensitivity.

Third, *Christians should rejoice at the privilege of being persecuted for the name and words of Jesus.* That's exactly what Jesus said should be our response to persecution (Matt. 5:11–12). As we have seen, overt and covert persecution is occurring in every corner of our culture. Christians are condemned for believing that Jesus meant what He said about eternal punishment for those who reject Him. We also are not P.C. if we believe that faith in Jesus is the *only* way to be reconciled to God. We should not be surprised at such opposition. The world opposed Him; it will also oppose us (John 15:18–20).

We should not invite persecution by being obnoxious, offensive, or insensitive, but we ought to be happy that we are so closely associated with our Lord that when someone rejects Him we are also rejected. According to Paul, "Christ crucified" is either a stumbling block or foolishness to those who value the wisdom of this world (1 Cor. 1:23). But God has made foolish the wisdom of the world (v. 20), and He "has chosen the foolish things of the world to shame the wise" (v. 27). We have to make up our minds whether we want to be wise in the eyes of the world or wise in God's eyes. If we choose God's wisdom, we can expect the world to think that we are foolish. When it does, we should consider it a joy to be persecuted for our allegiance to Jesus. And whatever we do, we must never forsake Jesus just for the sake of being politically correct.

Fourth, *Christians should use every possible conversation, or occasion of persecution, as an opportunity to share the good news of Jesus.* We are not to respond to persecution and marginalization with anger or resentment, but with love. And the most loving thing we can do for people is to tell them what Christ has done for us and how they can come to know Him and the life He offers. If someone is sincerely politically correct in order to treat oppressed peoples with respect and empower them, then surely they will listen when we say, "I am a representative of the minority called Christians. Can you listen respectfully to what I have to say? And please understand that no amount of rejection will cause me to waver in my devotion to Jesus, who is my living Lord."

Centuries ago, a wealthy young Christian was in love and engaged to be married. He had everything going for him. But he lived in the Roman Empire, and the emperor had declared Christianity to be *religio illicita* (an illegal religion). Saying, "Caesar is Lord," like everyone else, would have made him politically correct, but he would not say it. Instead he said, "Jesus is Lord." He was, by virtue of his faith in Jesus, guilty of treason.

As the story goes, this young man was arrested in a crackdown against Christians. While awaiting execution in the arena, he wrote love letters to his fiancée. They were beautiful, passionate letters assuring her of his great love for her. But the two were never married, for in A. D. 269 the young man was put to death for being a Christian.

His name was Valentine, and the date of his execution was February 14. Christians have been politically incorrect for a long time.

Several years ago, I was asked to deliver an invocation at a public gathering. I was asked not to use the name of Jesus in my prayer, since some of the people present would not be Christians. I told the one who invited me that I would not pray in that manner. I am a Christian, and I believe that I must pray like a Christian. In fact, I believe that it is unfair to expect Christians to pray as if they are not. I told this gentleman that if he wanted someone to leave off the name of Jesus, he would have to ask someone else to pray. To make sure he understood my position and to express friendship to him, I wrote a note to him after our conversation. In it I wrote, "Along with millions of our Christian brothers and sisters before us, many of whom died for their allegiance to the name of Jesus, I choose to accept 'the offense of the cross' rather than acquiesce to false belief." I encourage you to do the same.

CHAPTER 5

Christians, God, and Government

*Then He said to them, "Then render to Caesar the things
that are Caesar's; and to God the things that are God's."*
—*Matthew 22:21b*

*Every person is to be in subjection to the governing
authorities.*
—*Romans 13:1a*

An old friend who is a Christian wrote a note to me expressing his
opinion that the government should not allow prayers at state-
supported events such as football games and graduation exercises. A
college student preparing for vocational ministry wrote, disparaging
a tradition in some churches of displaying a U.S. flag in the sanctuary.
When I made information available regarding candidates for civil election, another church member sent a note denouncing such "political"
activity.

Christians regularly debate with one another how we are to relate
to the government and the political process, and the heat of the debate is increasing. Charles Colson even suggested the possibility of the
church's open corporate rebellion against the government of the United
States of America because "the courts have usurped the democratic
process by reckless exercise of naked power." The Supreme Court has
done this, Colson wrote, by writing such decisions as *Casey v. Planned
Parenthood*, "which enshrined the right of abortion as a specifically
protected Fourteenth Amendment liberty" and lectured pro-lifers for

continuing to contest the abortion issue. Other decisions have created a zone in which pro-choice advocates can demonstrate, but pro-life advocates cannot, and overturned Colorado's prohibition of local civil rights statutes based on sexual preference and branded any citizen who disagreed with them, a bigot.

Colson warned that the time has not yet come for despair and open rebellion, but he stated, "It would be hard to imagine that a Christian in good conscience could swear to uphold the Constitution or laws of any nation that practices the horrendous offense against God of taking the defenseless lives of the weakest among us: babies, the elderly, and the sick."[1] Such revolutionary language will continue to be used as long as the justices of the U.S. Supreme Court and elected officials continue to invalidate laws based on a transcendent moral order, and enact laws based solely on current public opinion (or even on judicial fiat).

The Bible gives clear guidance in the matter of relating to the state. Though Christians may differ over how to respond to a particular initiative by the government, we should agree on fundamental principles in the Word of God. However, among Christians there is an astounding ignorance of those principles. Further, patriotism, or a particular interpretation of it, has become so important to some U.S. Christians that it compromises their commitment to the message of the Bible. They embrace a hybrid grafting of capitalistic democracy onto the worship of the one, true God and add the Constitution of the United States to the canon of Scripture. Their "Christian" faith has become so nationalized that it no longer resembles New Testament faith. Looking at the national flag may bring a tear to their eyes; looking at the cross does not. Christ has been eclipsed by country.

What We Believe

One goal that attends any effort to love God with our minds is to affirm what He affirms and deny what He denies. Developing a Christian worldview involves understanding biblical truth and adopting that truth as an ideological frame of reference. Here we cannot do justice to all of the biblical texts relating to a Christian's relationship to government, but we can review relevant principles found in those texts. I have attempted to limit this discussion to bedrock biblical truths that should be both conspicuous and nonnegotiable.

God Is the Ultimate Sovereign

First, *God is sovereign over every person and nation.* He is "King of kings" (Rev. 19:16), and He will share His position of absolute authority with no person and no nation. As Abraham Kuyper put it, "There is not a square inch in the whole domain of our human existence over which Christ, who is sovereign over *all,* does not cry: 'Mine!'"[2] God's sovereignty extends to human governments. And because He alone is God, He alone is to be worshiped as God. To do otherwise is to break the first of the Ten Commandments (Exod. 20:3). When Jesus said that we are to render "to God the things that are God's" (Matt. 22:21), certainly He was including in these "things" our worship and ultimate allegiance. These belong to God and to no other, including Caesar.

Christians who want to develop a Christian worldview must adopt the perspective that every government is under God. To the almighty God, "the nations are like a drop from a bucket, and are regarded as a speck of dust on the scales; behold, He lifts up the islands like fine dust" (Isa. 40:15). There is a tendency for Christians to be tempted to adapt faith in a way that either equates their country with God or even exalts their country over God. Some churches have "God and Country" services, and these may be conducted in a way that does not conflict with a biblical worldview. In some churches, however, they should be called "Country and God" services, because God takes a back seat and the country is exalted. Faith in God is presented as merely one facet of patriotism. Citizenship, not discipleship, is preeminent, and the latter serves the former. Christians who face such a temptation should remember that Isaiah goes on to say that "all the nations are as nothing before Him, they are regarded by Him as less than nothing and meaningless" (v. 17).

A human government can never commandeer the absolute

sovereignty of God. Psalm 2 describes a plot by the nations to defy God's authority and rebel against His laws. What is God's reaction to their schemes? Does He feel threatened or defensive? Does He scramble to develop contingency plans in case of a coup d'état? Does He wring His hands and bite His nails, worrying that the leaders of these nations may shanghai His sovereignty? No, "He who sits in the heavens laughs, the Lord scoffs at them" (Ps. 2:4). God is only amused by puny creatures who feel omnipotent because they can muster a standing army and write a book of laws.

The sovereignty of God over nations is made even more explicit in the book of Revelation. When John wrote this book, the Roman Empire was a world force that had conquered every people group it had faced in the Mediterranean world and beyond. That world government was persecuting and even executing Christians because they refused to acknowledge the emperor as divine. Circumstances seemed to suggest that Rome was sovereign, not God. Some in the church must have been tempted to wonder if God really had any power over Rome. John himself had been exiled to the island of Patmos. Is this the way God exercises His sovereignty? In these circumstances God showed John a vision of heaven. Just as the writer of Psalm 2 understood, John saw that the Roman Empire had not shaken God off His throne. In the center of heaven, God was on His throne and in control (Revelation 4). God showed John His plans for the demise of human empires and the eternal victory of His people. God is sovereign over nations.

God Sets Authority Structures in Place

A second bedrock biblical truth is that *God establishes governmental authority.* This fact is one expression of God's sovereign rule over the universe. Romans 13:1b states it succinctly: "There is no authority except from God, and those which exist are established by God." In verse 4, Paul twice calls the governing authority "a minister of God." It is comforting to know that God has given authority to governments to restrain evil behavior and protect innocent citizens. However, when the government itself becomes evil, this truth becomes problematic. What about the Hitlers and Husseins of the world? What about the governments that make conversion to Christianity a capital offense? Did God establish those governments?

When we consider two facts, such questions are easier to answer. First, not everything that happens in the world is within God's perfect will, but everything is within His permissive will. It may be God's perfect will for unrighteous governments to repent and turn to Him, but He *permits* them to pursue their own way. Even when rulers and nations turn their backs on God and His law, He still is ultimately in control.

In the late eighth century B.C., Assyria under King Sennacherib was the dominant world power. The Assyrians worshiped pagan gods, despite their erstwhile penitence under the preaching of Jonah. They were as powerful as they were pagan; their military might enabled them to conquer and annex surrounding nations. With power came corruption, and the Assyrians became known for their brutality against conquered peoples. They committed the worst kinds of atrocities with impunity. During the time of Isaiah, Assyria conquered the northern kingdom of Israel and was threatening the southern kingdom of Judah.

Strange as it may have sounded to Isaiah's contemporaries, through the prophet the Lord was calling Assyria "the rod of My anger and the staff in whose hands is My indignation" (Isa. 10:5). God's message to His people was, "You think that Assyria is evil and opposed to Me. You're right. But what Assyria doesn't know is that it has been My intention to judge My people for a long time, and I am using Assyria to do it. Assyrians have been railing against Me and claiming that their achievements have been accomplished in their own strength, but the truth is that I have been using them as My instrument to accomplish My will. Furthermore, when I finish using them, if they don't repent, I will judge them too."

It was a pretty amazing statement. Sennacherib thought he was acting as his own god, but the real God was actually using him as a rod in His hand. The book of Proverbs puts it concisely: "The king's heart is like channels of water in the hand of the Lord; He turns it wherever

He wishes" (Prov. 21:1). Yes, even evil governments are in place under the permissive will of God. They are also under His ultimate control.

Rulers Are Responsible Morally

A third basic biblical truth is that *every government is responsible to God and will give an account to Him.* The nation of Israel was responsible to keep the obligations of the covenant with God, and God held even pagan nations responsible for their sin (see Amos 1–2). God's moral laws are universal, and nations that ignore them invite His judgment. "Righteousness exalts a nation, but sin is a disgrace to any people" (Prov. 14:34).

Be Model Citizens

Fourth, *God calls His people to be exemplary participants in the society in which they live.* Numerous biblical passages demonstrate this fact. Consider just one. In the early sixth century B.C., the people of Judah were being carried into exile by the Babylonians, just as their brothers, the Israelites, had been exiled by the Assyrians a century and a half earlier. The Jewish people did not want to be exiled to Babylon. They were a conquered, captured people being dragged to the foreign homeland of their enemies. Families were divided as some left and some stayed, and those going to Babylon had to leave behind the sacred temple and a centuries-old way of life and freedom.

Yet as they left, the prophet Jeremiah gave God's instruction: "Seek the welfare of the city where I have sent you into exile, and pray to the LORD on its behalf; for in its welfare you will have welfare" (Jer. 29:7). The exiles were to become interested in promoting the well-being of Babylon. Babylon had been their enemy, but when they moved there they were to be model residents. Contemporary followers of Christ have the same responsibility, regardless of the nation in which they live.

Submit to Authorities

A fifth biblical truth is related to the fourth: *God's people are to be submissive to the authority of the government.* This follows from the truth that the government's authority is derived from God. Submission is explicitly called for in two New Testament passages.

> Every person is to be in subjection to the governing authorities. . . . Therefore, whoever resists authority has opposed the ordinance of God; and they who have opposed will receive condemnation upon themselves. For rulers are not a cause of fear for good behavior, but for evil. Do you want to have no fear of authority? Do what is good, and you will have praise from the same. . . . Because of this you also pay taxes, for rulers are servants of God. . . . Render to all what is due them: tax to whom tax is due; custom to whom custom; fear to whom fear; honor to whom honor.
>
> —Romans 13:1–3, 6–7

> Submit yourselves for the Lord's sake to every human institution, whether to a king as the one in authority, or to governors as sent by him for the punishment of evildoers and the praise of those who do right. . . . Honor all people, love the brotherhood, fear God, honor the king.
>
> —1 Peter 2:13–14, 17

These passages make it clear that God intends for His people to obey the laws of the land in which they live.

Obey God Before Government

But what if those laws contradict God's laws? This leads to a sixth biblical truth: *Christians may have to disobey the government in order to obey God.* Though God's people were to "seek the welfare" of Babylon, when the king commanded everyone to worship a golden idol, Shadrach, Meshach, and Abed-nego refused to do so (Daniel 3). When the king issued a decree that everyone was to refrain from praying to anyone but him, Daniel disobeyed (ch. 6). Daniel and his friends disobeyed the government in order to obey God. As a result, Daniel was thrown into the lions' den and his friends were thrown into the furnace. Evidently they feared God more than men.

Peter and John faced a similar situation when the Sanhedrin forbade them to speak about Jesus (Acts 4:17–18). Jesus had commanded them to speak about Him (Matt. 28:19; Acts 1:8), so they had a decision to make: Should they obey Jesus or the Sanhedrin? Peter and John responded to the Sanhedrin by saying, "Whether it is right in the sight of God to give heed to you rather than to God, you be the judge; for we cannot stop speaking about what we have seen and heard" (4:19–20). In effect, they were saying, "If you decide that what we are doing is wrong, arrest us and judge us. But we are not going to stop." When Peter and other apostles were arrested again later, they told the Sanhedrin, "We must obey God rather than men," and they proceeded to proclaim the resurrection of Jesus (5:27–32). Peter and John decided to obey God, not the government. Tradition says that Peter suffered crucifixion for his obedience to Christ, and John was exiled for a time to the island of Patmos.

Many other Christians in the first century died because of their civil disobedience. Through the centuries and still today, an army of Christians has practiced civil disobedience in order to obey God. Often the result has been persecution, arrest, and even death. Christians are killed for their faith every year. Persecution of Christians and other religious people is so common in the world that in 1998 the U. S. Congress established a Commission on International Religious Freedom. Every year this commission reports to the U.S. president on countries that are hindering religious freedom, and recommends policy changes based on their findings. The commission's report is readily available to the public. The media, however, though quick to sermonize about First Amendment rights in order to defend obscenity and pornography, virtually ignore this report that cites numerous instances of arrest, torture, and murder of religious people by oppressive governments.[3]

Many Christians remain uninformed about their brothers and sisters in Christ who are faithful to their Lord in the midst of persecution. Likewise, many have so identified obedience to their government with obedience to God that they will not even concede the possibility that civil disobedience may be necessary in order to obey God. This very question was part of a survey quoted in the December 1996 issue of *George* magazine. The result was that 41 percent of Americans said they would follow the "laws of religion over the laws of the land."[4] I wonder if that many people would actually follow through if they faced real consequences from such a choice. The biblical perspective is that submission to the authority of the government is taught by Scripture, and disobedience is mandated when obeying the government means disobeying God.

God Changes the Heart

A seventh biblical principle is less explicit, but nonetheless clear: *The hearts, and therefore the policies, of people are changed by God, not the government.* I do not believe that this biblical principle is justification for Christians to parrot the common shibboleth, "You can't legislate morality." This half-truth overlooks the power of the government to use law for right or wrong. The very concept of "law" implies the existence of an external standard of right and wrong beyond mere personal opinion. Those who enact laws will legislate either a moral or an immoral standard. Through the enforcement of just laws, a government can and should restrain evil behavior and protect right behavior. Governmental leaders must realize that they have the moral force of law at their disposal.

Nevertheless, the power of human governments and laws is limited. External authorities cannot change the minds and hearts of people. However, there are no limits to the power of God's Spirit to transform hearts. For this reason the primary task of the church has always been to proclaim Christ, not to promote a particular form of government. Jesus spent no time training His disciples in how to lobby Jerusalem or Rome for political change. When He sent His disciples out, He did not tell them to preach about the kingdoms of this world, but that "the kingdom of heaven is at hand" (Matt. 10:7). Jesus was in tune with the consistent message of the Bible—systemic, or societal, change is derivative. It results from change in human hearts. Societies are changed by changed people, and people are changed by God.

What Should We Do?

General biblical principles regarding God and government seem clear. Though some Christians would state the above principles differently, the overwhelming majority of orthodox Christians agree on these basic truths. However, there are significant differences of opinion regarding the more specific matter of active involvement in public life. What stands should we take? Which candidates should get our vote? To what extent should we be politically active? Should we be involved at all?

Some Christians believe that we should withdraw from public life. Politics, they say, is a hopelessly dirty business. Christians, therefore, are better off staying out of politics and devoting their energies to the mission of Christ through the church. The church's involvement in politics only corrupts the church. There is no good way to do it—those who are more liberal *compromise* the faith, and conservatives *corrupt* the faith by giving the impression that to be a Christian is to believe in a strong defense, a balanced budget, and smaller government.

Other Christians opt out of political involvement (or even political thinking) because of the apocalyptic nature of their faith. This world is not our home, so let's spend our time here getting ready for heaven. Society is not redeemable until God consummates this age; we wait for the millennium. This high level of interest in end times precludes interest in secular politics, unless the purpose is to scour the daily news for "signs of the times."

There is a more insidious reason why Christians stay away from engagement with the government. They wrongly assume that Christian truth is private truth. "Jesus in my heart," daily devotionals, and Sunday's sermon are all for the purpose of making me feel good, enjoy life, and obtain the blessings of God. This is a pathetic reduction of Christianity. Christian truth is universal truth—for every person and every society. It is not right only "for me"; it is *right.*

The absolute sovereignty of God is not a doctrine that simply reassures me; it is an unconditional truth that makes every person and nation accountable to Him. Christian faith has a personal aspect, but it is never private. Christ transforms persons, and then He thrusts them into the Christian community to live, and into the world to help transform. He commanded us to "make disciples of all the nations" (Matt. 28:19) and said, "Let your light shine before men in such a way that they may see your good works, and glorify your Father who is in heaven" (Matt. 5:16). This can hardly be done in the prayer closet.

If, then, the Bible teaches that Christians are to engage the public sector, and it does, then what exactly are we to do? I offer six imperatives. At the risk of sounding trite, each starts with the same letter.

1. Pray

First Timothy 2:1–4 states this truth clearly:

> First of all, then, I urge that entreaties and prayers, petitions and thanksgivings, be made on behalf of all men, for kings and all who are in authority, so that we may lead a tranquil and quiet life in all godliness and dignity. This is good and acceptable in the sight of God our Savior, who desires all men to be saved and to come to the knowledge of the truth.

This is nonpartisan activity, but it is not necessarily nonpublic. As Christians pray alone and with other Christians, they ought to include prayer for "all who are in authority." This passage makes several points about prayer for governmental officials.

Prayer is effective. The assumption is that there will be results—the government will protect a quiet, godly lifestyle.

Prayer should include "thanksgivings." Some people find it difficult to thank God for elected officials when they disagree vehemently with their policies. However, we may at least thank God that He has ordained these governmental authorities so that evil persons will be accountable to someone who has the force of law.

Prayer is unselfish in its purpose. We are not praying for government handouts but for the maintenance of a just society that protects "a tranquil and quiet life in all godliness and dignity." This is praying that the government would use its power to protect the good and punish that which is wrong and harmful. It is praying for laws that are based on truth and equity. It is praying against laws that are an affront to godliness.

According to 1 Timothy 2, *the purpose of our prayer should also be evangelistic.* We pray to a God "who desires all men to be saved." In His presence, certainly we will speak about the conversion of those for whom we pray. The best thing that could happen to someone in authority is to be redeemed and transformed by Christ.

2. Practice

Before Christians can expect to exert a positive influence on the government, they must have their own moral house in order. We must practice the faith we proclaim. If it is right, then it is right for us. Sadly, some who profess to be Christians practice the same sorts of sinful behavior as those without Christ. When Christians are not faithful to their marriage, when they break up a family with divorce, or end a baby's life with abortion, they undermine the integrity of the church's message. We should be *mending* homes, not tearing them apart. We should be *saving* lives, not taking them. We should be living in harmony with the high value of life and family that we believe and teach.

When the apostle Peter wrote about the relationship between Christians and the state, he included exhortations about our behavior.

> For such is the will of God that by doing right you may silence the ignorance of foolish men. Act as free men, and do not use your freedom as a covering for evil, but use it as bondslaves of God.
>
> —1 Peter 2:15–16

Make sure that none of you suffers as a murderer, or thief, or evildoer, or a troublesome meddler; but if anyone suffers as a Christian, he is not to be ashamed, but is to glorify God in this name.

—1 Peter 4:15–16

If the church wants the government and society as a whole to change, then *the church* must be filled with changed people. We are called to show the world what it looks like to live what Paul calls "a tranquil and quiet life in all godliness and dignity" (1 Tim. 2:2). The church should outshine the government in doing good. If we believe that women should carry crisis pregnancies to term, then we should open our homes and churches and pocketbooks to help them do so. If we believe that it is not healthy for persons to live off governmental largesse, then churches should be organized to provide emergency assistance to the poor, the homeless, and the hungry. We should not expect the righteousness, compassion, and benevolence of the general public to exceed our own. Paul wrote the following to Christians in Philippi:

Prove yourselves to be blameless and innocent, children of God above reproach in the midst of a crooked and perverse generation, among whom you appear as lights in the world.

—Philippians 2:15

David Gushee has stated this principle well:

When we are racially inclusive without having to be told to be, abstain from sex outside of marriage, stay married for life and are glad to do so, relate respectfully to each other as male and female, do not resort to abortion as a form of birth control, support those in crisis pregnancies, care for our aged with respect, honor, and concrete help, feed the hungry and house the homeless and empower the poor, communicate in loving truthfulness, and offer grace to the broken and despairing and abandoned, we offer a radiant public witness that carries political implications and creates political opportunities. . . . This may be the source of our greatest influence—only if, though, the church is characterized by obedient and joyful following of the Way of Jesus Christ.[5]

3. Participate

The early church lived and ministered in the context of a monarchical form of government. Caesar's power was virtually unlimited. The ordinary citizen had few rights and no voice. Furthermore, the majority of residents in the far-flung Roman Empire were conquered peoples who were not even regarded as citizens. American Christians, on the other hand, live and minister in the context of a representative democracy. No biblical example shows us how to participate in a democratic process, since the early Christians did not live in a democracy. However, we do have biblical principles that guide us. That is, the principles of relating to a world without Christ should apply regardless of the governmental structure in which one lives.

Entire books have been written on whether, how, and when Christians should participate in the political process.[6] We cannot cover here all the nuances of this issue. However, it is important to clarify two points. First, we should remember that Christians take their marching orders primarily from Scripture, and only secondarily from the laws of the land. That means that our decisions about involvement in politics should be predicated on Scripture, not the law or public opinion of our nation.

In the case of the United States, the debates about whether and how Christians should be involved in public discourse have tended to appeal to the First Amendment to the U.S. Constitution, which rules against laws that establish or infringe upon free religious expression. People also elevate Thomas Jefferson's comment about a "wall of separation" that should exist between church and state. Various interpretations are offered to oppose or defend Christian involvement. The arguments are just as complex and contentious in relation to governments that have an established or de facto state-promoted religious heritage.

Ultimately, Christians have to provide a cogent explanation of their position in the light of such ideas. However, the prior question for Christians is, "What guidance does the Bible provide in the matter of involvement in governmental issues?" Not all Christians live in societies governed according to democratic political principles, and the Bible does not specifically address involvement in a democracy. But whatever the government context, Scriptural directives do speak of how to influence others for God and for good. A democracy is ostensibly ideal in that it offers Christians the opportunity to speak more openly and freely. Christians should ask themselves whether they can possibly be salt and light (Matt. 5:13–16) in society and avoid involvement in issues that affect the political process. If we do not confront our culture with the truth in the public sector, we can never hope to resemble the church described in Acts that spoke openly before religious, civil, and philosophical leaders concerning spiritual and moral matters.

A second point to clarify is that Christian participation in public life should be based upon a Christian worldview. Many nominal Christians involved in various levels of political life do not know or care to know biblical teaching on the very issues concerning which they are legislating. They consider economic concerns, personal prejudices, or provincial interests. When such matters overshadow Christian principles, neither voters or those in authority exert influence as Christians. Rather they are simply disgruntled taxpayers, businesspersons, whites or blacks, women or men, or residents of a particular area. When Christians vote according to interest blocs, these ways of identifying themselves eclipse their identity as Christians. Theology has not informed their politics. When this is the case, the church loses the opportunity to speak with a unified voice, because its message has been diluted by concerns more petty than divine. The result is a public policy that seems *ad hoc* to government officials. As Michael Cromartie has written,

Christian conservatives' involvement in politics has been reactive and not proactive. They see themselves as defendants, and not the aggressors, in the culture war. As a result, they become involved in politics for cultural reasons without seeking theological justification for that involvement until after the fact. One gets the impression that the underlying public philosophy for such activism is constantly evolving and is still being framed from election to election and issue by issue.[7]

The people of God need a fully developed theology of cultural engagement. And Christians should be motivated to political participation by such biblical truth, and not by "after the fact" reactions to cultural concerns. Then, once Christians vote or lobby on issues that have moral or spiritual implications (and many do), their first impulse should be to ask, "What does God say about this issue?" and "How can I glorify God with the way I vote or act on this issue?" (see 1 Cor. 10:31). Such questions are just the beginning point for political participation that deserves to be called Christian.

4. Persuade

Proper persuasion refers more to what we do *not* do than to what we do. The means of our cultural engagement is limited to personal persuasion and excludes coercion or force. It has not always been so for Christians. After Constantine converted, Christianity enjoyed majority status in the Roman Empire. Once the church was backed by the state, it had the power to impose its belief and practice on every citizen by force of law. The church did just that, at times compelling every person to attend church and outwardly espouse certain beliefs. This wedding of church and state declined in importance in Western cultures, although some still maintain the trappings of a state church. Virtually all Christian historians and philosophers agree that such power led to corruption. Coerced faith was not Christian faith, because it was not exercised voluntarily.

A small movement in conservative Christian circles in the United States has proposed a return to closer ties between state and church, to something resembling the theocratic principles of Old Testament Israel. This movement, variously called Christian reconstruction, theonomy, or dominion theology, calls for the systematic reorganization of American society around biblical principles. Jim Burgin, a student of the movement, explains that theonomists "want American government to be theocratic in nature, directly ruled by God through His people."[8] Reconstructionists find biblical support for their philosophy only in fallacious interpretations of Old Testament passages. Neither Jesus nor the apostles referred to the establishment of any form of government.

Thankfully, reconstructionists are a tiny minority among Christians. But the existence of this position makes it important to state that *Christians do not believe that the kingdom of God should be extended by forcing our ideas on a reluctant public.* Instead, we believe in personal persuasion. We believe that moral power, not political power, is the superior force. "The weapons of our warfare are not of the flesh, but divinely powerful for the destruction of fortresses" (2 Cor. 10:4). The enforcement of civil law can control behavior, but only God can change hearts. God may use His people to bring about this change through books, campaigning for righteous laws and officials, the use of media, teaching in universities, public debates, and personal conversations. But whatever the means chosen, the goal is not coercion but persuasion.

5. Proclaim

Throughout biblical history, God's people played a prophetic role in their societies. They did not recoil from speaking out to support the right and oppose the wrong. Our models are men like John the Baptist who plainly told Herod that he should not be married to his brother's wife (Mark 6:18), and the prophet Isaiah who freely advised kings to follow God's direction. Sometimes the kings listened to the prophets, and sometimes they did not. Other examples are Elijah (1 Kings 17–18), Micaiah (22:5–23), and Jeremiah (Jer. 32:1–8), each of whom was hated by governmental leaders because they spoke God's truth against current policy.

Biblical examples are plentiful, as are contemporary models. While not inspired in the sense of the prophetic authors of Scripture, the number of Christians who speak from a biblical perspective against wrongs in society is growing. Such prophetic voices face persecution and misunderstanding. The popular media sometimes misinterprets their words. They may be imprisoned or killed if they live in a society where they are less welcome to express their beliefs in public forums. Nevertheless, some call for a reentry of the Christian perspective in public debate. For example, Yale professor Stephen L. Carter, in *The Culture of Disbelief*, argues for more openness to traditional religious viewpoints in the public sector.[9] If Christians speaking Christian truth are welcomed by some secular philosophers into the public market, the church community certainly should applaud the effort. The church must not lose its prophetic voice, for, as Martin Luther King Jr. said, "The church is not the master or the servant of the state, but rather the conscience of the state."[10]

What will happen if Christians do not exercise this prophetic role? If the church does not cry out against governmental and political wrongs, it will fail to distinguish itself from the insipid, convictionless, benevolence-at-large civil religion. Governments throughout history have had professional religious advisors. Pharaoh had his priests, the kings of the East their magi, and kings of Israel and Judah had royal prophets on the payroll to prophesy only good news. In a compromised church, the leaders of the United States would have uncritical supporters to sing "God Bless America" on cue. Christians with a biblical worldview certainly want God to bless their homeland and pray for His blessing. However, they also may wonder whether God *can* bless any of today's national governments without compromising His holiness.

We must be careful not to silence our prophetic voice. To do so makes the church too close a friend of the world and binds the body of Christ to a temporal system. In Western nations that tends to be a democracy that regards public opinion but does not look to transcendent truth as it orders society. We should not imagine that the government may grant special favors to such a collaborating church. To the contrary, an innocuous church consigns itself to a future of irrelevance.

Of course, Christians should do more than proclaim the flaws of secular society. We should also proclaim the solution offered by Christ. After the worship of the living God, this is the first duty of the church. Jesus gave us the commission to "make disciples of all nations" (Matt. 28:19) and said that "repentance for forgiveness of sins would be proclaimed in His name to all the nations" (Luke 24:47). Christians are to proclaim the good news about Jesus in every society in which they find themselves. The reconciliation to God entailed in this good news transcends mere political solutions.

6. Prioritize

Each of the above actions is important. However, if Christians only express truth in the political realm, we will have failed to fulfill Christ's commission. We should align ourselves with political candidates and policies that are nearest to what is right and good. But we must also put such temporal matters in perspective. Political solutions are temporary. Philip Yancey has pointed out that Lyndon Johnson's "War on Poverty" was supposed to bring an end to poverty in the United States. The reality is that more poor people require help from the government now than was the case in the 1960s. Sex education was supposed to reduce the number of unwanted teenage pregnancies. The result of aggressively informing children about their sexuality has been a rise in the pregnancy rate and in teenage abortions. The central factor in such failures is not that they were bad policies. The main problem is that "whatever human beings touch goes wrong. Politics, especially, runs according to the Law of Unintended Consequences."[11]

Ultimately every political platform rots and crumbles. Bill Clinton's "Covenant for a New Century" and "Bridge to the Future" and the Republicans' "Contract with America" were all doomed to the same fate of obsolescence. Even U.S. citizens who read these words may already have forgotten those public initiatives. Carl F. H. Henry, a popular spokesman for evangelical theology in the late twentieth century, even asked if democracy itself has "had its day."[12]

However, the primary message that Christians have for the world will never become obsolete. Reconciliation with God through Christ is eternal; therefore it is more important. Our priority should be on eternal things. Jesus gave to the church a spiritual commission, not a political program. We are called to make disciples, not Republicans or Democrats or whatever the political parties might be. Christ did not come to endorse any secular agenda; rather He set a new agenda for worship, discipleship, and offering people abundant and eternal life through repentance from sin, and faith in Him. We could lobby the nation's capital for a decade and still not have the influence we would have if we had spent our time leading some of our governmental leaders to follow Jesus as Lord.

People need Jesus more than they need anything a government can give them. Let us do what only the church can do. If we don't, no one else will do it, and we will have abandoned an essential part of a Christian worldview.

CHAPTER 6

The Narcissus Myth: The Danger of Self-Love

[Jesus said,] "I am gentle and humble in heart."
—Matthew 11:29b

I say to everyone among you not to think more highly of himself than he ought to think. . . . Do not be haughty in mind, but associate with the lowly. Do not be wise in your own estimation.
—Romans 12:3, 16

Many evangelical leaders and some seminaries have fought the battle over the inerrancy of the Scriptures, and they have fought it well. However, victory seems strangely empty as apostasy sweeps the church. Inerrancy seems only to be of academic interest as we ignore the Word as a doctrinal base for our teaching. Scripture may be inerrant, but it seems the church does not intend to shape its thinking by it. Certainly this refusal to do so is nowhere more evident than in the acceptance of the thesis that man's most basic need is for a sense of personal worth, a better self-image, and higher self-esteem. . . . This idea is not only foreign to Scripture, but it is also the very antithesis of biblical teaching.[1]
—Gary Almy and Carol Tharp Almy

According to ancient Greek mythology, Narcissus was the son of the river god Cephisus. He was so handsome that many girls were interested in him, but he paid no attention to them. Echo was one nymph who loved Narcissus, and she was hurt so badly by his rejection that she gradually faded away until only her voice was left. But Narcissus' downfall was his love for himself. One day he looked into a pool of clear water and saw the reflection of his face. He was so much in love with his appearance that he could not leave the pool. He stared at the reflection until he finally died. The apparent cause of death was starvation, but the real cause of death was self-love. If at any point Narcissus' infatuation with himself had abated, he could have left the pool and survived.

The mythical Narcissus died, but the love of self for which he is known is alive and well. Self-love continues today, and at no time in history has it been so accepted and encouraged as at this time in Western culture. "Looking out for number one" is presently viewed as a fundamental and immutable law of the universe. If we are serious about loving God with our minds, we will examine such a perspective in the light of what God has said in His Word. We will learn to think correctly about ourselves. Is "me-ism" or self-love, the Christian way to think about ourselves? If not, we must make a conscious decision not to think like the culture, but to have the mind of Christ in reference to ourselves.

I had conversations with two men during the same week that illustrate the vast difference between self-centered narcissism and Christ-centered thinking. Both of these men are professing Christians, but their perspectives about themselves are poles apart. The first man was young and had his life before him. In our conversation, I alluded to the difference between focusing one's life on self and focusing on Christ. He interrupted me to say that one of the things that was really important to him was to be sure that his career was not for himself or even just to provide for his wife. He wanted to shun self-honor to make certain his life was pleasing to the Lord.

The second man was financially successful. He was also involved in immoral activities, and he was beginning to reap the consequences of his sin. When I spoke to him about his need to reorder his life to be pure and obedient to Christ, he responded, "I see what you mean. I need to do things that will make me feel better about myself so I will be more prepared to deal with the stresses in my life." He didn't get it. Somehow my "Do what's right" became his "Do what makes me happy." It was as if a translator liberally altered my words to fit the accepted dogma of a foreign culture. In this case, the accepted dogma was the centrality of the self.

There is an enormous difference between these two men. The first was God-centered; the second had a hard time leaving his reflection in the pool. Sadly, he's not the only Narcissus in our midst.

Rarely has self-centeredness risen to the level of legitimacy it enjoys in England, Canada, the United States, Australia, and other relatively prosperous countries at the beginning of the twenty-first century. We should not be surprised that self-centeredness has attained such a prominent status in Western culture. Every major worldview described in chapter 2 encourages self-centeredness. Naturalism erases transcendent principles and asserts that reason is competent to construct an adequate system of right and wrong. Therefore, the individual is left as his or her own god. Hedonism's goal is individual pleasure, a concept that is inherently self-centered. Relativism, with its absence of absolute truth, allows individuals to invent their own "truth" according to personal preference. Pluralism also denies absolute status for any system of truth and makes the individual a "values chef" who adds ingredients at whim to cook up his or her own religion. Each of these systems makes *self* the center of the universe. No wonder, then, that self-centeredness is so prominent and so readily accepted.

It is no longer argued that self is the center of the universe; it is *assumed*. In 1976, Tom Wolfe wrote an article titled "The 'Me' Decade and the Third Great Awakening."[2] The designation "The 'Me' Decade" has now been used by various writers with reference to the 1960s, 1970s, 1980s, and 1990s. It should be evident that me-ism is not a decade-long phenomenon. It is ingrained into our cultural psyche as part of the *zeitgeist,* the worldview lens through which twenty-first century Westerners interpret everything.

This cultural assumption has been abetted, perhaps even spawned, by the presuppositions and practices of modern psychology. Many in the psychotherapy industry claim that thinking much of ourselves (self-esteem, self-love, self-actualization, self-acceptance, or the "I'm Okay" perspective) is necessary for good mental health, and a lack of such self-regard is a central cause of a host of psychological pathologies. No evidence exists to prove the truth of that assertion. In fact, much research has *disproved* it, and even some who assume its truth admit that the evidence shows no consistent correlation between self-esteem and mental health.[3]

Unfortunately, however, many Christian psychologists, writers, and even pastors have absorbed the assumptions of the psychological community to the extent that their goal in counseling is the fulfillment of the self, not the glory of God achieved through the obedience of the counselee.[4]

The focus on good feelings about the self, or self-esteem, has had a major impact on public schools, and therefore on our children. Teachers spend class time doing exercises that communicate to students how wonderful and important they are. For example, when Loren Miller Elementary School in Los Angeles decided to take action to improve test scores, they spent part of each day in "I Love Me" lessons. Students completed the phrase, "I am . . ." with words such as "beautiful, lovable, respectable, kind, or gifted." Then they memorized the sentences instead of memorizing their school work.[5] What is the result of such an approach? As one might expect, students feel better about themselves, even when they have poor academic performance. A 1989 study of math skills compared students in eight countries. Korean students ranked highest in math performance, and United States students ranked lowest. The researchers also asked students to rate how good they were at mathematics. The U.S. students ranked highest in their valuation of their own math skills, whereas the Koreans ranked themselves lowest. Those who tout self-esteem as essential to mental health and performance claim that only those who feel good about themselves will perform well. This study, however, demonstrated an inverse relationship between self-esteem and academic performance. Other studies have shown similar results.[6]

The assumptions of me-ism are also behind most North American media advertising. We are told that we should buy the advertised products to be good to ourselves, to satisfy our desires, and because we deserve the best. Condoms are promoted among young unmarrieds instead of abstinence, since it would be useless, or at least bad form, to suggest that persons place any limits on their personal pleasure. Self-fulfillment and self-pleasure also drive the entertainment industry. North Americans are spending more money on sports and leisure activities. Especially in U.S.–Canadian sports, fans ruminate about the inequity in the incredible wealth of entertainers and athletes, as they type their charge card number on an Internet ticket agency Web site. They continue to purchase tickets so that they may be entertained as satisfactorily as their neighbors. It is no exaggeration to say that many Americans work at their play and play at their work. And at the heart of a culture that is driven by consumption and obsessed with entertainment is a self-centered worldview. Christopher Lasch, in *The Culture of Narcissism*, summarizes, "Self-absorption defines the moral climate of contemporary society."[7]

This worldview has affected Christians for decades. Twenty-five years ago, John Piper observed that in many churches,

> Today the first and greatest commandment is, "Thou shalt love thyself." And the explanation for almost every interpersonal problem is thought to lie in someone's low self-esteem. Sermons, articles, and books have pushed this idea into the Christian mind. It is a rare congregation, for example, that does not stumble over the "vermicular theology" of Isaac Watts's "Alas! And Did My Saviour Bleed": "Would He devote that sacred head/For such a worm as I?"[8]

Five years after Piper made this analysis, California megachurch pastor and television preacher Robert Schuller wrote *Self-Esteem: The New Reformation*. It is an understatement to say that the philosophy expressed by Schuller in this book is self-centered.

To be born again means that we must be changed from a negative to a positive self-image—from inferiority to self-esteem. . . .

When we are adopted as children of God, the core of our life changes from shame—to self-esteem. And we can pray, "Our Father in heaven, honorable is *our* name." So, the foundation is laid for us to feel good about ourselves! . . .

We might even conclude—at least have reason to suspect—that the level of the Lordship of Christ in a life can be measured by the rising level of Christian self-worth. . . .

What is our Lord's greatest passion for his church today? I believe that he wants his followers to respect themselves as equal children of God and to treat all other human beings with that same respect.[9]

Evidently Schuller believes that our Lord has altered His "greatest passion," because Jesus said that the greatest commandment is to love God, not to respect ourselves. Schuller's perspective is so acclimated to our culture that it is out of touch with biblical truth.

In 1982, the same year Schuller's *Self Esteem* was published, Paul Brownback wrote *The Danger of Self Love: Re-Examining a Popular Myth*. On the first page, Brownback flatly states, "From beginning to end the focus of Scripture is the exaltation of God and not man."[10] In the 1980s, Dave Hunt wrote two books, both of which identified the current exaltation of self as a cultural ideology that is "seducing" Christianity.[11] The combat over this issue continues unabated, and the current battleground is the local church. The pressing question is, "Will churches determine their mission by discovering what people want or by discovering how the Bible defines a church?" Perhaps the question could be answered easily after we answer the question: "Which is central to biblical thinking—God or man?"

What, then, is the biblical perspective about the self? Consider three statements in answer to that question:

- The Bible calls people to humility, not self-exaltation.

- The Bible calls people to service, not self-fulfillment.
- The Bible emphasizes sacrifice, not selfishness.

Let's take a closer look at each of these.

The Bible Calls People to Humility

According to the Bible, human beings have worth because we are created in the image of God (Gen. 1:26–27, 31). God trusts us with the task of caring for the world He created (2:15). God loves us (John 3:16), and we have the potential to grow into the likeness of Jesus Christ (Rom. 8:29; 2 Cor. 3:18). In the Christian worldview, these facts are connected to the structure of reality and the way God made us. Feeling better or worse about ourselves does not change these facts.

Another component of a biblical view of persons is the fact that God's image in us has been marred by sin. This sin makes us "helpless," "ungodly," "sinners," and "enemies" of God (Rom. 5:6–10). We need reconciliation with God, and God has provided this in Christ. When a person receives Christ, he or she becomes "a new creature" (2 Cor. 5:1), capable and responsible to become all that God intends.[12]

This biblical portrait of the self hardly leaves room for self-exaltation. Yes, we are valuable, but our value derives from what God has done—His creation of us, investment of worth, and salvation from sin. Therefore, this perspective humbles us, even as it affirms our worth. Biblical truth about the self leads us neither to self-glorification nor to masochism or self-loathing. It challenges us to obey and glorify the sovereign Creator who has the authority to command.

In spite of this clear biblical picture of the self, the effort to Christianize me-ism has spawned numerous expeditions into Scripture to find supporting texts. Psalms of praise have been transformed into positive self-affirmations. Covenant promises are used to try to bind God to give us what we want. Other "positive confessions" have been found to offer good words about "me." As a result, some pulpits are occupied by preachers immersed in a popular psychology loosely related to out-of-context Scripture texts. They speak more of self-image, self-love, and self-fulfillment than of self-sacrifice, self-denial, and self-control. They speak of faith as if it were a magic wand, and of God as if He would rather give us what we want right now than teach us to be holy. This perverts biblical truth.

Another perversion reinterprets the crucifixion of Jesus to support a high view of self. It is said that God paid a price to redeem us, and that price was the very life of His Son. That much is true, for we were redeemed (set free) "with precious blood" (1 Peter 1:19). However, those who wish to exalt the self go on to say that, because the life of Christ was the price for our redemption, *His* life is the measure of *our* worth. "So," the reasoning goes, "if you want to know how much God values you, just look at what He paid for you—His own Son!" This is a logical extension of the facts, but not a biblical assertion.

Actually, the Bible says the opposite. The fact that Jesus had to die for our redemption does not measure our worth; it demonstrates our sin. "While we were yet sinners, Christ died for us" (Rom. 5:8b). *Orthodox Christian theology has always pointed to the cross to remind us of our sin, not our self-worth.* His death was a sacrifice for our sin, not a proof of our great significance. God allowed Isaiah to see this over seven hundred years before the birth and death of the Messiah: "He was pierced through for our transgressions, He was crushed for our iniquities" (Isa. 53:5a). This is a far cry from Jesus' death as an expression of our great worth.

The biblical word for self-exaltation is pride. Consider the following words about pride:

- "The fear of the Lord is to hate evil; pride and arrogance and the evil way and the perverted mouth, I hate" (Prov. 8:13).
- "Everyone who is proud in heart is an abomination to the Lord; assuredly, he will not go unpunished" (Prov. 16:5).
- "A man's pride will bring him low, but a humble spirit will obtain honor" (Prov. 29:23).
- "Everyone who exalts himself will be humbled, but he who humbles himself will be exalted" (Luke 18:14b).
- "Clothe yourselves with humility toward one another, for God is

opposed to the proud, but gives grace to the humble" (1 Peter 5:5b).

Our great models for godly living in the Bible were humble, not proud. Jesus Himself said, "I am gentle and humble in heart" (Matt. 11:29). Paul called himself the "foremost" of sinners (1 Tim. 1:15). "Moses was very humble, more than any man who was on the face of the earth" (Num. 12:3). When Isaiah saw a vision of God in the temple, he did not respond by thinking, "I must be really special for God to reveal Himself to me." Instead he saw his sinfulness more clearly than ever and said, "Woe is me, for I am ruined! Because I am a man of unclean lips" (Isa. 6:5).

One night Jesus' disciples fished all night and caught nothing. The next day, Jesus told them to cast the nets once more; the resulting catch strained the nets. When Simon Peter saw what happened, he did not say, "Jesus did this miracle because I am so important. Now I see how much I'm worth to God and to myself." Nor did he say, "This is great, Jesus! Go fishing with me *every* day, and we'll make a fortune!"

Instead he saw his sinfulness in the presence of Christ's holiness and much like Isaiah he said, "Depart from me, for I am a sinful man, O Lord!" (Luke 5:8).

This dichotomy of thinking about the self has been recognized by Christian leaders. The historic Christian doctrine has been to eschew pride, or self-exaltation. For example, John Calvin wrote,

> For so blindly do we all rush in the direction of self-love that everyone thinks he has a good reason for exalting himself and despising all others in comparison. For there is no other remedy than to pluck up by the roots those most noxious pests, self-love and love of victory. This the doctrine of Scripture does. For it teaches us to remember that the endowments which God has bestowed upon us are not our own, but His free gifts, and that those who plume themselves upon them betray their ingratitude.[13]

Perhaps the ingratitude of which Calvin wrote is the root of pride. Instead of acknowledging that "every good thing bestowed and every perfect gift is from above" (James 1:17), the proud imagine that they are in some way responsible for the gifts they have. They presume that they deserve some credit for them, so they feel a complacent sense of satisfaction, or as Calvin put it, they "plume themselves upon them."

The Bible Calls People to Service

Jesus said of Himself, "The Son of Man did not come to be served, but to serve" (Matt. 20:28). Later, Paul wrote about Jesus:

> Have this attitude in yourselves which was also in Christ Jesus, who, although He existed in the form of God, did not regard equality with God a thing to be grasped, but emptied Himself, taking the form of a bond-servant, and being made in the likeness of men. Being found in appearance as a man, He humbled Himself by becoming obedient to the point of death, even death on a cross. For this reason also, God highly exalted Him, and bestowed on Him the name which is above every name.
> —Philippians 2:5–9

Before Jesus was born as a man, He was with God and was God (John 1:1). Yet, when it was time for Him to leave the glories of heaven for the pain of earth, He did not grasp for the comfort of the perfect fellowship within the Trinity. Instead, He emptied Himself and gave Himself away as a humble servant, even dying for undeserving sinners.

If Jesus' chief concern had been His own self-interest and comfort, He never would have exchanged heaven for earth, the worship of angels for the persecution of evil men. But His chief concern was divine glory and the plan of salvation, so He served. When He had the opportunity to act for His own benefit, He chose instead to give Himself away in service to others. Paul writes in Philippians 2:5 that Christ's followers are to have the same humble servant attitude. Jesus Himself taught us to serve as He served. One day, after He had served the disciples by washing their feet, He said to them, "If I then, the Lord and the Teacher, washed your feet, you also ought to wash one another's feet. For I gave you an example that you also should do as I did to you" (John 13:14–15).

A notable contrast to the life and words of Jesus is found in the humanistic psychologist and writer Carl Rogers. Rogers's wife was terminally ill. She needed the attention of her husband in her final days, but he virtually abandoned her. He explained, "I realized that it was necessary for my survival to live *my* life, and that this must come first, even though Helen was so ill."[14] This is simply the consistent ethic of a value system that places self-fulfillment over others. Just think of all the works of benevolence—from hospitals to hot meals—that never would have been done if the priority had been "to live *my* life." Rogers's life provides a bold contrast with Christ's. For Christians with a biblical worldview, self is no longer the central concern. Instead, at the center of life is Christ and others. Loving and serving—these become the twin goals of life, not satisfying self. As Paul put it, "Through love serve one another" (Gal. 5:13).

During the first months of our marriage, my wife and I read Thomas à Kempis's *The Imitation of Christ* together. Thomas wrote in the fifteenth century, so he was unaffected by the modern emphasis on self-love that has infected the church. I'm glad we chose to read that book, because it helped us to begin our marriage by thinking about selfless service instead of self-exaltation and self-fulfillment. Every Christian should read such works to balance the philosophical biases of our time. Thomas à Kempis wrote:

> It is great wisdom and high perfection to esteem nothing of ourselves, and to think always well and highly of others. . . . Vain is he that setteth his hope in man, or in creatures. Be not thou ashamed to serve others for the love of Jesus Christ; nor to be esteemed poor in this world. . . . I would I could serve Thee all the days of my life. I would I were able, at least for one day, to do Thee some worthy service. . . . O how humbly

and meanly ought I to think of myself! How ought I to esteem it as nothing, if I should seem to have aught of good![15]

What if such words were written today? One of our contemporaries who had been steeped in current self-oriented prejudices would
pity Thomas as psychologically unhealthy, even masochistic. Such a
person is crippled in serving God and others because he is too inse-
cure and has not learned to love himself. To the contrary, Thomas à
Kempis has long been regarded as a spiritual example for Christians.
So much for the necessity of self-love. Thomas was only reflecting the
biblical emphasis on humility and service over self-exaltation and self-
fulfillment.

The irony is that those whose goal is to please the self are never
fully satisfied. So many people who have lived in wealth and ease have
been profoundly unhappy with their lives and have only longed for
more. They have never found a purpose for living beyond themselves,
and the self-life is simply too small a purpose to bring fulfillment. On
the other hand, those who give themselves away in service to others
find fulfillment in the worst of circumstances.

Corrie ten Boom and her sister, Betsie, were imprisoned in the
Ravensbruck concentration camp during World War II. While there
they experienced the worst kind of inhumanity at the hands of Nazi
guards. They were herded like cattle, regularly stripped in public, forced
to do hard manual labor eleven hours a day on a starvation diet, and
made to sleep in a bed with five women and countless fleas. Human
misery, pain, and death were all around them. All of that would not
bring pleasure to the self-life. It did not bring pleasure to Corrie and
Betsie. However, in the midst of their suffering, they found joy. This
joy did not derive from the opportunity to pursue personal pleasure
or from the comfort of their surroundings. They had neither. Nothing that is coveted by lovers of self was available to them. Instead, they
found joy in service to others. By a miracle, they had been able to
bring into the camp with them a Bible, and every day women in the
barracks gathered to listen to them read it aloud. This became the
reason to live for Corrie and Betsie. If self-love had been their goal,

they would have been grievously disappointed. However, in serving others, they found lives of purpose. Corrie wrote later:

> As the rest of the world grew stranger, one thing became increasingly clear, and that was the reason the two of us were here. . . . From morning until lights-out, whenever we were not in ranks for roll call, our Bible was the center of an ever-widening circle of help and hope. Like waifs clustered around a blazing fire, we gathered about it, holding out our hearts to its warmth and light. The blacker the night around us grew, the brighter and truer and more beautiful burned the word of God. . . . Life in Ravensbruck took place on two separate levels, mutually impossible. One, the observable, external life, grew every day more horrible. The other, the life we lived with God, grew daily better, truth upon truth, glory upon glory."[16]

This is the irony—God created us in such a way that we find fulfillment and joy as we give them away, not as we seek them for ourselves. Jesus was right: "He who loves his life loses it, and he who hates his life in this world will keep it to life eternal" (John 12: 25).

The Bible Emphasizes Sacrifice

Romans 12:1 is a classic exhortation to self-sacrifice: "Therefore I urge you, brethren, by the mercies of God, to present your bodies a living and holy sacrifice, acceptable to God, which is your spiritual service of worship." Christians are to lay themselves on the altar and give themselves to God for His service. We are to offer ourselves to be burnt up in the service of the living God. Not only does that contrast with the me-ism of our culture; it also contrasts with the experience of many Christians. A great number of Christians give God some money, some time, or some small part of their lives. However, Romans 12:1 is a call to present our *bodies,* which is all of self. When we present our bodies to God as living sacrifices, He has it all.

Jesus again is our. example in giving ourselves away. "Though He was rich, yet for your sake He became poor, that you through His poverty might become rich" (2 Cor. 8:9). Sacrifice for the sake of others is the opposite of selfishness, and it is the calling of Christ.

When I think of Christ's sacrifice and the sacrifice to which Christians are called, I think of the Christians who have been killed for their service to God. Through the centuries, many thousands have chosen to die rather than deny their faith. Their decision was the opposite of self-service. Polycarp was one of the earliest to made such a choice. During the Empire-wide persecution under Marcus Aurelius in the second century, Polycarp, the bishop of Smyrna, was arrested, stood before the proconsul, and was condemned to be burned at the stake. But first he was urged to recant, to deny Christ. His reply was, "Eighty and six years have I served him, and he never once wronged me; how then shall I blaspheme my King, Who hath saved me?" At that the fire was lit around him.[17] That is sacrifice, not selfishness.

The "health and wealth" theology that appeals so strongly to selfishness has nothing to say in situations like those faced by Polycarp and the ten Boom sisters. It is a theology tailored for a small segment of the world's history and population—primarily nominal church members in the modern West. If this theology of selfishness is not true for all the world, then it is not true for any part of the world. People like Polycarp are the heroes of faith, not those who serve God with the assumption that faithfulness will accrue dividends of personal blessing. After all, we follow the example of the One who owned nothing and gave away everything, including His life's blood.

The Bible makes explicit this connection between Christ's death and ours. One example is the testimony of the apostle Paul: "I have been crucified with Christ; and it is no longer I who live, but Christ lives in me" (Gal. 2:20a). Paul's self-life had been put to death, so self-love was dead, and he no longer concerned himself with his comfort, popularity, wealth, or image. Dead people don't worry about such things. The self-life is meant to die, not be reformed. It is not that we need *change*, but rather *exchange*—our lives for Christ's life in us. "It is no longer I who live, but Christ lives in me."

It is not that Christ's presence obliterates our personalities. Paul went on to write in the rest of Galatians 2:20, "And the life which I now live in the flesh I live by faith in the Son of God, who loved me, and delivered Himself up for me." We still live, but we live a different kind of life in intimacy with Christ. "Christ lives in me."

This "exchanged life," as some have called it, produces two marvelous effects. First, one's perspective about everything changes. We no longer approach life with the questions "What's best for me?" "What will I get out of it?" "What will people think of me?" Instead, we think in terms of giving ourselves away. That is what Jesus did, and He lives in us. Second, we are delivered from many stresses that plague us daily. For example, we no longer beat ourselves up trying to perfect the self, because the self is dead. Instead, we will focus on the joy of fellowship with Christ. We will not fret ourselves over what others think of us, because self is just not that important. Instead, only what people think of Christ will matter.

This is not a book about intimacy with Christ; it is about developing a Christian worldview. But at some point, perhaps at this point, we should mention that Christianity is not just a set of ideas. Christianity is a living relationship with the living God who has manifested Himself in His only Son, Jesus Christ. The New Testament describes that relationship with numerous word pictures (reconciliation, new birth, adoption, salvation. . . .), but the reality is the same. All these terms describe the same experience with God that is available only because of His seeking grace expressed in the Person and work of Jesus. Once we place our faith in Jesus, we have a desire to please our Master, to do His will. We develop a mindset or worldview that is in accord with His will as expressed in His Word. An essential aspect of that biblical worldview is thinking about ourselves in a way that reflects who He has created us to be—nothing more, nothing less.

In the fourth century A. D., Augustine expressed well the Christian view of the self. In *The City of God,* he wrote, "Two cities have been formed by two loves; the earthly by the love of self, even to the contempt of God, the heavenly by the love of God even to the contempt of self. The former, in a word, glories in itself, the latter in the Lord."[18] Christians in every age of the church have adopted this perspective. It originated with Christ. Christians of the twenty-first century would do well to return to such a view of the self. We have stared at our reflection in the pool too long. We should leave it before we begin to feel the hunger pangs.

CHAPTER 7

The Midas Trap: A Biblical Perspective on Money

Do not store up for yourselves treasures on earth, where moth and rust destroy, and where thieves break in and steal. But store up for yourselves treasures in heaven, where neither moth nor rust destroys, and where thieves do not break in and steal; for where your treasure is, there your heart will be also.

—Matthew 6:19–21

You cannot serve God and wealth.

—Matthew 6:24b

None of you can be My disciple who does not give up all his own possessions.

—Luke 14:33

What a man most needs is not a knowledge of how to get more, but a knowledge of the most he can do without, and of how to get along without it. The essential cultural discrimination is not between having and not having or haves and have-nots, but between the superfluous and the indispensable.[1]

—Wendell Berry

Another figure of ancient Greek mythology, Midas, was said to be the king of Phrygia in Asia Minor. Whether a historical model for Midas actually lived, the story about him is that Midas once did something that pleased the god Dionysus. So Dionysus gave to Midas a special power—everything he touched turned into gold. At first, Midas's miraculous power pleased him, but it wasn't long before the blessing became a curse. Midas quickly learned that many things are more valuable than gold, and without them gold is worthless. Even Midas's food turned to gold when he touched it. He longed to be free from his new power. It had been nice, but what good was gold if he couldn't live? Midas was told to bathe in the river Pactolus. He did so, and the magic touch left him. That, according to the myth, is why the sand on the banks of the Pactolus River has a golden hue.

Greeks used the story of Midas to teach that some things are more important than money. It's nice to be rich, but what if you had the Midas touch, with all the gold you wanted, but no food? What if you had enormous wealth but poor health? What if you had unimaginable possessions, but broken relationships with friends and family? What if you owned a dream house with a bank account to match, but the work of increasing wealth so obsessed you that you could not enjoy the palace? What if making money so preoccupied you that there was no time to consider weightier matters, such as your relationship with God? These are not hypothetical situations. They exist all around us.

We all know people caught in "the Midas trap," the life-consuming desire for more money—money to make, to spend, and to save for the next generation to spend. One day the person caught in the trap realizes that life has been used up on trivialities. The Greeks wrote about this materialistic syndrome thousands of years ago, so it is hardly a new phenomenon. Plato classified the pursuit of money as an "unnecessary" appetite, and stated that the man of understanding will not "heap up riches to his own infinite harm."[2]

The most stringent warnings and most rigorous standards concerning the love of money come from the Bible. Jesus told a parable about a man caught in the Midas trap (Luke 12:16–21). This man with the

Midas touch had more grain than barn space for storing it. So he tore down his barns and built larger ones. Once they were filled, his plan was to retire and devote himself to a life of leisure. He gave no thought to spiritual things, only material things. "But God said to him, 'You fool! This very night your soul is required of you.'" He suddenly found himself at the end of his life instead of the beginning of the good times, and he had neglected his soul, which was the only thing that now meant anything. Jesus concluded the parable by stating that all materialistic people are as foolish as this man: "So is the man who lays up treasure for himself, and is not rich toward God."

The Way Things Are

Jesus' warning, like the warnings of the Greeks, has been forgotten by an affluent, materialistic society. We have much, but we want more. Richard Foster has described the situation in which "compulsive extravagance is a modern mania. The contemporary lust for 'more, more, more' is clearly psychotic; it has completely lost touch with reality. The chasm between Third World poverty and First World affluence is accelerating at an alarming rate."[3]

Western self-identity and even self-worth are determined by how much we possess and consume. We want a larger house and more expensive car, not because the space is needed or the transportation more dependable, but because these things will move us up the ladder of societal esteem. We have been taught that we should do all we can to move up the materialistic ladder. Those in the Hindu caste system are bound to remain in a class or socioeconomic level. The rest of us can trade in a compact car for a luxury model, or move from costume jewelry to fashion jewelry to diamonds and pearls. People in the United States and Canada in particular accept this progression as the natural order of things, though materialism long has been a hallmark of Eastern cultures in Japan and Hong Kong. To question the right of social progression is cultural heresy. Yet, the Bible promotes a different attitude and lifestyle.

It will be easier to understand and respond to our current situation if we are aware of how materialism developed. Conspicuous consumption and unbridled covetousness have not always been the order of the day. One illustration will exemplify how far we have come.

> In 1635 a Puritan merchant named Robert Keayne left London to take up residence in the new settlement at Boston. From humble circumstances, he had risen through hard work and careful planning to a position of some prominence. In the New World he prospered further. But four years later his ship of fortune ran aground. The elders of the First Church in Boston, of which he was a member, brought charges against him for dishonoring the name of God. Soon after, he was tried and found guilty by the General Court of the Commonwealth as well. Writing his memoirs some fourteen years later, he was still stung by the disgrace of the event. His sin was greed. He had sold his wares at a 6 percent profit, 2 percent above the maximum allowed.[4]

We shake our heads in disbelief at such a story. In today's market, Keayne would be respected as a shrewd businessman for his ability to "earn" fifty percent more than the going margin of profit. His church, far from bringing charges of greed against him, would be grateful for the additional offerings and would likely place Brother Robert at the head of the finance committee.

How did our culture make the journey from the regulation of profit margins and restriction of greed, to today's insatiable covetousness on the corporate and personal levels? Perhaps American Protestant theology made an unwitting contribution to the development of consumerism. Rodney Clapp has written that the "Protestant work ethic" made business, and the profit that resulted, an acceptable, even a holy, calling. The famous dictum of John Wesley was, "Earn all you can, save all you can, give all you can." Such an encouragement to industry, frugality, and generosity was well suited to Wesley's eighteenth-century environment in England. Yet, Wesley himself worried about the application of his statement. He later wrote:

I fear, wherever riches have increased (exceeding few are the exceptions), the essence of religion, the mind that was in Christ, has decreased in the same proportion. Therefore do I not see how it is possible, in the nature of things, for any revival of true religion to continue long. For religion must necessarily produce both industry and frugality; and these cannot but produce riches. But as riches increase, so will pride, anger, and love of the world in all its branches.[5]

Protestantism's emphasis on individual decision and personal fulfillment may have fertilized the soil of consumerism, but the primary impetus came from industry, not theology. It should be remembered that, until the twentieth century, most U.S. homes were sites of production as well as consumption. "Even as late as 1850, six out of ten people worked on farms. They made most of their own tools; they built their homes and barns; they constructed their furniture; they wove and sewed their clothes; they grew crops and animals, producing food and drink; they chopped wood and made candles to provide heat and light."[6]

The Industrial Revolution changed all that as it moved from England to the post-Civil War U.S. From 1859 to 1899, the number of factories in the United States grew from 140,000 to 512,000. The new factory system resulted in mass production and drove people from farm production to wage labor. Production of goods took a quantum leap, and suddenly the new economic system was producing more goods than the population could consume.

How was this gap between production and consumption closed? Since the momentum of factory production was already underway, *manufacturers decided to increase consumption rather than decreasing production.*[7] Thus was born modern consumerism, and advertising was the midwife. Manufacturers used advertising to convince consumers to buy goods they had never owned or even thought they needed. Sellers realized that advertising must go beyond catering to existing needs, to create new needs. That is the way consumerism works. People see an advertisement. Suddenly they want something that they could have done without had they never seen the advertisement. Many advertising messages, explicit and implicit, seem ludicrous when we analyze what they are really saying, yet they are effective. If only we will use the right toothpaste, we will suddenly be popular and attractive. If we drink the right brand of beer, the opposite sex will be drawn to us like bears to honey. If we buy a particular brand of car, we will leap with joy. Personally, I have never had that feeling after forking over so much money.

Advertising has created a cultural ethos that defines the good life with reference to how many new goods and experiences one is able to acquire and consume. Advertising has had help. George Monsma has reviewed four other influences on the spending habits of North Americans. First, Monsma observed that the average family's perceived needs rise as the level of consumption increases. The goal is to "keep up with the Joneses," and the Joneses keep spending more.

Second, the spending "standard" is constantly being raised by the affluent, and individuals must spend more just to maintain their relative status. Monsma called this "positional" spending. Third, as technology becomes more complex, previously unanticipated expenditures become more important. A good example of this phenomenon is the computer. So many people in the marketplace have one, and so much work is done on computers, that owning (and upgrading) a system has become increasingly important. Thorstein Veblen reversed a once-popular saying to describe this process: "Invention is the mother of necessity."[8] This complexity factor also includes the issue of "planned obsolescence," a manufacturing/marketing strategy in which model changes ensure that a product will soon become obsolete unless it is upgraded or replaced.

Fourth, Monsma analyzed the pervasiveness of advertising and the availability of credit. Credit makes it easier to indulge our desires for immediate gratification, putting off the actual expenditure of money. Especially in North America, easy credit led to record high levels of consumer debt and personal bankruptcy.[9]

Monsma sees four basic pressures to be materialistic:

- *peer pressure.* We want to "keep up with the Joneses."
- *position pressure.* We spend to establish or maintain social position.
- *progress pressure.* We spend in order to stay current with newer, better technology.
- *pace pressure.* Easy credit artificially speeds the pace at which we can acquire.

All of these reasons for increased spending could easily serve as rationalizations for Christians to capitulate to materialism as an inevitable consequence of living in this country. Before we do so, however, we should heed Rodney Clapp's warning:

> The fact that it [materialistic capitalism] cannot be changed wholesale immediately is no excuse (at least not for Christians) for failing to engage it critically, understanding it as best we can, and resisting its ill effects wherever and as vigorously as we can. . . . Consumer capitalism, both for good and for ill, is a pervasive and foundational reality of our day, yet people can significantly respond to it and potentially change its course.[10]

How resistant are Christians to materialism's "ill effects"? Not very. Robert Wuthnow's research on Americans' attitudes toward money, cited in *God and Mammon in America*, finds that 86 percent of weekly churchgoers say greed is a sin. However, 79 percent of the same group say they wish they had more money. Wuthnow concluded, "Most churchgoers can thus deplore the greed they see in others but remain insensitive to its impulses in themselves." Perhaps this trend is understandable in light of the fact that only 16 percent of these same weekly churchgoers say they were ever taught that wanting a lot of money is wrong.[11]

The statistics Wuthnow cites help to explain the results of a study on giving by John and Sylvia Ronsvalle. The Ronsvalles show that from the 1920s to the 1990s, per capita income in the United States increased by 250 percent in real dollars. Per capita income increased by 90 percent from the late 1950s to the late 1990s. However, from the late 1950s to the end of the century, the average giving per member for the group of Protestants the Ronsvalles studied declined from 3 percent of income to 2.5 percent. Yet, over three-quarters of pastors said that the most frequent reason offered by church members to explain why they cannot give more is that they cannot afford it. Further, the Ronsvalles show that churches are giving less money to mission causes and keeping more for local congregation benefit.[12]

As those in the World War II generation pass from the North American scene, approximately $7 trillion is passing into the hands of the next generation, the greatest transfer of wealth in the history of the world. However, much of that wealth will not go to the offspring of the deceased. Many in the older generation, accustomed as they are to the virtues of saving and giving, are reticent to leave their wealth in the hands of children who live by cultural standards marked by self-indulgence and greed. They would rather leave their money to charitable causes than see it selfishly squandered by their children. Charitable organizations, of course, are wisely pursuing such funds.[13]

Some church leaders have spoken out against the materialism that has gripped the church in America. John Haughey has named it "mammon illness."[14] R. Albert Mohler has called it "nothing less than the financial apostasy of the American church."[15] John White used a biblical analogy, referring to the church's materialism as worshiping "the golden cow":

> God's ancient people worshiped the Baalim: we worship a materialistic golden cow. At heart many of us have a greed for things. We have made the world's agenda of status seeking our own. Unquestioningly we have adopted the world's techniques of gaining influence and security. . . . If our behavior (as distinct from our verbal profession) is examined, many of us who call ourselves Christians begin to look more like materialists. We talk of heaven but we strive for things.[16]

The Way Things Ought to Be

Western Christians live in a materialistic culture where more is better and greed is good. That fact is no real tragedy. Christians have always lived in cultures opposed to biblical principles. It is unrealistic to expect those without Christ to act like Christians; they are not. So when they act like pagans, we should not be surprised; they *are* pagans. However, the tragedy lies in the extent to which Christians have been caught in the materialistic trap of secular culture. It's time for us to set ourselves apart from the world by our attitude and actions regarding material things. It's time for us to heed the biblical admonition to "conduct yourselves in a manner worthy of the gospel of Christ" (Phil. 1:27a). Such *behavior* starts with biblical *thinking* about possessions. The church today is in need of a worldview that includes a theology of things. We need a view of possessions that is thoroughly biblical and unaffected by the influence of our materialistic culture. With that goal in mind, consider ten biblical principles concerning possessions.

First, *God created and owns everything.* The first verse of the Bible affirms God's creation: "In the beginning God created the heavens and the earth." Genesis 1:21 establishes the inherent worth of material things: "God saw all that He had made, and behold, it was very good." It's clear that the Bible teaches that material things are good, not bad. Throughout history, various religions have propagated the idea that spiritual things are good but material things, or the flesh, is bad. The biblical perspective, however, is that the natural order was created by a good God and is itself good. We should not think, therefore, that money, houses, land, or other possessions, are of themselves evil and ownership should be shunned. These things are good, even to be enjoyed.

Genesis 2:9a shows that this was God's original intention: "The Lord God caused to grow every tree that is *pleasing* to the sight and *good* for food" (emphasis mine). In other words, God intended for humankind to enjoy created things (as well as to care for them, according to 2:15). However, we are to do so with the recognition that we are ultimately only managers under God, the Owner. "The earth is the Lord's, and all it contains, the world, and those who dwell in it" (Ps. 24:1).

Second, *Christians are to be givers not takers.* God's people are to give, both to Him in acts of worship and to others in acts of generosity. For example, the Old Testament teaches the requirement to give the tithe to the Lord (for example, Lev. 27:30; Mal. 3:8–10). Jesus upheld this standard. With reference to the tithe, He said, "This you ought to have done" (Matt. 23:23c).

However, Jesus also expanded the concept of giving. His norms for discipleship included giving up everything to follow Him (see Luke 9:23, 57–62; 14:33). Statements that indicate that no one can be a disciple who does not give up all his own possessions shock moderns. We have grown comfortable with a cultural gospel eviscerated of the more demanding features of Jesus' teaching. But if we are going to be disciples of Jesus, we must come to Him on His terms, not ours. He is the Owner of everything that we consider to be ours, and we are only managers, or stewards.

When we give, we are to do so "not grudgingly or under compulsion; for God loves a cheerful giver" (2 Cor. 9:7b). That is, giving is not dutiful obedience to a resented law; it is happily releasing our grip on material things so that they may be used for the ministry of the gospel. This was the way of the early church, where "they began selling their property and possessions, and were sharing them with all, as anyone might have need" (Acts 2:45).

Jesus emphasized giving to the needy. He closely associated Himself with the poor, so much so that He said when we give to those who are hungry, thirsty, naked, sick, and imprisoned, we are giving to Him (Matt. 25:35–40). In this, He was continuing the Old Testament theme of giving to the poor. The Israelites were to give special consideration to strangers and to the poor, remembering that they also had been destitute sojourners in Egypt. If we are to develop a biblical perspective on this point, we would do well to heed the challenge of Peter Davids: "No Christian should rest comfortably with his or her lifestyle so long as it allows life with surplus while a brother or sister somewhere in the world is suffering relievable want."[17]

Third, *when we give things to God, we are returning to Him what is His.* This truth is a corollary of the first. If God owns everything, including us, it is absurd to imagine that in giving to God we are supplying some need in God. To the contrary, we are only returning to Him what is His. When King David challenged the people of Israel to give provisions to build the temple in Jerusalem, they responded by giving generously. David then verbalized this truth beautifully in a prayer.

> Both riches and honor come from You, and You rule over all, and in Your hand is power and might; and it lies in Your hand to make great and to strengthen everyone. Now therefore, our God, we thank You, and praise Your glorious name. But who am I and who are my people that we should be able to offer as generously as this? For *all things come from You, and from Your hand we have given You.*
> —1 Chronicles 29:12–14 (emphasis mine)

Fourth, we *are not to make possessions first in our lives or worship them.* Jesus urged His disciples not to worry about material concerns such as food and clothing (Matt. 6:25–32). His followers are to live by faith, not fear, when it comes to material needs. He said that we should "seek first His kingdom and His righteousness; and all these things will be added to you" (v. 33). Fretting over financial matters reveals that these matters are too important to us. Jesus chided His followers against worrying about *essentials.* Western Christians should take this to heart. Our worry about stock market investments or pension plans reveals our materialism and lack of trust in God to provide.

Material things that take on undue importance have become the objects of our worship. Jesus said, "No one can serve two masters; for either he will hate the one and love the other, or he will hold to one and despise the other. You cannot serve God and *wealth*" (Matt. 6:24b, what some older Bible versions have called "mammon"). There is nothing wrong with *using* wealth, but we must not *serve* mammon. Richard Foster has helped us to define the distinction between the two.

> We are using mammon when we allow God to determine our economic decisions. We are serving mammon when we allow

mammon to determine our economic decisions. . . . Do we buy a new car because we can afford it, or because God instructed us to buy a new car? If money determines what we do or do not do, then money is our boss. If God determines what we do or do not do, then God is our boss. . . . Most of us allow money to dictate our decisions: what kind of house we live in, what vacation we will take, what job we will hold. Money decides.[18]

The first of the Ten Commandments is, "You shall have no other gods before Me" (Exod. 20:3). If money "decides" for us, then money has taken the place of God as the object of our worship. We are committing idolatry, or as John White wrote, we are worshiping the golden cow.

Fifth, *money will neither satisfy nor bring fulfillment.* The best biblical example of this truth is the testimony of the writer of Ecclesiastes. He had accumulated enormous wealth, but it all was "vanity and striving after wind and there was no profit under the sun" (Eccl. 2:11b). This kind of testimony has been repeated countless times through the centuries. Those who have amassed great wealth have acknowledged that it does not make them happier. In fact, at times they feel that they would be happier without their wealth.

Some people believe that the accumulation of money will cure their covetousness. However, greed is not a material problem; it is a spiritual problem. No matter how much we have, if greed is in our hearts we will still want a little more. The writer of Ecclesiastes said it well: "He who loves money will not be satisfied with money, nor he who loves abundance with its income. This too is vanity" (Eccl. 5:10).

Sixth, *we are happier when we give.* The book of Proverbs states, "Happy is he who is gracious to the poor" (Prov. 14:21b). Paul quoted Jesus as saying, "It is more blessed to give than to receive" (Acts 20:35b). Do we believe that? Are we happier when we give than when we receive? Personally, I would rather be the benefactor than the needy recipient. I would rather be the one giving a blessing than the one receiving it. Numerous benefits accrue to those who give.

Seventh, *covetousness or greed is sin.* The tenth commandment reads, "You shall not covet your neighbor's house; you shall not covet your neighbor's wife or his male servant or his female servant or his ox or his donkey or anything that belongs to your neighbor" (Exod. 20:17). Coveting means selfishly wanting what someone else has. In practice, it is usually synonymous with the love of money or greed. The Bible magnifies the seriousness of this sin: "The love of money is a root of all sorts of evil" (1 Tim. 6:10a). The Bible also identifies several dangers associated with loving money. For example, many who have loved money have "wandered away from the faith, and pierced themselves with many a pang" (v. 10). Greed also causes us to trust in money instead of in God.

> Instruct those who are rich in this present world not to be conceited or to fix their hope on the uncertainty of riches, but on God, who richly supplies us with all things to enjoy. Instruct them to do good, to be rich in good works, to be generous and ready to share, storing up for themselves the treasure of a good foundation for the future, so that they may take hold of that which is life indeed.
> —1 Timothy 6:17–19 (cf. Prov. 11:28)

Greed also leads us to base our lives upon wealth. Jesus spoke of "the deceitfulness of riches." When we covet, we are easily deceived into believing that wealth is an adequate foundation for life, but the truth is that it is an unstable foundation: "Do not weary yourself to gain wealth, cease from your consideration of it. When you set your eyes on it, it is gone. For wealth certainly makes itself wings, like an eagle that flies toward the heavens (Proverbs 23:4–5).

Covetousness may also cause us to become proud ("The rich man is wise in his own eyes"—Prov. 28:11) and ungrateful. Moses warned the Hebrew slaves that when they settled in the Promised Land and acquired some wealth they would be tempted to become proud and "forget the Lord your God who brought you out from the land of Egypt, out of the house of slavery" (Deut. 8:14). Covetousness is spiritually dangerous. It can even affect our giving (2 Cor. 9:5). This kind of greed is particularly difficult to detect and admit, but it is nonetheless pernicious. To quote Richard Foster again, "When greed is tied to giving, it is particularly destructive because it appears so good, so much like an angel of light. When we give out of a spirit of greed, an all-pervasive attitude of paternalism poisons the entire enterprise. When greed motivates our giving, we are still trying to profit from the transaction."[19]

Eighth, *we are blessed when we give.* This truth is stated in numerous ways in the Bible. For example, when the Lord called the people of Malachi's day to tithe, He promised to "open for you the windows of heaven, and pour out for you a blessing until it overflows" (Mal. 3:10b). Jesus said, "Give, and it will be given to you. They will pour into your lap a good measure—pressed down, shaken together, and running over. For by your standard of measure it will be measured to you in return" (Luke 6:38). In a lengthy passage on giving, Paul tells the Corinthians, "Now He who supplies seed to the sower and bread for food will supply and multiply your seed for sowing and increase the harvest of your righteousness; you will be enriched in everything for all liberality, which through us is producing thanksgiving to God" (2 Cor. 9:10–11).

From these and other passages, it is clear that God will bless His people when they give. What is not found in the Bible, the claims of health and wealth preachers notwithstanding, is a *quid pro quo* promise that each gift will be matched by a specific financial reward from God. Such preachers are like those "men of depraved mind and deprived of the truth, who suppose that godliness is a means of gain. But godliness actually is a means of great gain when accompanied by contentment" (1 Tim. 6:5–6). The key ingredient here is contentment. The "gain" does not result from "seed faith" that invests in the kingdom to receive a greater return. The "gain" comes to godliness that gives with contentment; that is, with no desire for return.

Ninth, *Christians are to be content.* Contentment is almost an anachronism in contemporary culture. We are constantly under financial and time pressure. Advertising exposes us to more ways to spend our money and pursue pleasure than we could possibly accomplish in three lifetimes. Therefore, we are confronted with a basic economic problem of chasing unlimited opportunities with limited resources. So we are hurried and harried as we seek to experience and own everything expected of us. All of this, of course, is driven by market forces and societal pressure, not biblical principle. We need to hear again Paul's testimony regarding his lifestyle.

> I have learned to be content in whatever circumstances I am. I know how to get along with humble means, and I also know how to live in prosperity; in any and every circumstance I have learned the secret of being filled and going hungry, both of having abundance and suffering need. I can do all things through Him who strengthens me.
> —Philippians 4:11b–13

> For we have brought nothing into the world, so we cannot take anything out of it either. If we have food and covering, with these we shall be content.
> —1 Timothy 6:7–8

Those caught in the Midas trap reason, "If only I had a little more, I could be content." That is self-deception. Contentment, like greed, is a spiritual condition, not a financial one. Whatever the economic level of our material lives, we can decide to be content, or we can decide that we want a little more. The former is the way things ought to be; the latter usually is the way things are.

Tenth, *material things should be placed in proper perspective.* God's people are to live with a constant awareness that this world is not all there is. All that we see will one day burn. "The day of the Lord will come like a thief, in which the heavens will pass away with a roar and the elements will be destroyed with intense heat, and the earth and its works will be burned up" (2 Peter 3:10).

On the basis of this understanding of the future, Peter asks, "What sort of people ought you to be in holy conduct and godliness?" (v. 11b). Peter answers that "we are looking for new heavens and a new earth, in which righteousness dwells" (v. 13). If so, the focus of our lives is not on what is below but on what is above. We are "aliens" (1 Peter 1:1) in this world, "for our citizenship is in heaven" (Phil. 3:20a).

When this worldview sets us apart from the materialism of our culture and we feel like square pegs in a round world, Paul writes,

> We do not lose heart, but though our outer man is decaying, yet our inner man is being renewed day by day. For momentary, light affliction is producing for us an eternal weight of glory far beyond all comparison, while we look not at the things which are seen, but at the things which are not seen; for the things which are seen are temporal, but the things which are not seen are eternal.
>
> —2 Corinthians 4:16–18

In 1994, I went on a short-term church mission trip to St. Maarten. I spent a week teaching children in Bible school, going door to door inviting people to crusade services, and preaching in the evenings. After the week of service, the mission team spent one day sightseeing, while I returned home alone to preach for the Sunday service. I remember standing in line to check my baggage at the airport with the American tourists returning home. They had been on the island to gamble, party, and play on the beach. I could not help but notice the expensive luggage, clothes, and jewelry of these rich Americans. I was quite a contrast. My back-of-the-closet mission trip clothes looked frumpy next to their designer travel wear. My plain suitcase had been given to me by a friend. I had been in St. Maarten not to play, but to serve God and the people. Instead of gambling, I had spent just enough to buy a few presents for family members. The only suit I had taken on the trip had remained on the island with the local pastor, who happened to wear the same size.

Some might have thought that these external differences might denote my deep spirituality. However, what was going through my mind was far from spiritual. I began to envy the vacationing Americans, wondering what it might be like to own such things and to be able to travel to exotic places for the sole purpose of indulging myself. But as we showed our passports, I realized that they were returning home, but I was not. Heaven is my real home. I realized with fresh force that I am really giving up nothing to serve God. The things I will do without in this life are not worthy to be compared with the glories of heaven. When I reach that place, I will finally realize just how trivial and vain were the coveted possessions of this world.

A Final Challenge

Christians have no built-in immunity to the Midas trap. We are just as susceptible as anyone else to the sin of materialism. However, we have a lot of spiritual and practical help available through the presence of the Holy Spirit in us and the teaching of Scripture before us. I have been exploring how to love God with our minds. The goal is to be more equipped mentally to live the Christian life, more dedicated to the truth of God's Word, and more committed to use our minds to bring glory to God. If we are to reach that goal, surely we must honestly address the way we think about money. As we do so, we must also be prepared to think and live differently from the culture around us.

There are three defining differences between the Christian worldview and a secular worldview with regard to possessions. First, the difference between the Christian and secular worldviews is *the difference between consumption and contentment.* The spiritual formula in 1 Timothy 6:6–8 is: *godliness + contentment = great gain.* The gain is not some financial windfall that inevitably results from living right. Godliness is not used as leverage to gain more things. The object of our pursuit is godliness, not gain. When we pursue godliness with contentment, there *is* a windfall, but only God knows its form and timing.

Are you really content with "food and covering" (1 Tim. 6:8)? Jesus was. In fact, He didn't always have food and covering, but still He was content. At least once He fasted for forty days, and He once said, "The foxes have holes, and the birds of the air have nests, but the Son of Man has nowhere to lay His head" (Luke 9:58). Jesus was a homeless person. It's an uncomfortable picture for those of us who speak often of being like Jesus while longing to build that study or jacuzzi onto our house. Jesus was an itinerant preacher who sometimes did not know where He would lie down to sleep. How odd He would seem in our consumer-driven, consumption-oriented culture. A fundamental principle upon which our economy is built is that what we own determines our identity and significance. It's strange to think that the most significant Person in the history of the planet owned nothing. The unavoidable message of our culture is that we will never be content until we acquire a "satisfactory" level of income and consumption. The message of the Bible is that contentment is possible only when we *stop* striving for more.

A second difference between the Christian worldview and a secular worldview is *the difference between positive thinking and faith.* Of course, Christians have a lot to be positive about. But in many cases the positive thinking movement has substituted a positive mental attitude for faith in God. "Whatever you can conceive, you can achieve." The mind becomes the tool that is able to work the miraculous. It is true that our thinking has a powerful effect on how we act, but a positive mental attitude (PMA) is not the same as biblical faith. We can *not* achieve everything we can conceive, nor should we want to do so if what we conceive is outside the will of God for us. Faith is acting upon what God has commanded and promised; anything else is not faith but presumption. And there's a lot of presumption going around these days. Mike Bellah described the situation this way:

> We have entertained great expectations of financial independence, of comfortable and painless living, of quick and easy spiritual victories, and of a Christian entitlement to enjoy the visible trappings of success in the world. We have intensely held these expectations, believing that merely holding them fervently (our PMA) would help bring them about.[20]

In the kind of approach to faith that Bellah has described, which is a common one, faith means that I believe God is capable of fulfilling my expectations for life. But to the contrary, biblical faith is believing that God will do what *He* said He will do. God has never promised to serve as a celestial vending machine so that we may have whatever we want as long as we believe that we will have it. For us to pretend otherwise is merely to prove our own greed.

A third difference between the Christian worldview and a secular worldview is *the difference between greed and giving.* Most people without Christ think in terms of getting, not giving. Greed is a part of our sinful nature. It starts early. A toddler is in his playpen playing with a toy. Another toddler is put in the playpen and begins to play with another toy. What does the first toddler do? He bops the other toddler on the head with his toy and takes both toys. He wants all he can get. As we get older, we learn that bopping people on the head is anti-social behavior, so most of us don't do that anymore. Still, in our hearts, we want what the other person has. We do not grow out of our greed.

A divine change in our hearts is needed. Only when Christ changes us can we comprehend that the love of money is the root of all sorts of evil. When Christ makes us new, the crass materialism of our culture loses its attraction. We no longer desire what Madison Avenue tells us to desire. As children of God, we are "being led by the Spirit of God" (Rom. 8:14). We no longer think only about what we want. Christ empowers us to pray, as He did, "Not My will, but Thine be done" (Luke 22:42). Billy Graham has said, "God has given us two hands—one to receive with and the other to give with. We are not cisterns made for hoarding; we are channels made for sharing. If we fail to fulfill this divine duty and privilege we have missed the meaning of Christianity."

Don't miss the meaning of Christianity. Don't get caught in the trap.

CHAPTER 8

Sex and the "Wicked Bible"

The one who commits adultery with a woman is lacking sense;
He who would destroy himself does it.
Wounds and disgrace he will find,
And his reproach will not be blotted out.
                                        —Proverbs 6:32–33

"You have heard that it was said, 'You shall not commit
adultery'; but I say to you that everyone who looks at a
woman with lust for her has already committed adul-
tery with her in his heart."
                                        —Matthew 5:27–28

"From the beginning of creation, God made them male
and female. For this cause a man shall leave his father
and mother, and the two shall become one flesh; so they
are no longer two, but one flesh. What therefore God
has joined together, let no man separate."
                                        —Mark 10:6–9

The first edition of the King James Version of the Bible was printed in 1611. Another edition was printed in 1631. In the later edition, possibly the most scandalous mistake in the history of the printing press was made. The word "not" was left out of the seventh commandment, so that it read, "Thou shalt commit adultery." Archbishop William Laud was so enraged that he fined the printers 300 pounds—a lifetime's income. Thereafter, the 1631 edition came to be known as the "Wicked Bible." Some people, no doubt, would prefer that *not* would remain out of the seventh commandment permanently. In Aldous Huxley's novel, *Brave New World*, he does just that, reversing sexual standards so that promiscuity becomes a virtue. Written in 1932, this was Huxley's vision of the future.

Sex as the National Religion

It seems that Huxley was not too far afield in his predictions of the future. Though promiscuity may not have achieved the rank of virtue, it has certainly been promoted from the rank of vice. Illustrations of this abound. My wife and I saw a television show in which a young female character had never been married, but had been promiscuous. However, her latest sexual partner had broken up with her, and she was feeling a little down. This, of course, is standard fare for television today. Of the frequent depictions of sexual seduction on TV, by far the majority are outside marriage. What was different about this episode was that a minister was involved. The woman goes to a minister to ask him what to do to feel better. The minister never mentions that what the woman has done is wrong, and he seems unconcerned that the woman feels no shame about her fornication. He makes no reference to sin or to the Christian faith. Instead, he tells her that music cheers him up when he feels blue, so the two of them sit on the organ bench together and sing an upbeat song. By the time the program breaks for a commercial, the woman feels much better. Apparently, those who write and produce such television shows either do not know or would like us to forget that Christian ministers are to help us follow God's instructions regarding sex, so they depict ministers as settling for helping people feel better, whatever their sexual choices may be.

Those sexual choices resemble Huxley's *Brave New World* more every day. The Centers for Disease Control (CDC) report in a 2001 study that 45.6 percent of high school students in the United States stated that they had engaged in sexual intercourse, 60.5 percent of high school seniors admitted to past sexual intercourse, and 21.6 percent had had more than four sexual partners.[1] Not surprisingly, there were 896,000 teen pregnancies in 1997, a rate of 2455 a day.[2] Such widespread sexual activity outside marriage has also resulted in a proliferation of sexually transmitted diseases. In the U.S., for example, the CDC reported that in 2000 there were 31,575 cases of syphilis, 702,093 cases of chlamydia, 358,995 reported cases of gonorrhea,[3] and 40,421 reported cases of HIV.[4] The situation led R. Albert Mohler to write, "America has transformed sex into its national religion, complete with high priests, sacraments, and eager ushers at the door. These days, it does a big business in funerals."[5]

Meanwhile, bizarre sexual antics are advancing closer to society's mainstream. Sadism, masochism, and even bestiality are regarded as alternate sexual choices, and we are encouraged not only to tolerate them, but to celebrate them. Pedophilia, formerly regarded as child abuse, now is more benignly called "adult-child sex" and "intergenerational sex." Journal articles and books are being written to support this practice.[6] And when Harris Mirkin, a professor at the University of Missouri at Kansas City, wrote an article in the *Journal of Homosexuality* suggesting that pedophilia is really not so bad after all, the chancellor of the university defended him by implying that those who disagreed were living in the Dark Ages.[7] The Internet has proven to be a propitious ally for this sexual obsession. Millions of people post dating ads, complete with their physical dimensions, making themselves available to anyone who will consent and can click a mouse. This is a dehumanizing reduction of courtship by which people become commodities. Principled courtship, by contrast, rests on such virtues as unselfish love, commitment to build a lasting relationship, emotional and spiritual intimacy, and regard for the other person's character. These virtues are, according to the university chancellor, medieval.

For those who are less social, the Internet provides a cornucopia of pornographic images convenient for their leering. About 20 percent of American adults, as many as 40 million, visit sexually explicit Web sites.[8] And the Internet is only one facet of the enormous pornography industry. In 1996, Americans spent more than $8 billion dollars on various kinds of pornography. That's more money than

Hollywood's annual domestic box office receipts, and more than all the revenues generated by rock and country music recordings. In the same year, every night between 9 P.M. and 1 A.M., an average of 250,000 Americans made calls to commercial phone sex lines, spending between $750 million and $1 billion.[9] Sex, of course, is also used by conventional businesses as a marketing tool. Sex sells to the extent that a return to Christian virtue likely would cause a recession.

When American culture had something closer to a moral consensus, Judeo-Christian values were the moral assumptions. Not everyone lived by those values, but people generally agreed about what was right and wrong. If someone was shown to have committed adultery, most people agreed that he had wrongly given in to temptation. Usually he felt guilty about it. Today it is claimed that anything is okay between two consenting adults. It seems to be almost expected for a man going through a mid-life crisis to have an adulterous affair as a means of regaining his self-esteem and sense of virility. Women are incessantly told that sexual emancipation and power are part of the package of women's rights.[10] If Christians say that sex outside of marriage is wrong and the good old days would be an improvement over today's anything-goes, amoral system of ideas, we are branded as hypocritical Victorians who are anachronistic and unrealistic. We are told, "Wake up and smell the coffee. This is the way it is these days. The days of *Ozzie and Harriet* are gone forever."

More's the pity. What was so bad about *Ozzie and Harriet*? Did people used to say, "Gee, I wish just once one of them would commit adultery"? Are we really better off watching dysfunctional families live out their selfishness, anger, and rebellion?

The Dismal Testimony of the Church

The saddest fact of all in this sex-obsessed culture is the extent to which the church of Jesus Christ is capitulating to its influence. Randy Alcorn has summarized the situation well: "Nothing so hamstrings the believer's spiritual potency as sexual compromise—and never has the church in America been so compromised as now."[11]

A study conducted by Josh McDowell reported that 43 percent of teenagers who attend evangelical or fundamental churches have experienced sexual intercourse by age nineteen.[12] According to a survey of those who read *Christianity Today,* an audience made up of people identifying themselves as evangelical Christians, 23 percent admitted to extramarital intercourse, and 45 percent said that they had done something sexually inappropriate with the opposite sex. Even more astonishing, 12 percent of pastors said they had had extramarital intercourse since they began local church ministry, and 23 percent said that they had done something sexually inappropriate with the opposite sex.[13] A. W. Richard Sipe, a former Benedictine monk, studied sexuality among Catholic priests. Over a twenty-five-year period, he interviewed some fifteen hundred priests and laypersons. Sipe estimates that half of the fifty-three thousand Roman Catholic priests in the U.S. break their vows of celibacy.[14]

I suppose such behavior is the reason for the existence of organizations like The Interfaith Sexual Trauma Institute, which is devoted to "the building of healthy, safe, and trustworthy communities of faith."[15] This group publishes a newsletter and sponsors regional workshops to teach about wrong (sexual) uses of religious authority. The very existence of such an organization is the worst kind of testimony about the church.

The reason for such poor sexual behavior on the part of the church is wrong thinking about sex. As we see in Proverbs 23:7a, "as he thinks within himself, so he is." A few examples make this wrong thinking very clear. A young man and woman were living together outside of marriage. When they came to my office, they seemed sincere when they said, "Our parents told us that living together is wrong, but they never told us why. Their generation didn't live together, but a lot of people are doing it now. Does the Bible say this is wrong, and what *does* the Bible say about sex before marriage? We'd like to know." They both claimed to be Christians, but their worldview was so inadequate that it did not even include basic biblical information about sex. I opened the Bible and showed them what is written about the subject. Interestingly enough, the woman came to me later and confessed that, although she had been outwardly religious in the past, she had never personally received Christ as Savior. She did so and became a Christian for the first time.

This couple's lack of biblical perspective concerning sex is common. In a survey among Episcopalians, 75 percent of the nearly twenty thousand Episcopalians surveyed said a faithful Christian can live with someone of the opposite sex without marriage. Seventy percent said that faithful Christians can be sexually active gays and lesbians.[16] It's the "Wicked Bible" all over again, except this time on purpose.

A sexuality report produced by a Special Committee on Human Sexuality for the Presbyterian Church (USA) advocated full acceptance, including ordination, of practicing homosexuals. The report stated, "Coming of age about sexuality requires affirming a diversity of responsible sexualities in the church, including the lives of gay men and lesbians, as well as new patterns among nontraditional families." The chairman of the committee, John Carey, stated, "We don't feel that marriage, by itself as a legal entity, ought to be the sole norm for legitimizing sexuality." He defined fidelity as "concern for the total well-being of the spouse's partner."[17]

Orthodox Christians breathed an uneasy sigh of relief when the report was summarily rejected by the P.C.USA's general assembly— relieved that it was rejected, but uneasy that it could be drafted by the committee in the first place. Such realities in the church make a strong case that it is urgent for today's Christians to construct a worldview with a thoroughly biblical view of sexuality.

A Christian View of Sex

Right behavior begins with right thinking. Sexual behavior is not an exception to this rule. The battlefield for sexual purity is the mind. What goes on in our minds affects our feelings, and usually we act according to our feelings. Many Christians have sub-Christian sex lives because they have never constructed a Christian view of sex. They have allowed themselves merely to soak in their culture's perspective on sex and have ignored biblical teaching, if they know that the Bible addresses it at all. Randy Alcorn has underscored this fact:

Practical advice about sex must be built on a proper foundation of right thinking about sex. Without this foundation, the practical help can at best engender a superficial morality (superior to immorality, but far less than ideal). . . .

The majority of believers simply do not have this moral foundation upon which to build. . . . The photographic plates of our minds have been exposed so long and so thoroughly to the world that the Word doesn't seem to sink in.

There is much wrong sexual behavior among Christians, to be sure, but *wrong thinking is at the root of the wrong behavior.* Because we fail to identify this wrong thinking and its sources—and fail to eliminate or reject them—we continue to indiscriminately buy the antibiblical sexual propaganda foisted on us by the world, largely through the media. This leads to more wrong thinking and, eventually, more wrong behavior."[18]

Seven biblical truths about sexuality establish a foundation for a Christian worldview perspective:

First, *God created sex.* This is difficult for many people to grasp. Teenagers with lustful thoughts picture sexual expression as something they have discovered. Adulterers and pornographers conceive of sexuality as that which must be expressed behind God's back. Many think of sexual intercourse as something a prudish God frowns upon and a puritanical church disdains as a necessary evil. Yet the Bible plainly states that God made sex.

God made humankind in a dual form—male and female (Gen. 1:27). God also commanded the male and female to "be fruitful and multiply" (v. 28a). Sexual intercourse is God's given means of this fruitful multiplication. After God created the world, including the bodies of humans who were to engage in sex, He concluded that it was "very good" (v. 31). The second chapter of Genesis provides greater detail regarding the order and means of the creation of the first male and female. God created the man first and declared, "It is not good for the man to be alone; I will make him a helper suitable for him" (2:18). God created the woman and brought her to the man (v. 22).

The biblical conclusion was, "For this reason a man shall leave his father and his mother, and be joined to his wife; and they shall become one flesh. And the man and his wife were both naked and were not ashamed" (vv. 24–25). Consider the following facts that derive from the biblical story of creation:

1. God created males and females.
2. God intended for the female to be a companion to the male.
3. God created the bodies of males and females to complement one another anatomically.
4. God brought the woman to the man.
5. God commanded the man and the woman to reproduce children.
6. God established the fact that the two were to become "one flesh."
7. God excluded all shame or censure from their nakedness and oneness.

Clearly, God's intention is for one man and one woman to be companions and to become one flesh. This, according to God, is "very good." The Bible also makes it clear that men and women are to have only one sexual partner. Having sex with another partner destroys the oneness between a man and woman and is condemned in the Bible as adultery. When some Pharisees asked Jesus about divorce, Jesus returned to the Genesis account of creation as the model of marriage, and He made explicit something that is only implicit in Genesis: "What therefore God has joined together, let no man separate" (Matt. 19:6). The biblical model is one man for one woman for life.

Second, *God's original purposes for sex were unitive and procreative.* This is made clear from the passages cited above. Sex unites a man and a woman in a dynamic way. They are not merely two bodies enjoying a pleasurable experience with one another; they are "one flesh" (Gen. 2:24). This is not only physiological; it is also ontological, even spiritual. That is the reason Paul argued against adultery by stating that if a Christian "joins himself to a prostitute," he is joining Christ to that prostitute (1 Cor. 6:15–17). The logic works like this:

- A Christian has united his life with Christ, so that Christ is part of his essence, or being.
- In sex with a prostitute, a man unites his essence, or being (not just his body), with the prostitute.
- Therefore, to have intercourse with a prostitute is to join Christ to that prostitute.

This, Paul argued, is what makes adultery so serious a sin. Not only does it shatter the marital unity that is according to God's design, it also drags the presence, or nature, of Christ (in the Christian) into the sinful relationship.

Sex is also God's chosen way to fill the earth (Gen. 1:28). In fact, God *commanded* the first man and woman to multiply. Some have suggested that this is the only command that humankind has ever consistently obeyed.

Third, *God intends sex to be pleasurable for husbands and wives.* It should not be overlooked that this is the context in which God forbids extramarital sex. William Frey observes that the pleasure of sex is reserved for marriage and ruined outside marriage:

> When we say no to promiscuity or other substitutes for marriage, we do so in defense of good sex. It is not from prudery that the Bible advocates lifelong, faithful, heterosexual marriage, but out of a conviction that the freedom and loving abandon that are necessary for sexual ecstasy come only from a committed marital relationship.[19]

The biblical book of the Song of Solomon is a poetic tribute to the joys of sexual attraction and experience. Some of the language in that book is quite passionate and explicit.

> "Your stature is like a palm tree,
> And your breasts are like its clusters.
> I said, 'I will climb the palm tree,
> I will take hold of its fruit stalks.'

Oh, may your breasts be like clusters of the vine,
And the fragrance of your breath like apples,
And your mouth like the best wine! . . ."

"I am my beloved's,
And his desire is for me.
Come, my beloved, let us go out into the country,
Let us spend the night in the villages.
Let us rise early and go to the vineyards;
Let us see whether the vine has budded
And its blossoms have opened,
And whether the pomegranates have bloomed.
There I will give you my love."
—Song of Solomon 7:7–9a, 10–12

This erotic poetry appears in the context of holy Scripture. It was originally written in the context of Israel, the people of God. Contemporary people of God should learn from this the appropriateness of expressing full devotion to God while at the same time having a passionate love life with one's spouse.

A similar message is found in the book of Proverbs.

Let your fountain be blessed,
And rejoice in the wife of your youth,
As a loving hind and a graceful doe,
Let her breasts satisfy you at all times;
Be exhilarated always with her love.
For why should you, my son, be exhilarated
    with an adulteress?
—Proverbs 5:18–20

These words counsel the people of God to express their sexuality within the context of their marriages and not seek fulfillment elsewhere. The words *satisfy* and *exhilarated* further underscore the validity of pleasure experienced in sexual love.

If anyone has the idea that God is prudish or that the Bible discourages sex, they also should consider 1 Corinthians 7:3–5:

> The husband must fulfill his duty to his wife, and likewise also the wife to her husband. The wife does not have authority over her own body, but the husband does; and likewise also the husband does not have authority over his own body, but the wife does. Stop depriving one another, except by agreement for a time, so that you may devote yourselves to prayer, and come together again so that Satan will not tempt you because of your lack of self-control.

These verses encourage, even command, husbands and wives to have sexual relations regularly. They are not to deny one another's desire for sex. If they abstain for awhile for the purpose of prayer, after this "fast" they are to resume regular sexual relations. This emphasizes that the purpose of marital sex is broader than procreation; it is the God-given outlet for the expression of the God-given sex drive, which is pleasurable.

Studies on sexual fulfillment indicate that faith in Christ enhances enjoyment of sex. For example, Archibald Hart, dean of the School of Psychology at Fuller Theological Seminary, polled a group of men, 85 percent of whom were conservative, religious Protestants. More than 80 percent said that their faith had increased their understanding of the role of sex in life and their respect for women. Those who were dissatisfied with their sexual relationships were more likely to come from nonreligious homes.[20] Contrary to Hollywood's portrayal of religious people as uptight, repressed prudes who are sexually unfulfilled, Christians enjoy sexual expression within marriage, as God intended from the beginning.

Fourth, *sexual relations between unmarried partners is wrong.* When I was pastor of a church in a rural area, I enjoyed watching my farmer neighbors prepare the soil and plant their fields with corn, soybeans, and other crops. As I drove by the freshly tilled fields, I remember thinking how beautiful it was. Dirt is beautiful in its place. However, the same dirt on my living room carpet is no longer beautiful. It is dirty. It's the same way with sexual expression. God created it. It is beautiful in its rightful place, and that place is marriage. When taken out of that environment, it is dirty.

The biblical word for sex between persons who are married, but not to one another, is *adultery,* and unless one is reading a copy of the "Wicked Bible," the seventh commandment still prohibits adultery. The biblical word for sex between unmarried people is *fornication.* When that young man and woman who were living together asked me what God had to say about their sexual relationship, I read 1 Thessalonians 4:3–5 to them:

> This is the will of God, your sanctification; that is, that you abstain from sexual immorality; that each of you know how to possess his own vessel in sanctification and honor, not in lustful passion, like the Gentiles who do not know God.

The term *vessel* refers to the physical body. The same term is used in 1 Peter 3:7a in reference to a spouse's body: "Dwell with them with understanding, giving honor to the wife, as to the weaker vessel" (NKJV). The point here is that the wife's body, or vessel, is weaker. It is uncertain in 1 Thessalonians 4 whether Paul was using *vessel* to refer to the bodies of those he was addressing or the bodies of their spouses. In other words, am I to possess my own body in sanctification and honor, or am I to possess my spouse's body in sanctification and honor? Either way, Paul's point is that honor, not lustful passion, should characterize the way we relate to human sexuality.

The word translated "honor" is significant in constructing a Christian view of sex. The same term is used with reference to marital sex in Hebrews 13:4: "Let marriage be held in honor among all, and let the marriage bed be undefiled." As with the term *vessel* in 1 Peter 3:7, *honor* is also used with reference to wives: "Show her honor as a fellow heir of the grace of life" (v. 7b). The Greek term translated "honor" can also be translated "esteem," "dignity," "value," or "worth." It refers to the process of giving something significance, or weight.[21] In the New

Testament, it is used of honoring parents (Matt. 15:4; 19:19; Mark 7:10; 10:19; Luke 18:20; Eph. 6:2), honoring widows (1 Tim. 5:3), honoring Jesus more than Moses (Heb. 3:3), and honoring God (1 Tim. 1:17; 6:16; Rev. 4:9). Christians become useful to God for service when they are vessels "for honor, sanctified" (2 Tim. 2:21). Christians will receive honor as a final reward for being faithful to God (Rom. 2:7; 1 Peter 1:7).

It is important to review the meaning and use of *honor* because this quality is to characterize marital sex. Putting together 1 Thessalonians 4:4, 1 Peter 3:7, and Hebrews 13:4, Christians are to have this sense of honor, esteem, or dignity for their bodies, their spouses, and for marriage in general. The idea of honor in reference to sex and marriage precludes the philosophy of sex that is most prominent in culture today. This common philosophy views sex as a form of recreation or entertainment in which partners may engage solely for the purpose of bringing physical pleasure to one another. Sexual intercourse, according to this view, is like a back rub punctuated with a pleasurable muscle spasm at the end. Not so, according to the Bible. Instead, the biblical perspective is that sex is reserved for marriage and deserves honor. Like valuable china and crystal, it is beautiful but not intended to be used in just any circumstance; it is reserved for the special occasion of the marital relationship. Thus, it is honored.

In some translations of 1 Thessalonians 4:3–5, the translation used instead of "sexual immorality" is "fornication." The original Greek term is the same word from which the English *pornography* is derived. It is the general term for sexual misconduct.

First Thessalonians 4:3–5 also emphasizes the separateness of Christians from "Gentiles," or unbelievers. A clear contrast is drawn between "you"—Christians in Thessalonica—and the Gentiles. This contrast is defined as the difference between "sanctification and honor" on the one hand, and "lustful passion" on the other hand. The Greek word translated "sanctification" is the noun form of the adjective that is translated "holy." The idea of this word is separateness, or difference. In this context, the message is that Christians are to be different, or separate, from non-Christians in the way they handle their sexuality.

The reason for this difference is that the Gentiles "do not know God." First Thessalonians 4:3–5 makes it clear that the conflict between popular worldviews and a Christian worldview will be expressed in our ideas and practices regarding sex.

Fifth, *illicit sex is harmful.* This fact is missing from most fictional portrayals of recreational, do-it-if-it's-what-you-feel sex. Nevertheless, the pain resulting from fornication and adultery is a reality, and the Bible states this fact clearly.

> Or can a man walk on hot coals,
> And his feet not be scorched?
> So is the one who goes in to his neighbor's wife;
> Whoever touches her will not go unpunished. . . .
> The one who commits adultery with a woman is
>   lacking sense;
> He who would destroy himself does it.
> Wounds and disgrace he will find,
> And his reproach will not be blotted out.
> —Proverbs 6:28–29, 32–33

The message could not be more straightforward: The one who engages in sexual sin will experience pain. Therefore, it is stupid ("lacking sense") to do it.

The evidence of this is all around us. Sexual sin is multiplying human misery. In my years as a pastor, and now as dean of students, no one has ever come to me to extol the joys of an illicit sexual relationship. Instead they have come to me emotionally broken and sometimes physically diseased, having been caught in the undertow of sexual impurity. They had looked over their marital fence and thought the grass was greener on the other side. But they found it to be strewn with the dry bones of those who tried to survive sexual impurity. Instead of finding bliss, they inflicted pain on their families, friends, church, and on themselves.

Marriages are being disintegrated by sexual sin. Adultery ruins trust between a husband and wife because it always involves deception. It spoils the exclusive intimacy of marital sex; in biblical terms, the one-ness of husband and wife is shattered as one spouse is "joined" to someone else (1 Cor. 6:16). Adultery creates emotional misery for the one who commits it and for the victimized spouse. Those who are guilty of it will struggle with guilt for the rest of their lives. They will be plagued by self-hatred, self-disgust, and perhaps by disease.

Children are also hurt by adultery. Adultery sends a message to them that the adulterous parent (or relative or friend) is a liar and a cheat, and that honor, character, and faithfulness are not as important as pleasure. It also screams to them that the innocent parent is not valued or loved as much as selfish indulgence. When Christians commit adultery, they also hurt the church. The church is robbed of its holi-ness, spiritual power, and moral integrity before the world. Newer Christians in the church are given a wretched example of what it means to live the Christian life.

The Bible also addresses the financial and physical results of adultery. God's people are warned against it, lest "strangers will be filled with your strength and your hard-earned goods will go to the house of an alien" (Prov. 5:10). How many people have involved themselves in an adulterous affair with the result that they forfeited a house and were forced to pay alimony and child support? Their "hard-earned goods" are going to their ex-spouse's new house and new family.

Proverbs 5:11 adds another consequence of sexual sin: "And you groan at your latter end, when your flesh and your body are consumed." This expresses the physical suffering that results from physical sin. God said long ago that we will suffer if we involve ourselves in sexual sin. Can there be any doubt that the reason there are so many more sexually transmitted diseases is because there is so much more sexual sin? Remember Proverbs 6:32: "He who would destroy himself does it."

And contrary to the popular "safe sex" ideology, condoms don't help much. Studies indicate that condoms have a 15 to 30 percent failure rate in preventing pregnancy. To prevent the spread of HIV or other venereal diseases, they are less reliable, since a woman is fertile only part of each month, but she can contract a disease at any time. How can the safe sex establishment possibly think that it's helpful to say to people about to jump off a skyscraper, "Here, use this para-chute. It works 70 to 85 percent of the time."? Why don't they try to dissuade them from jumping?

In 1987, eight hundred sexologists gathered for a conference in Heidelberg, Germany. When Dr. Theresa Crenshaw asked how many would have intercourse with the AIDS-infected partner of their dreams, relying on a latex condom for protection, not one of them raised a hand.[22]

Robert C. Noble is an infectious-diseases physician and professor of medicine at the University of Kentucky College of Medicine. His words underscore what the Bible said centuries ago:

> Unmarried people shouldn't be having sex. . . . There's no cure for AIDS. There's no cure for herpes or genital warts. Gonor-rhea and chlamydial infection can ruin your chances of ever getting pregnant and can harm your baby if you do. . . . There is no safe sex. . . . If the condom breaks, you may die.[23]

It turns out that "free sex" is not free at all. Some people think that God commanded us not to participate in illicit sexual relations be-cause He wanted to withhold pleasure from us. Actually, the opposite is true. He wanted to withhold misery, sorrow, and suffering from us. He does not intend to keep sex *from* us; He wants to keep it *for* us. He wants us to enjoy it, not be destroyed by it. He wants us to build happy families, not destroy them. When people face sexual temptation, they ought to realize that, no matter what the cost of holiness, the cost of sexual sin is always higher.

Sixth, *Christians can and should resist sexual temptation.* It is im-possible to live in American culture without being faced with sexual temptation. Enticement to lust is all around us in the forms of adver-tisements, television shows, immodest dress, suggestive songs, and pornography. God does not hold us accountable for what we see through no fault of our own, but we are responsible for taking the second look. Furthermore, when we are tempted, we do not have to succumb to that temptation. God's commands are not unreasonable, and they are certainly not impossible to obey. "Thou shalt not commit adultery" is not an exception. He has not commanded us to do something that we are incapable of doing.

How do we win the battle with sexual temptation? We must *control our environment*. What we read, what we look at, and what we think about has a powerful effect on us. We are sitting ducks for a sexual fall if we expose ourselves to lascivious material and allow ourselves to fantasize about sexual sin. Our goal is "to be wise in what is good, and innocent in what is evil" (Rom. 16:19). That is, we will know a lot about what is right and good, but we will be naive or ignorant when it comes to sinful things.

We can also control our social environment. It is possible to communicate in direct and subtle ways that we are committed to sexual purity. Single Christians can let people know of their commitment. They can also take their Bibles and pray during their dates. Married Christians can let people know of their commitment to their spouses. They can refrain from the lingering stare and the caring touch. They can steadfastly avoid being alone with a member of the opposite sex, even in the car on the way to a business lunch. Take away the opportunity to build an intimate relationship. We cannot commit sexual sin if there is no opportunity to do so.

To resist sexual temptation it is necessary to *commit to our spouse*. The Good News Bible interprets Proverbs 5:15, "Be faithful to your own wife and give your love to her alone." The passages cited earlier in this chapter from Song of Solomon and 1 Corinthians 7 encourage us to keep the grass green on our side of the marital fence so that everybody else's grass looks brown by comparison. A decision married people should make is, "If my spouse is going to have a good lover, it will be me."

It is helpful to *consider the consequences* of sexual sin. When men have come to me to talk about sexual temptation, I have cited for them what I review when I face such temptation.

- My prayer life will be ruined if I capitulate to sexual temptation. I will not be motivated to pray, and the Bible says, "If I regard wickedness in my heart, the Lord will not hear" (Ps. 66:18).

- My purity will be spoiled. My moral integrity and spiritual power are based on purity, but that is destroyed by sexual sin.
- My passion for my wife will be diminished. Physically, I will be less absorbed with my wife because of sexual energy given to someone else. Emotionally, our intimacy will be reduced because of my guilt and involvement with another woman.
- People who look to me as an example will be hurt immeasurably. There are people in every Christian's life who look to him or her as an example of what a Christian is supposed to be. Don't disappoint them.
- I will experience pain as a result of sexual sin. In every case of sexual temptation, Proverbs 6:33 should flash into my mind: "Wounds and disgrace he will find, and his reproach will not be blotted out."

Seventh, *there is more to life and love than sex.* The greatest thing in life is not sex. In fact, the greatest thing in life is not marriage or even serving God. The greatest thing in life is having a love relationship with the almighty, all-loving God of the universe. That's why Jesus said the greatest commandment is to love God. That's why Paul wrote, "I count all things to be loss in view of the surpassing value of knowing Christ Jesus my Lord" (Phil. 3:8a). That's why Jesus told a woman who was busily serving Him that sitting at His feet was more important (Luke 10:38–42).

It's not that postmoderns in our sex-obsessed culture don't worship. They do. Many of them worship the god of orgasm, or the god of the "perfect" female body, instead of the one true God. But there is more to life than sex. That's the message the Bible presents in a hundred ways. Our culture is preoccupied with sex, but God intends for us to be preoccupied with Christ, who came to give us life in abundance (John 10:10) and "who is our life" (Col. 3:4).

There is also more to love than sex. Love is a prominent theme in the Bible. Jesus said that loving God is the greatest commandment and loving others is the second greatest commandment. Loving people is exalted in the Bible over eloquent spiritual speech, prophecy, knowledge, faith, generosity, and self-sacrifice (1 Cor. 13:1–3). Sex is never glorified in that way. So, if the Bible elevates love over sex, why aren't we preoccupied with love instead of sex?

Love is described many times in the Bible with no reference to sex. Consider the following description:

> Love is patient, love is kind, and is not jealous; love does not brag and is not arrogant, does not act unbecomingly; it does not seek its own, is not provoked, does not take into account a wrong suffered, does not rejoice in unrighteousness, but rejoices with the truth; bears all things, believes all things, hopes all things, endures all things.
>
> —1 Corinthians 13:4–7

All of these attributes of love may be manifested without a physical relationship. If the Bible does not equate love with sex, why do people in our culture assume that one will lead to the other? Why do people refer to sex as "making love"? Sex cannot make love, though it is a beautiful and intimate expression of marital love.

Our culture is obsessed with sex instead of love. People with a biblical worldview enjoy marital sex, but they are obsessed with loving God and others. There will always be people who prefer to live by the "Wicked Bible." However, a Christian worldview begins with reference to the real Bible, including what it teaches about sex.

CHAPTER 9

Homosexuality and the Christian Worldview

For they exchanged the truth of God for a lie, and worshiped and served the creature rather than the Creator, who is blessed forever. Amen. For this reason God gave them over to degrading passions; for their women exchanged the natural function for that which is unnatural, and in the same way also the men abandoned the natural function of the woman and burned in their desire toward one another, men with men committing indecent acts and receiving in their own persons the due penalty of their error.

—Romans 1:25–27

Do you not know that the unrighteous will not inherit the kingdom of God? Do not be deceived; neither fornicators, nor idolaters, nor adulterers, nor effeminate, nor homosexuals, nor thieves, nor the covetous, nor drunkards, nor revilers, nor swindlers, will inherit the kingdom of God. Such were some of you; but you were washed, but you were sanctified, but you were justified in the name of the Lord Jesus Christ and in the Spirit of our God.

—1 Corinthians 6:9–11

W hy should a chapter on homosexuality be included in a book on constructing a Christian worldview? Homosexuality is "an issue so important that it increasingly appears to be the battleground for all the forces seeking to give shape to the world for the next century."[1] To continue the martial analogy, if Christians do not think and act in a Christian way with regard to every cultural issue, then we have not even shown up for the battle. The result is that we lose the opportunity to "give shape to the world for the next century" by default. Some Christians may regard homosexuality as a distasteful subject and wish that it would go away. It will not, at least not anytime soon. Discussion of this issue is everywhere in our culture. The question is not *whether* we will think about homosexuality, but *what* we will think about it.

If Christians are to develop Christian ideas about homosexuality, they must not limit themselves to the study of secular literature. Christians must stop and listen to the Word of God on the subject. Orthodox Christians traditionally have not uncritically adopted the conventional thinking of the society around them. Instead, they have built a worldview by subjecting cultural ideas to the critique of holy Scripture. On the basis of the teaching of the Bible, Christians either reject or accept the opinions they encounter in society—rejecting that which conflicts with its teaching and accepting that which coincides with its teaching.

Another reason to consider our view of homosexuality is that it affects the witness of the church. When conversations at the water cooler or between classes turn to the ethics of homosexual practice, the nearest Christian may be called to the witness stand and asked, "What does the Bible say about that?" or "Why does the church say homosexuality is wrong?" or the more pejorative "Why are Christians so homophobic?"

Since people on both sides of the homosexuality debate are presently so touchy, even violent, about the subject, I should announce my disposition at the beginning toward those who participate in homosexual behavior. First, I have no political motives. A wide array of political issues relate to homosexuality—same-sex marriages, gays in the military, the rights to adopt and collect insurance benefits, inclusion of information about homosexuality in public sex education curricula, and ordination to ecclesiastical office, to name a few. I am not out to push the legislation du jour. The problem is deeper than political programs. It has to do with the way we think about God's ordering of His creation and His intention for our bodies. That is my subject. I recognize, however, that when the church thinks correctly on this issue, there is cultural impact, and new cultural thought sometimes expresses itself in legislation.

Also, I do not approach the subject with any sense of superiority or personal hatred. Christians are to love every person as God does. All of us, homosexuals and heterosexuals, are sinners. The doctrine of total depravity asserts that every part of us has been tainted by sin, and that includes our sexuality. As Merville Vincent of the department of psychiatry at Harvard Medical School, has written, "In God's view I suspect we are all sexual deviants. I doubt if there is anyone who has not had a lustful thought that deviated from God's perfect ideal of sexuality."[2] Only Jesus has remained sexually sinless in thought and deed. Further, sexual sins are not the only sins, so Christians are never without guilt before God as they speak on any issue. They must not approach homosexuals with a "holier than thou" attitude. We should, however, approach life with a desire to be holy. And part of being holy is thinking and acting in a way that is pleasing to God, including the way we think and act concerning homosexuality. To that end I will explore three facets of this issue.

The Bible and Homosexuality

Genesis 1–2

The place to begin a discussion about homosexuality is not Sodom but creation. God created us male and female. Gender was part of His original plan. Therefore, Christians should dismiss the idea of a unisex society as a violation of God's design. Consider how and why the first woman was created. God said that all of His creation was good.

However, He also said that it was *not* good that man was alone, so God said, "I will make him a helper suitable for him" (Gen. 2:18b). God created the animals and Adam named them, but none of them was suitable as his mate. So God put Adam to sleep, took one of his ribs, and fashioned a woman. When God brought her to the man, he recognized immediately that she was the fitting complement for him. He said, "This is now bone of my bones, and flesh of my flesh; she shall be called Woman, because she was taken out of Man" (v. 23).

The Hebrew of Gen. 2:23 is in the form of a poem. The first poem of human love was written by the first man for the first woman when he first saw her. The Bible responds to this love poem, "For this reason a man shall leave his father and his mother, and be joined to his wife; and they shall become one flesh" (v. 24). Note that "a man" and "his wife" are singular, which indicates that marriage is an exclusive union between one man and one woman. "Shall leave his father and mother" means that a new family unit is about to be formed, and a public social occasion is in view. We call that occasion a wedding. "Shall be joined to his wife" indicates that marriage involves a commitment to a person of the opposite sex. "They shall become one flesh" establishes that marriage is consummated in sexual intercourse. Again, it is between a man and a woman, and as yet there is no shame or sin connected with that marital act.

Often those who argue for support of homosexuality state that Jesus never spoke on the subject. That is true, but Jesus quoted the above verses as evidence that a lifelong union between a man and a woman was God's intention from the beginning, and He added, "What therefore God has joined together, let no man separate" (Mark 10:9). So Scripture makes it plain that God established marriage as a relationship of heterosexual monogamy, and He provided no alternative. Wherever homosexuality may have originated, it was outside the Garden of Eden, and therefore outside God's design for humankind.

Genesis 19

The first time homosexuality is mentioned in the Bible is in the story of the destruction of Sodom.

> Before they lay down, the men of the city, the men of Sodom, surrounded the house, both young and old, all the people from every quarter; and they called to Lot and said to him, "Where are the men who came to you tonight? Bring them out to us that we may have relations with them." But Lot went out to them at the doorway, and shut the door behind him, and said, "Please, my brothers, do not act wickedly. Now behold, I have two daughters who have not had relations with man; please let me bring them out to you, and do to them whatever you like; only do nothing to these men, inasmuch as they have come under the shelter of my roof."
>
> —Genesis 19:4–8

Genesis 19 is a straightforward narrative that relates how Lot invited two angelic messengers into his home in Sodom, and after offering polite resistance (v. 2), they accepted the invitation. The men of the city then demanded that Lot bring his visitors out to them. The purpose of this demand is the interpretive crux of this passage. Literally, the Hebrew verb is "that we may *know* them." This verb was used of sexual intercourse; hence the New American Standard Bible's translation "that we may have relations with them." Until recently this has been the only interpretation given to this passage.

More recently, however, two reconstructions of the story have been offered. First, some have pointed out that *know* refers to intercourse in the Old Testament only ten times out of hundreds of occurrences. Therefore, *know* should be understood in the sense of "interrogate." This would fit the context, it is claimed, and would make the sin of the men of Sodom inhospitality or discourtesy, not homosexuality. After all, a list of the sins of Sodom is in Ezekiel 16:49, but homosexuality is not mentioned.

However, there are at least two textual impediments to such a reinterpretation (besides the difficulty of believing that God incinerated Sodom because of a breach of ancient Near Eastern etiquette). First, Lot referred to the intention of the men as acting "wickedly." Notwithstanding the high standards of hospitality at the time, it is unlikely such a strong term would have been used to refer to the act of interrupting dinner to ask the men some questions. Indeed, such a use of this Hebrew word is unprecedented in the Old Testament. It is difficult to picture Lot resolutely refusing to allow the men to go outside, apparently risking his life in so doing, to prevent a social faux pas. It would make more sense to understand the demand of the men of the city as threatening imminent harm to the visitors.

Second, as an alternative to sending his visitors out to the men of the city Lot offered his daughters, who had not "had relations with man" (Gen. 19:8). The same Hebrew word—*know*—is used here with reference to Lot's daughters. It is hardly possible to interpret this occurrence of the term as a reference to interrogation; the obvious sense is sexual. Lot's offer to the men to "do to them whatever you like" makes this clear, whatever it may say about Lot's morality. The meaning that for centuries has been clear enough is that Lot offered sex with his daughters because it was sex that the men of the city were demanding. Finally, though Ezekiel 16 does not refer explicitly to sexual sin, the word *abominations* is used, and this word describes sexual sin in the same chapter (Ezek. 16:22, 58) and in Leviticus 18:22 and 20:13.

Another recent reinterpretation of Genesis 19 is that the sin of the men of Sodom was not homosexuality per se. The sin was that the men were attempting to *force* the visitors to have sex with them ("They pressed hard against Lot and came near to break the door," v. 9b). Thus, the sin was not homosexuality but homosexual rape, and gang rape at that. Such an interpretation would, conveniently, help to validate consensual homosexuality. I am willing to grant, with Thomas Schmidt, that perhaps these men "attempted male rape as a means to humiliate the suspected spies."[3] However, like Schmidt, I do not regard as irrelevant that early on, "sodomy" came to refer to all homosexual activity, not just homosexual rape.

Further, Jude 7 defines the sin of Sodom as sexual, but makes no reference to rape: "These indulged in gross immorality and went after strange [literally "other"] flesh." The sin mentioned by the inspired writer is not violence but homosexuality.

Leviticus 18 and 20

> You shall not lie with a male as one lies with a female; it is an abomination.
>
> —Leviticus 18:22

> If there is a man who lies with a male as those who lie with a woman, both of them have committed a detestable act; they shall surely be put to death. Their bloodguiltiness is upon them.
>
> —Leviticus 20:13

The meaning of these verses is clear. Their applicability to the New Testament church, however, is disputed. After all, many of the regulations in Leviticus are no longer regarded as normative. For example, we no longer kill animals as sacrifices to God; we don't put children to death if they curse their parents (v. 9); it's okay to wear clothes of "two kinds of material mixed together" (19:19); and even if we believe homosexuality is wrong, we do not advocate executing those who practice it (20:13). So, are we to regard the censure of homosexuality as just one more outdated ordinance?

Two important principles of interpretation come into play here. One is the principle of *repetition*. That is, if a law is repeated in the New Testament, it is applicable to today. The prohibition against homosexuality is repeated in 1 Corinthians 6 and 1 Timothy 1, as we will see. This repetition makes the law against homosexuality binding under either of the extreme interpretations of Old Testament law. Classic covenant theology declares that all the Old Testament applies except what the New Testament repeals; and classic dispensationalism avers that none of the Old Testament applies except what the New Testament repeats.[4]

The second relevant issue is *classification.* Old Testament laws have been generally classified in three categories: civil laws, ceremonial laws, and moral laws. In which category is the law against homosexuality? The command to execute the one who is guilty of homosexuality surely must be classified as civil law; it was the prescribed public response to the crime. However, it is difficult to imagine someone classifying a law that relates to personal sexuality as anything other than moral law.

Nevertheless, Peter Gomes has done just that in writing that homosexuality is condemned in Leviticus because it is "ritually impure."[5] The only possible evidence for such a claim is that these rules are in the "Holiness Code" (Leviticus 17–27) which contains many stipulations for the maintenance of ritual purity. However, in that same code are laws that indisputably pertain to personal morality. Examples are incest (18:6–18), adultery (v. 20), bestiality (v. 23), stealing and lying (19:11–13), hatred (v. 17), and cheating (vv. 35–36). It is true that each of these wrongs, including homosexuality, made Israelites ritually impure. But in these cases they were ritually impure *because* they had committed an immoral act.

Some argue that the law against homosexuality is in the Holiness Code simply because homosexual prostitution was practiced in connection with pagan Canaanite worship. Therefore, according to this argument, homosexuality was prohibited because it would have caused the Israelites to resemble the pagan Canaanites, and thereby become ritually unclean.

However, it is absurd to claim that all of the personal behaviors in the Holiness Code are prohibited merely because they were found among the Canaanites, so that the laws are not binding for Christians. This claim is also inconsistent, since no one will apply this reasoning to behaviors such as incest, lying, and adultery. It leads one to wonder why some are willing to apply it to homosexuality.

Romans 1

In the first chapter of Romans, Paul begins his argument for the total depravity of humankind, which prepares the way for his emphasis on salvation by grace through faith in Christ. Paul mentions homosexuality as one evidence that humankind had turned away from God and His design. Marion Soards writes,

To summarize Paul's main argument: All humans are under the power of sin; not one sin or sinner is better off than another; God's grace freely redeems all humankind through the faith of Jesus Christ. . . . Homosexuality was one vivid indication of the real problem of sin, and Paul states bluntly that all humans are sinners.[6]

Paul also "states bluntly" that homosexuality is sin. The terms he chooses makes this abundantly clear: *degrading passions*, *unnatural* (literally, "against nature"), and *indecent* (which can be translated "shameless"). The unanimous testimony of the church through the centuries has been that Romans 1:26–27 (quoted at the beginning of the chapter) clearly denounces homosexuality as sin. In fact, upon reading the words it is inconceivable to understand Paul in any other way. However, some have attempted to reinterpret him. I will summarize three such "interpretations":

No heterosexuals allowed. Some have claimed that Romans 1 condemns only homosexual acts committed by heterosexual persons. The text says they *"exchanged* the natural function." Therefore, the sin is heterosexuals exchanging their heterosexuality for homosexuality; it does not apply to persons who are "naturally" of homosexual orientation. Richard Hays's response to this interpretation shows it to be nonsensical:

> Neither Paul nor anyone else in antiquity had a concept of "sexual orientation." To introduce this concept into the passage (by suggesting that Paul disapproves only those who act contrary to their individual sexual orientations) is to lapse into an anachronism. The expression *para physin* ("contrary to nature"), used here by Paul, is the standard terminology in dozens of ancient texts for referring to homoerotic acts. The fact is that Paul treats *all* homosexual activity as *prima facie* evidence of humanity's tragic confusion and alienation from God the Creator.[7]

Reformed homosexuality. According to this innovative reading, "degrading passions" and "indecent acts" referred only to taking advantage of the passive partner, or female role, in homosexual sex. According to Gomes, it also referred to "the most disagreeable form of homosexual activity known to Paul and his contemporaries, pederasty," in which an adult male exploited a younger male for sexual purposes. "All Paul knew of homosexuality was the debauched pagan expression of it."[8] This, Gomes would have us believe, is in contrast to the normal Christian expression of it. Gomes's interpretation is wishful thinking. The point of Romans 1 is that any homosexual act is by definition, unnatural. Contrasting "debauched" homosexuality with "acceptable" homosexuality creates a distinction found nowhere in the Bible. According to Scripture, homosexuality *is* debauched.

Disappearing homosexuality. This approach to the biblical passages that deal with homosexuality is really the consequence of the other interpretations that attempt to detour the plain meaning of Scripture. Gomes offers this explanation for Romans 1:26–27: "The first thing to be remembered here is that Paul is not writing about homosexuality in Romans—neither about homosexuality as he would have understood it nor about homosexuality as we now understand it." Gomes also denies that 1 Corinthians 6:9 is "about homosexuality."[9] Such attempts at interpretive sleight of hand fool only the most gullible or the most prejudiced. The reality is that both of these passages include information about homosexuality, and Gomes offers no convincing reasons why they do not.

This effort to redefine the debate brings to mind the scene from *The Wizard of Oz* when Dorothy and her friends enter the presence of the great Oz. Only a few moments pass until they notice the man hiding behind the curtain, who is plainly manipulating the imposing image before them. "Pay no attention to that man behind the curtain!" he says into the microphone, making it even more obvious that he is pretending to be Oz. Similarly, writers who claim that the above passages are not about homosexuality are saying, "Pay no attention to what the text is saying; listen to what we tell you it is saying." Discussions about Roman society and distortions of the meaning of Greek terms do not change the clear message of the texts. The attempts to change the message are only obfuscating smoke and noise.

1 Corinthians 6

In 1 Corinthians 6:9–10 and 1 Timothy 1:9–10, the wrongness of homosexuality is not argued; it is assumed. In either passage, homosexuality is included in a long list of sins. In 1 Corinthians 6, homosexuals are placed alongside fornicators, idolaters, adulterers, thieves, covetous, drunkards, revilers, swindlers. In 1 Timothy 1, they are in the company of the lawless, rebellious, ungodly, sinners, unholy, profane, murderers, immoral men, kidnappers, liars, and perjurers, along with "whatever else is contrary to sound teaching." The burden of proof rests on those who wish to show that homosexuality is not a biblical sin, and the appearance of *effeminate* and *homosexuals* in these lists of sins adds a heavy weight. What to do?

The response to these verses has been to contend that the terms translated "effeminate" and "homosexuals" were intended to refer to pederasts and their preadolescent companions, or to solicitors of prostitutes and the prostitutes themselves.[10] If this is correct, only those specific practices are listed as sins and therefore these verses may be omitted from the contemporary discussion about consensual homosexuality. The attempt to assign such meanings to the term translated "homosexual" arises from the fact that this term does not appear prior to the New Testament and is not used again for two centuries. However, in 1984, David Wright demonstrated that this term was taken from the Greek translation of the Old Testament, specifically Leviticus 18:22 and 20:13.[11] It is a compound word, combining two words used in both Leviticus verses. Taken together, the words refer to a man lying with a man. The fact that Paul borrowed his terminology from Leviticus is highly significant for the interpretation of both Old and New Testament passages. First, it underscores that Paul regarded the levitical laws concerning homosexuality to be moral laws, not ceremonial or civil. Second, since the verses in Leviticus make no distinction between particular forms of homosexual behavior (i.e., unacceptable pederasty or prostitution versus acceptable homosexuality) it is unlikely that Paul, who was relying on Leviticus terminology, intended such a distinction. Third, this use of shared vocabulary establishes continuity and consistency in the biblical witness—homosexuality is invariably denounced as sin every time it is mentioned in Scripture.

Interpretation or Inspiration?

When one reads the way pro-homosexual literature employs the Bible in service of an ideology, it becomes clear that something larger than homosexuality is at stake. The real question is, *How shall we regard the Bible?* What kind of book is it? Is it from God or is it from man? Is it revelation from God that is applicable to every generation, or is its message so hopelessly rooted in a bygone culture that scholars must dislodge it from the ancient Near East and modernize it before its kernel of spiritual truth can be uncovered? Should its words be believed at face value, even though they conflict with ideas common in modern cultures, or should we declare that it is inspired and helpful only insofar as it supports the agenda that is currently politically correct? As one reads scholarly and popular literature on homosexuality and the Bible, it becomes obvious that authors answer these questions in vastly different ways.

Perhaps this is why Soards begins his book on the Bible and homosexuality with an entire chapter on biblical authority. At the end of his book he returns to the issue of the Bible's authority to write,

> Increasingly, however, persons who have religious or social sensibilities that lead them to advocate accepting homosexual behavior simply dismiss the normative role of scripture in Christian life. . . . In part, people take this position because they react to the all-too-real abuses of the authority of scripture. They have heard the phrase "the Bible says" used as a cudgel in such outrageous ways that they have come to blame the Bible for its misuse by mean-spirited interpreters. The abuse of the Bible is no reason, however, to discard the scrip-

tures as the norm of Christian life. . . . Recognizing the authority of scripture means that we do not pick the parts that please us and ignore—or, perhaps worse, imaginatively remake—the sections that we find difficult or unacceptable.[12]

I have chosen three examples to illustrate this problem of reinventing the nature of the Bible. First, Marilyn Bennett Alexander and James Preston, in We Were Baptized Too, devoted only two pages to the consideration of Scripture in an ostensibly Christian book about homosexuality. In their brief summary of the message of Romans 1, they state, "Paul is not specifically singling out homosexual acts, but he borrows a standard Hellenistic list of moral failings. Homoerotic acts were considered evil in a Hellenistic culture because they were thought to be motivated by lust."[13]

The point being made by Alexander and Preston is that since (or if) Paul borrowed the list from a Hellenistic source, this passage expresses Hellenistic disapproval of homosexuality, but not necessarily Pauline disapproval, and certainly not divine disapproval.

It is true that Paul is not "specifically singling out homosexual acts." He listed such acts as sins within a long list of other sins. However, the hypothesis that Paul used a standard list of "moral failings" has no bearing on whether the list is authoritative or not. The Ten Commandments have points of contact with other laws recorded in the Near East (such as Hammurabi's Code), but no one suggests that the Ten Commandments are not applicable on that basis. The orthodox Christian position has always been that, in the writing of the Bible, if there was such "borrowing," the Holy Spirit superintended the process with the result that every word of the Bible is "God-breathed" (2 Tim. 3:16).

Alexander and Preston do not explain that they are adopting a new approach to the inspiration of the Bible, but that is exactly what they are doing. This new strategy says that passages including vocabulary similar to other documents are not divinely inspired, but are rather "borrowed." Such an approach is not compatible with historic Christian orthodoxy, which affirms that "all Scripture is inspired" (2 Tim. 3:16) and that "no prophecy was ever made by an act of human will, but men moved by the Holy Spirit spoke from God" (2 Peter 1:21).

Another example is Mahan Siler's attempt to justify his pastoral decision to conduct a worship ceremony to bless a homosexual "union"—something similar to a wedding. Siler writes, "The Bible does not condone homosexuality. Every instance of homosexual behavior is denounced, regarded as sinful." So far, so good. Then Siler goes on to say, "If homosexual persons are accepted and affirmed, it must be in faithfulness to the higher biblical norm of God's justice for all persons."[14] These words were written in the context of blessing the union of two homosexuals, so Siler is not writing of merely "accepting" and "affirming" the *people* involved in sinful activity; he is suggesting that the church accept and affirm, or "bless," the way they have chosen to express their sexuality. This should be done, Siler maintains, in deference to "the higher biblical norm of God's justice for all persons."

Is there precedent for this sort of interpretation? When the Bible explicitly prohibits a specific kind of behavior, as in the case of homosexuality (which Siler admits), are there instances when such moral prohibition has been said to have been superseded by a "higher biblical norm"? No, this has not been done in all of Christian history. Imagine a Christian group teaching that professing and unrepentant adulterers should be accepted and affirmed in their adultery because of biblical concepts like equity ("Adulterers are equal, not inferior, to the sexually faithful!") or freedom ("Claiming that adulterers are wrongdoers is repressing them!"). Imagine the same thing happening with regard to murderers or thieves. Such an idea is absurd, yet Siler has applied that sort of reasoning to the biblical text with regard to homosexuality. Only the most biblically illiterate or the most ideologically prejudiced could be swayed by such an argument.

It is significant that no explicit moral prohibition of the Bible has been reversed in the history of the church. Further, no "interpretation" has been successful in explaining such texts as optional, prejudicial, or misunderstood. That leads us to the crux of the matter. The real issue is inspiration, not interpretation. Those who try to justify homosexuality have lowered their view of the inspiration of the Bible.

They engage in telling the Bible what it can teach instead of humbly hearing and submitting to its truth. Keith Hartman, a secular journalist unhindered by scholarly or Christian considerations of specific texts, expresses this approach well:

> At some point we have to start questioning if all this stuff really comes directly from God, or if maybe some of the prejudices and cultural biases of the authors placed limits on their ability to understand Him. It can be very comfortable to assume that the Bible is perfect and definitive, because then you don't have to think for yourself about what's right and wrong.[15]

Hartman's first sentence brazenly contradicts classic Christian doctrine regarding the inspiration of the Bible. His second sentence assumes that acceptance of the Bible's perfection precludes the possibility of thinking for oneself. Simon LeVay, whose research is cited below, expresses the same sentiment. Responding to the effort to reinterpret the Bible so as to annul its teaching on homosexuality, he writes,

> I'm not a biblical scholar, but I must say I find this kind of argument unconvincing. Sexual intercourse between people of the same sex is condemned quite explicitly in both the Old and New Testaments as well as in other sacred books. Rather than attempt . . . to explain away all these passages through etymological quibbling, wouldn't it be more sensible to ask whether the moral codes that were promulgated by the authors of those books are still appropriate two or three millennia later?

LeVay proceeds to recommend the abandonment of religion altogether, for "there are plenty of societies that flourish without God."[16] LeVay and Hartman should be given credit for their honesty in admitting their perspective about the contents of the Bible, and for the fact that they understand the choices. Either accept the Bible as true, including its message about homosexuality, or reject it all. Unfortunately, LeVay and Hartman make the wrong choice. We should not be surprised at such a choice from people who are not Christians. The fact that the same ideas are being believed and promoted in the church underscores the absence of a biblical worldview, and it reveals how the church is beginning to accept a redefined concept of truth.

Treatments of the issue of homosexuality that reveal a low view of the inspiration of Scripture are abundant. For example, Christine Gudorf writes, "The Bible is *a* [not *the*] primary resource for Christian ethics." Not surprisingly, she goes on to suggest acceptance of homosexual practice in the church.[17] Similarly, Phyllis Bird calls the Bible, "the starting point of the church's conversation, not the end, a conversation partner, not an oracle." Bird goes on to argue that the Bible was written by, and primarily about, males, so "the conversation of Scripture is both incomplete and biased. This means, I believe, that the testimony of Scripture may not be absolutized, or viewed as final revelation."[18]

This demotion of Scripture is typical of modern liberal Protestantism. One must keep in mind that this recent and errant view of the Bible contrasts sharply with the orthodox position of the believing church. This position is summarized in the Reformation idea of *sola Scriptura*—only Scripture is the rule of faith and practice. As Martin Luther declared, "We dare not give preference to the authority of men over that of Scripture! Human beings can err, but the Word of God is the very wisdom of God and the absolutely infallible truth."[19] Luther once referred to the Bible as a queen, and wrote, "This queen must rule, and everyone must obey, and be subject to, her. The pope, Luther, Augustine, Paul, an angel from heaven—these should not be masters, judges, or arbiters but only witnesses, disciples, and confessors of Scripture. Nor should any doctrine be taught or heard in the church except the pure Word of God."[20]

Homosexuality and the Church

Compliance with the Culture

The exposition I have provided of the relevant sections of the Bible are not original or unique. Throughout twenty centuries of Christian interpretation of the Bible, the unchanging position of the church has been that the Bible identifies homosexual behavior as sin. Following the Bible's lead, the church has always believed that homosexuality is unnatural and has always taught against its practice.[21]

Until now. Today, examples of the abandonment of the Scriptures abound. Consider just a few examples. As mentioned earlier, Siler led his congregation (Pullen Memorial Baptist Church in Raleigh, North Carolina) to bless the union of two gay men. About ten years later, the same church, under a new pastor, called a self-avowed lesbian to be copastor.[22] Nearby, Binkley Memorial Baptist Church in Chapel Hill, North Carolina, ordained a homosexual to the Christian ministry. Such actions are rare for Baptists, but not for the American church as a whole. Seminaries have lifted bans on same-sex relationships between ministerial students.[23] Denominations have pro-homosexual caucuses that lobby for the ordination of homosexuals and the acceptance of same-sex unions.

The Episcopal denomination is a case in point. In 1991, the Episcopal general convention affirmed the traditional teaching that sexual expression is appropriate only within the confines of heterosexual marriage, but the same convention acknowledged "the discontinuity between this teaching and the experience of many members of this body." The accuracy of that statement was subsequently confirmed when several dioceses ordained openly homosexual priests and performed liturgies for blessing same-sex unions.[24] A group of Episcopalian bishops drafted a Statement of Koinonia in which they made such breathtakingly heretical statements as the following:

> We believe that both homosexuality and heterosexuality are morally neutral. . . . We also believe that those who know themselves to be gay or lesbian persons, and who do not choose to live alone, but forge relationships with partners of their choice that are faithful, monogamous, committed, life-giving and holy are to be honored.

On June 15, 2001, delegates to the General Assembly of the Presbyterian Church (U.S.A.) voted 317 to 208 to lift a ban on the ordination of homosexuals.[25] A United Methodist conference refused to discipline a homosexual minister. Their own regulations prohibit "self-avowed practicing homosexuals" from serving as ordained pastors, and the minister publicly announced that he was "proudly as much a practicing gay man as [he was] a practicing United Methodist."[26] This inaction came after other United Methodist conferences suspended a Methodist minister in 1999 and took away the ordination of another in 2000 because they presided over the blessing of homosexual unions.[27]

The Vancouver, British Columbia, diocese of Anglicans voted to permit the blessing of same-sex unions. Conservative Anglicans walked out of the meeting.[28] An entire denomination, the Metropolitan Community Church, openly affirms the homosexual lifestyle. This denomination has about three hundred congregations with a membership of 250,000, about 95 percent of whom are active homosexuals.[29]

I know of none who call themselves evangelical Christians who affirm homosexual behavior as acceptable. If any do, they would not fit the term *evangelical*. The label usually is used to refer to those who hold a high view of the inspiration and authority of the Bible. However, some evangelical groups are feeling the tremors of the shift in society's sexual standards, and some evangelicals are becoming sympathetic to the liberal Protestant acceptance of homosexuality, forgetting that such acceptance was possible for liberals only after sacrificing the authority of the Bible.

Homosexual debates have arisen on the campuses of historically evangelical schools such as Calvin College, Eastern College, Gordon College, and Wheaton College.[30] All of this should by no means be seen as majority acceptance of homosexuality by the confessing church. Only the most liberal denominations have adopted pro-homosexual beliefs or practices as normative. However, the very fact that such an issue is a point of contention within some church bodies is evidence of the extent to which the prevailing winds of the culture have blown the church from her biblical moorings. Churches are compromising on the issue of the morality of homosexuality as a concession to a corrupt culture. Such compromises are never made by the church, however, without great sacrifice. In this case it is truth that is being sacrificed.

Homosexuals at Church

Are homosexuals welcome in the church? Of course they are welcome. As sinners they are not unique. All people have sinned, and sinners are welcome to come and hear about Christ in church. This right answer is not always given in churches today. There are "homophobes" who make homosexuals feel unwelcome. That is tragic, since Christ welcomed sinners, transformed them, and died for them. The church is imperfect, and one challenge of today's church is to become more like Christ in welcoming sinners and offering Christ's redemption to them.

Several years ago, as a pastor I spoke to the church I served about the issue of homosexuality. I referred to some of the Scripture passages mentioned above to demonstrate how God views homosexuality. I then added,

> If it is our intention to lead unbelievers in our area to faith in Christ, the ministry of our church will have to focus on grace, forgiveness, and help, not judgment, condemnation, and exclusion. We want [a homosexual] to feel that he is among friends here, not that he is intruding in a meeting of a secret fraternity where he does not know the passwords or handshakes. The message he hears should show how faith in Christ works; it should be winsome and full of hope.

I believe those are needed words in the church of Jesus Christ today. We must not compromise God's commands concerning homosexuality. Neither can we compromise God's commands that we minister to hurting and sinful people. Is it possible to "hate the sin but love the sinner"? I hate a lot of things I do, but that doesn't mean I hate myself. And my love for homosexuals causes me to hate their sin all the more, because I know it is blocking them from experiencing God's best for their lives.

Yes, homosexuals should be welcomed to church. But they should be in church for the same reason all of us are there—to be healed. All of us have sinned. My sins may not be listed in Romans 1 or 1 Corinthians 6, but they are named elsewhere in Scripture, and I am guilty. The Bible gets no argument from me. I admit my sin with humility and sorrow, and I call out to God for His forgiveness and cleansing. Therefore, I find salvation, help, and healing. God offers the same grace and healing to those who have committed the sin of homosexuality. Such cleansing is predicated on our confession, so the worst thing that could happen is for some Christian to tell homosexuals that what they are doing is okay. If they believe that message, they will fail to confess their sin and thereby miss out on God's cleansing, and that is a tragedy with eternal consequences.[31]

This was expressed well by a homosexual friend of Richard Hays, the Duke ethicist. Hays's friend was dying of AIDS, and Hays quoted his friend's words as he neared death. The fact that these words come from a homosexual gives them special force: "Are homosexuals to be excluded from the community of faith? Certainly not. But anyone who joins such a community should know that it is a place of transformation, of discipline, of learning, and not merely a place to be comforted or indulged."[32]

When we go to a medical doctor for an examination, we want him to tell us the truth about our physical condition, even if it's bad news. If a doctor told you that you had cancer, it would not be because he did not love you. To the contrary, it would be because he *did* love you. Only when an accurate diagnosis is made can effective treatment be prescribed. In order to find help we must face the fact that there is a problem. The church should love homosexuals enough to do the same. That does not make us gay bashers or homophobes. It simply means that we agree with God that such behavior is wrong and harmful.

Several years ago, a young man who was visiting the church I was serving, confided to me that he felt he was a homosexual. When he told me, I realized that he was trusting me with a secret known only by a few people, so I told him I was honored to be brought into his confidence. But I also told him that he would never experience the abundant life God had planned for him if he chose a homosexual lifestyle. I told him that I wanted him to experience God's best, and I would help him. But I also told him that homosexual behavior is not God's best, and it would hurt him. I told him all of that not because I didn't love him, but because I *did* love him.

Some people today defend the homosexual lifestyle by saying that Jesus would love and accept homosexuals, and so should we. Certainly Jesus would love them. He loves all of us sinners so much that He died for us (Rom. 5:8).

But Jesus also had great reverence for the Word of God. He said, "Whoever then annuls one of the least of these commandments, and so teaches others, shall be called least in the kingdom of heaven; but whoever keeps and teaches them, he shall be called great in the kingdom of heaven" (Matt. 5:19). Jesus never compromised or relativized God's moral law in order to affirm someone who insisted on violating it. When the Pharisees caught a woman in adultery, they were surprised when He did not join them in condemning her. He saw *their* sin and condemned it. Even so, He said to the woman, "Go and sin no more" (John 8:1–11). Jesus refused to compromise on principle and never affirmed immorality. Jesus also loved people and ministered to their needs. He knew how to balance God's absolute standard with caring for persons.

Somehow the church must learn that balance. There are signs that the church is doing just that. Though I have heard of prejudice in the church against homosexuals, more often I have seen and heard of concern for and ministry to homosexuals. Christians are learning to look beyond the sin to the fact that homosexual people are usually hurting people.

Nature and Nurture

In *An Ounce of Prevention,* Don Schmierer presents compelling evidence that homosexuality arises from environmental factors. Such factors include a distant father, a controlling mother, media and culture, pornography, moral relativism, seduction by peers, parental adultery, chemical imbalances, and pedophilia and molestation. Schmierer's thesis is that environmental factors are primary in homosexual behavior, so homosexuality can be prevented by providing the proper environment.[33]

While Schmierer's thesis has much to commend it and is certainly worthy of consideration, I would like to respond to the opposite contention—that homosexual "orientation" is the result of nature or genetics, not nurture, or one's environment. What if science should prove that some people are born with a "homosexuality gene"? Would this not redefine the debate? Could it really be called "sin" if homosexuality is in fact an inborn trait, like blue eyes or brown hair?

Some interesting studies have been done on this subject. It is beyond the scope of this chapter to give any more than passing reference to them, but to understand the debate it is necessary at least to be aware of them. One such study was done by Dean Hamer of the National Cancer Institute. He studied families with a high proportion of gay men. Hamer focused on an examination of the X chromosome and found that thirty-three out of forty pairs of brothers who were both gay had a similar genetic structure in a particular area of the X chromosome.

A few caveats must be mentioned with regard to Hamer's study. First, linking specific behavior with a specific gene is considered a precarious venture by many geneticists. Second, several factors make the study far less than conclusive to scientists: the small sample size; the lack of a heterosexual control group; and the unaccounted finding that fourteen of the eighty alleged homosexuals did not have the marker.

Another study was done by Simon LeVay. After examining forty-one corpses, he found that in nineteen corpses of homosexuals who had died from AIDS, the neuron group next to the hypothalamus was smaller than that in heterosexuals. LeVay assumed the other sixteen male corpses and the six female corpses were heterosexual. Such an assumption, of course, makes his study far from conclusive. Further, most of the reporters who announced LeVay's experiments neglected to relate that LeVay himself acknowledged that his study falls far short of "proof" for a physical cause of homosexuality.[34]

It is highly unlikely that the nature-nurture debate will be resolved any time soon. Scientists in various disciplines have had the same discussions for decades regarding other areas of behavior with no resolution. Suppose, however, that Hamer or LeVay is right, or that someone else supplied irrefutable proof that homosexuality is genetically determined. Does that justify behavior the Bible describes as immoral?

As Hays concluded, "Surely Christian ethics does not want to hold that all inborn traits are good and desirable."[35] It may also be true that some people are more genetically inclined to alcoholism or violent behavior, but that does not lead to the conclusion that the Scriptures regarding drunkenness and murder have been superseded by science and now are hopelessly out of date. We simply say that the grace and power of God are more than adequate to prevent persons from acting on those inclinations to sin. Furthermore, it has long been asserted by the church (in accord with Ephesians 2:1–3 and other passages) that *all* of us are born with an inclination, or tendency, to sin. We are corrupt, totally depraved. Yet, the redemption Christ offers is sufficient for all of us, regardless of the identity of our sin. Does it take a miracle for avowed homosexuals to turn to celibacy or to heterosexual monogamy within marriage? Yes, but God is able to do miracles. He has also performed the miracles of turning wife abusers into good husbands, alcoholics into teetotalers, misers into givers, and so on.

Such miracles are not only possible; they are also needed. Statistically speaking, the homosexual lifestyle is a destructive lifestyle. Studies have shown that twice as many homosexual men abuse alcohol as heterosexuals, and seven times as many have a history of drug abuse. Depression is thirteen times more likely among homosexual men, and suicide attempts are six times as likely among homosexual men and twice as common among lesbian women.[36] This is in addition to the epidemic of sexually transmitted diseases among homosexuals. In fact, drug use and depression may amplify the spread of disease, since some gay men report that despair has moved them to engage in dangerous sexual practices.[37] My own limited experience in counseling homosexuals confirms these studies. The men to whom I have ministered were struggling with regret and self-condemnation. They felt guilty and were having great difficulty forgiving themselves.

The most significant fact in the nature-nurture debate is the transformation of homosexuals into heterosexuals. If homosexuals change and renounce their former lifestyle as wrong, then homosexuals aren't forced by their genetic make-up to practice homosexuality. The fact that homosexuals want to change and do change is so devastating to the arguments of pro-homosexual lobby groups that they have sought to stop those who would help homosexuals change their orientation, and they attempt to suppress reports so that no one will know that it is happening. In August of 1997, for example, the American Psychological Association adopted a resolution to limit treatment designed to change the behavior of homosexual men and women.

Perhaps this was done because that May, the National Association for Research and Therapy of Homosexuality released the results of a study among more than eight hundred people who were struggling to overcome homosexuality and of more than two hundred therapists who were treating them. After treatment, only 13 percent still perceived themselves to be exclusively or almost entirely homosexual, while 33 percent described themselves as exclusively or almost entirely heterosexual. Before treatment, 63 percent indicated they had frequent and intense homosexual thoughts, but only 3 percent said they had such thoughts after treatment. Ninety-nine percent said they believe treatment to change homosexuality can be effective and valuable.[38]

A beautiful example of such transformation is my friend Eric Garner. He had been a practicing homosexual for about ten years when he read in the Bible for the first time that homosexual behavior is wrong. He mentioned what he had read to his partner, who candidly acknowledged that he already knew that the Bible condemns homosexual behavior. The words of the Bible didn't bother Eric's friend, but they bothered Eric. He began to go to church to look for God and peace. Finally, in desperation he went to a Christian couple to ask for help. They offered their friendship and support, and eventually he moved in with them to start a new life. He received Christ as his Savior and began following Him as his Lord.

Eric readily admits the difficulty of completely breaking with his former lifestyle, and he describes it as spiritual warfare. Another friend who came out of the homosexual lifestyle also told me that he believed his fight against homosexuality had been warfare against demonic forces. Before long, however, God took away all homosexual desire from Eric and placed a wonderful Christian woman in his life. Heterosexual desire returned, and Eric and Kelly are happily married today with one child. They are two of the most delightful people I know, and both love Jesus Christ and live for Him. Their relationship is a model of what God intended for humankind from the beginning—one man and one woman, for life.

CHAPTER 10

The Myth of Disposable People

*And [Pharaoh] said, "When you are helping the He-
brew women to give birth and see them upon the
birthstool, if it is a son, then you shall put him to death;
but if it is a daughter, then she shall live." But the mid-
wives feared God, and did not do as the king of Egypt
had commanded them, but let the boys live.*

—Exodus 1:16–17

*Behold, children are a gift of the Lord;
The fruit of the womb is a reward.*

—Psalm 127:3

*For You formed my inward parts;
You wove me in my mother's womb.
I will give thanks to You, for I am fearfully and
    wonderfully made;
Wonderful are Your works,
And my soul knows it very well.
My frame was not hidden from You,
When I was made in secret,
And skillfully wrought in the depths of the earth.
Thine eyes have seen my unformed substance;
And in Your book were all written
The days that were ordained for me,
When as yet there was not one of them.*

—Psalm 139:13–16

I came to know Priscilla Ann Glassey when I was speaking at an Atlanta church where she was a member. While in Atlanta, I stayed in her family's home. Priscilla epitomizes the current struggle over abortion inside and outside the church. For that reason I begin this chapter by quoting from her story, as she wrote it.

> When I was about 10 years old I accepted Jesus Christ as my personal Lord and Savior. I told everyone about the new joy I'd found. But . . . not only did my peers seem unimpressed by my newly found Savior, they also seemed to scorn me. . . . A few years passed and the time came for me to enter high school. I was terrified! . . . I tried for the first two quarters to hang around the "jocks" and cheerleaders, but they usually ignored me and treated me as if I were scum. So, instead I began to hang around the druggies. . . . I listened to their advice, because for once I felt like I was popular. . . . From that point I found myself at parties every weekend. . . . I stopped praying and going to church. . . .
>
> Throughout my freshman and sophomore year, I drank, experimented with more drugs and went from one boyfriend to another. I had always thought sex was supposed to be special, but none of the guys had ever fulfilled all my inner desires; the most important was to be loved. I didn't realize that I was already loved by God, and each and every day I broke his heart by what I was doing.
>
> Then, in the summer of 1985, I met Mark. . . . We dated all summer and I thought I'd finally found true love, that is until I got pregnant. He'd always told me that he'd stand by me no matter what happened, but when I needed him the most, he was nowhere to be found. He offered to pay for an abortion. I made the appointment, but couldn't go through with it. I finally got the courage to tell my parents. . . . They sat down and talked things out with me. That night we decided I'd go to a maternity home to have my baby. They gave me the option to keep the baby, but I was only 17 and didn't feel like I could

handle the responsibility. I also wanted my baby growing up knowing who his father was. . . .

On May 22, 1986, I had an 8 lb., 4 oz. baby boy with strawberry blonde hair and deep blue eyes. . . . There in the hospital I cried and dedicated him to the Lord. . . . Even though I miss my son desperately, I don't regret my decision for one minute.

I am grateful that Priscilla made the choice to have the baby. That little fellow is becoming an adult himself now. It is sad, however, that many young women in crisis pregnancies make another choice. I have counseled with a family in almost exactly the same circumstances. They were petrified that someone might find out about the pregnancy and think less of them, so they disposed of the child by abortion as quickly and as quietly as possible. Such a decision is a tragedy. It is tragic because it does not erase shame, it only internalizes and postpones it. Even if abortion could make the pain of a wrong decision go away, the price is too high—it ends a human life.

As a child, I was told that in the United States human life is respected. This has never been the case in my lifetime. As I was growing up, men were sent to die in Vietnam in a war of ill-defined goals and unclear justification. Today, twenty thousand people are murdered every year. Drunk drivers kill seventy people a day, but companies are allowed to advertise alcohol. In the trials of Jack Kevorkian for assisting in the suicides of several people, the juries representing the people of the State of Michigan proved that they did not possess the moral backbone to enforce explicit laws to convict a man who participated in numerous "assisted suicides" (a contradiction in terms). In addition, the lives of approximately 1.6 million babies are ended every year by abortion, more than 39 million since the Supreme Court's Roe v. Wade decision in 1973.[1] Those who say that life is respected in either Canada or the U.S. are either thinking of some past era or they are simply mistaken. One of the manifestations of a lack of respect for life is abortion. As Francis Schaeffer and C. Everett Koop wrote, "Of all the subjects relating to the erosion of the sanctity of human life, abortion is the keystone.

It is the first and crucial issue that has been overwhelming in changing attitudes toward the value of life in general."[2]

A Review of the Facts

Abortion is the second most common surgical procedure in the United States, circumcision being the first. Fifty percent of pregnancies are unintended, and half of those unintended pregnancies are aborted, so about one out of four pregnancies ends in abortion.[3] Seventy-four percent of women who have abortions are unmarried. Women who claim no religious identification are about four times as likely to have an abortion as those who identify with a religion. However, about 20 percent of the women who have abortions describe themselves as "born-again" or "evangelical" Christians. Thirty-three percent of abortions are performed on women from twenty to twenty-four years old. Teenagers have nearly 22 percent of all abortions.[4]

As to why women are having abortions, the Alan Guttmacher Institute, Planned Parenthood's research arm, surveyed women seeking abortions and found that over 95 percent were performed for "societal" reasons or birth control. About three-fourths of the women surveyed said that having a baby would interfere with work, school, or other responsibilities. About two-thirds said they could not afford a child, and half said they did not want to be a single parent or have relationship problems.[5] Only between 1 percent and 3 percent of abortions are the result of incest or rape.[6]

And what does the public believe about abortion? Public opinion polls have been used by both sides of the abortion debate to demonstrate that public sentiment rests on one side or the other. The results of public surveys are largely determined by what questions are asked. For example, when people are asked to agree or disagree with a statement like, "I believe that abortion is morally wrong under all circumstances and should never be performed," only a small percentage will agree. That small percentage is then touted by pro-abortionists as overwhelming public support for their cause. But when people are asked to agree or disagree with a statement like, "I believe there are circumstances under which an abortion should not be performed," the response is correspondingly high. Pro-lifers tout that number as public support for their position. A survey that seems reliable, though now dated, was commissioned by Focus on the Family and the Family Research Council, and conducted by the Roper organization. A diverse group of two thousand adult men and women were polled. Respondents were asked, "Which of the following statements best reflects your view of abortion?" Ten choices were then supplied. The results are below.

1. Abortion is wrong under any circumstances (19 percent).
2. Abortion is wrong except to save the life of the mother (7 percent).
3. Abortion is wrong, except to save the life of the mother, and in cases of rape or incest (18 percent).
4. Abortion is wrong, except in instances of rape or incest; to save the life of the mother; and in cases of infant deformity, disease or retardation (11 percent).
5. Abortion is wrong, except in instances of rape or incest; to save the life of the mother; in case of infant deformity, disease or retardation; and where the child is unwanted and will not have a good quality of life (11 percent).
6. Abortion is permissible for any reason the woman chooses until the fetus can survive outside the womb (9 percent).
7. Abortion is permissible for any reason, except as a way to select the sex of the child (4 percent).
8. Abortion is permissible for any reason the woman chooses, at any time during the pregnancy; and no legal restrictions should be imposed, including no parental notification or no delay for informed consent (7 percent).
9. Abortion is permissible for any reason the woman chooses at any time during the pregnancy; there should be no legal restrictions of any kind; and the government should pay for the procedure if a woman cannot afford the expense (6 percent).
10. Don't know (8 percent).[7]

A later poll was conducted that focused on the connection between religious affiliation and views on abortion. The data was compiled by sociologist Christian Smith of the University of North Carolina. The results of Smith's study are revealing, but probably not that surprising.

Among evangelicals:
6 percent believe abortion should be legal in all cases.
6 percent believe abortion should be legal in most cases.
50 percent believe abortion should be legal in a few cases.
38 percent believe abortion should be illegal in all cases.

Among fundamentalists:
9 percent believe abortion should be legal in all cases.
9 percent believe abortion should be legal in most cases.
51 percent believe abortion should be legal in a few cases.
32 percent believe abortion should be illegal in all cases.

Among those in mainline denominations:
16 percent believe abortion should be legal in all cases.
15 percent believe abortion should be legal in most cases.
53 percent believe abortion should be legal in a few cases.
16 percent believe abortion should be illegal in all cases.

Among those in groups identifying themselves as liberal:
22 percent believe abortion should be legal in all cases.
21 percent believe abortion should be legal in most cases.
42 percent believe abortion should be legal in a few cases.
14 percent believe abortion should be illegal in all cases.

Among Roman Catholics:
11 percent believe abortion should be legal in all cases.
13 percent believe abortion should be legal in most cases.
59 percent believe abortion should be legal in a few cases.
17 percent believe abortion should be illegal in all cases.

Among those not holding any Christian identification:
31 percent believe abortion should be legal in all cases.
17 percent believe abortion should be legal in most cases.
36 percent believe abortion should be legal in a few cases.
16 percent believe abortion should be illegal in all cases.[8]

Babies are aborted by several different methods. Two methods are preferred for abortions in the first trimester of pregnancy—dilation and curettage (D&C) and suction. When D&C is used, the mother's cervix is dilated and the surgeon scrapes the wall of the uterus, cutting the baby's body to pieces and removing the placenta. Suction is often used in conjunction with D&C. Suction involves the use of a suction tube about twenty-eight times stronger than a home vacuum cleaner. The tube is inserted into the womb and it sucks the baby and the placenta from the uterus into a jar. With both these methods, it is possible to identify human arms and legs.

Saline injection is the most common method of abortion during the second trimester. D&C and suction cannot be used this late in the pregnancy because of the danger of hemorrhaging in the mother. In saline abortions, a long needle is inserted into the sac of liquid surrounding the baby. Some of the fluid is removed and a solution of concentrated salt is injected. The baby swallows the salt and is poisoned. Often skin is burned in the process, which explains why many of the pictures of aborted babies show skin that looks charred. It takes about an hour for the solution to slowly kill the baby. About a day after the procedure, the mother goes into labor and delivers a dead, shriveled baby.

Hysterotomy and partial birth abortion are used in the final trimester. Hysterotomy is the delivery of a child by cesarean section, except that a C-section is done to save the baby, and a hysterotomy is done to kill the baby. The baby is allowed to die of neglect or is killed through some deliberate action. Partial birth abortion is an example of such a deliberate action. In this procedure, which has been the subject of much political controversy, the baby is breech-delivered alive so that the entire body except for the head is outside the mother's womb. The head remains in the birth canal while the abortionist kills the baby by making a hole in the skull and inserting a suction device into the skull and suctioning out the brain. Far from being rare, an estimated forty thousand to fifty thousand partial birth abortions are performed each year.[9]

A Review of Biblical Principles

If those in the church of Jesus Christ knew and submitted to the truths in the Word of God concerning pre-born human life, the statistics cited above would dramatically differ. There are three primary reasons the church is not unanimously opposed to abortion. First, Christians are ignorant of biblical teaching that relates to abortion. The blame for this must be laid ultimately at the feet of individual Christians who have not studied the Bible for themselves, though ministers who do not teach or do not believe the Bible are also to blame.

Second, the church has been infected by opinions common in the culture that conflict with the Bible. Theologian Timothy George has stated that the reason for the failure of the church to respond prophetically to abortion is "the erosion of doctrinal substance" and "the failure to think through theologically the great issues of our time."[10] This error in the church can be blamed on lazy thinking and the failure to build a worldview that is consistently Christian.

A third reason the church is divided concerning abortion is that God's people have been satisfied to trust their own notions on this issue instead of seeking and submitting to God's truth.

The solution for each of these three problems is knowledge of the truth of the Bible and submission to that truth. The starting point of some who argue in favor of abortion is to say that the Bible says nothing about abortion. The Bible also does not mention cocaine, chemical warfare, or the Ku Klux Klan, but a convincing case against these things can be made using principles contained in the Bible. As we read the Bible, the point is not to find words of disapprobation against the medical procedure of abortion; the point is the nature and origin of the fetus, and the biblical perspective on ending that kind of life.

As you read the passages cited below and the explanations offered, consider whether you are willing to believe God's Word, or whether you will choose the wisdom of the world or your own moral judgment. If you do not choose the first, you are abandoning any hope of developing a worldview that is consistently Christian.

What Is the Origin of Pre-born Human Life?

From whence does human life come? On November 19, 1997, septuplets were born to Bobbi and Kenneth McCaughey of Carlisle, Iowa. The successful birth of seven children was truly amazing, so the news media predictably gushed over this phenomenon. But the McCaughey family did something highly controversial, and to some, unacceptable. Doctors counseled them to abort some of the fetuses in order to increase the likelihood of the survival of the others, but they refused, believing that each life was a precious gift from God. Furthermore, though they used fertility drugs, they explicitly and publicly attributed the births to God. This, also predictably, exposed the McCaugheys to criticism and resulted in abundant ruminations about the origin of life.

For example, one journalist, referring to the McCaugheys' use of fertility drugs, wrote, "Even the use of the drugs leads some to wonder whether society is beginning to see life not as a gift from God but as a human product that can be refined, manipulated, and improved." No doubt those who base their opinions on naturalist or secularist assumptions have concluded that manipulation and improvement are human prerogatives. The reporter also asked, "In the dazzling world of reproductive technology, where does the hand of man stop and the hand of God take over?"[11]

That is an important question, and for those who are willing to listen, the Bible answers it clearly. In Psalm 139, the Bible says that God was the One forming the psalmist in the womb. Job said to the Lord, "Thou hast granted me life" (Job 10:12). Isaiah 44:24a states, "Thus says the Lord, your Redeemer, and the one who formed you from the womb, I, the Lord, am the maker of all things." And the psalmist asserts, "It is He who has made us, and not we ourselves" (Ps. 100:3).

The message of those verses is clear; God is the Author of life. It is not appropriate for humans to claim credit for the formation of human life. A man and a woman may choose to have sexual intercourse, but they are incapable of choosing to conceive. In fact, a man and a woman may have sexual relations many times with no conception. Then one day God sovereignly chooses for a sperm cell to be attached to an egg, and He causes life to be conceived. The man and the woman may no more claim that they had the creative power to begin that life within the woman than they can claim the final authority to end it. Laboratory personnel may "artificially" inseminate or place sperm and egg together in a test tube, but what causes it to "take"? God creates life. The logical and biblical corollary to that truth is that only God should have the prerogative to end life.

The advance of cloning technology also demonstrates that Western culture does not accept the sovereignty of God over human life. When we clone, we insert human preference into the process of childbirth. Children become commodities to be manipulated, and procreation becomes manufacture. Cloning is an effort to design a child according to one's desires, which is at best a perversion of parenthood and an expression of selfishness. And it is a short step from believing that every child should be a "wanted child," the slogan used to defend abortion, to believing that the child exists to satisfy our desires. If the child is not satisfactory, we resort to genetic engineering to fulfill our desires with an acceptable "product."

What Is the Nature of Pre-born Human Life?

One of the classic texts that answer this question is the one cited at the beginning of this chapter: "For You formed my inward parts; You wove me in my mother's womb. . . . My frame was not hidden from You, when I was made in secret. . . . Your eyes have seen my unformed substance" (Ps. 139:13, 15a–16a). David wrote Psalm 139 in praise of God who formed him and knew him in the womb. According to this passage, what was in the womb? It was not a blob of tissue; it was David, and God knew him in the womb. "In Your book were all written the days that were ordained for me, when as yet there was not one of them" (v. 16b). God had a plan for David's life, and this plan was not formulated the day he was born but while he was still in the womb.

Furthermore, "You wove me" indicates that God was actively involved in the development of the baby during gestation. The Bible teaches that God is sovereign and His sovereignty extends to every part of the universe; the uterus is not an exception to that. He cares for the child in the womb, and He is the One who forms this tiny body.

Another text that teaches the same truth is Jeremiah 1:4–5: "Now the word of the Lord came to me saying, 'Before I formed you in the womb I knew you, and before you were born I consecrated you; I have appointed you a prophet to the nations.'" God said that He knew Jeremiah before he was formed in the womb. He had a plan for Jeremiah's life before he was born. An abortion would have canceled God's design for his life. God knows who we are and what we will be, and He knows this while we are still in utero. If God relates to a fetus as a human being, shouldn't we?

Paul Simmons is one of those who denied the truths of Jeremiah 1:4–5 regarding pre-born human life. He wrote that these verses apply only to Jeremiah and may not be understood to be stating general principles regarding the nature of human life in the womb. "Jeremiah declared that God *knew* him, *formed* him and *consecrated* him. He is making no similar claim for everyone."[12] There are problems with Simmons's interpretation. First, in this text God is doing the declaring, not Jeremiah. Perhaps the fallacy of attributing the words of God to a man is the source of Simmons's interpretive flaws.

Second, Simmons states that this text "deals with calling not conception."[13] That is, the purpose of these verses is to explain Jeremiah's call, not to convey information about his conception and birth. Jeremiah's pre-born state is mentioned only to support Jeremiah's divine call. However, the text deals with both conception *and* call. Evidently, Simmons is prepared to accept only what the text says about Jeremiah's call, so he conveniently concludes that the text contains no information about Jeremiah's conception. His point, of course, is that what the text states about Jeremiah's conception is present *only because* it supports Jeremiah's call. Therefore, since it is not the main point of the text, its message about a baby in the womb can be ignored.

It is true that the nature of pre-born human life is not the main point of this text. However, does relating *incorrect* information about a baby in a womb really support Jeremiah's divine call to prophesy? Further, the fact that the words about Jeremiah's pre-born state are not primary does not mean they are not true. Is it a valid interpretation principle to state that the primary point of a biblical text is true but secondary and tertiary points are not? No, if the Bible is indeed the Word of God, we can believe that the information it contains concerning the nature of pre-born human life is accurate even though it may not be the main point of a particular passage.

A third problem with Simmons's interpretation of Jeremiah 1:4–5 is that it necessarily places limits on the knowledge of God. Orthodox Christian theology has traditionally asserted that the knowledge of God is both complete and prior. That is, God knows of every event and He knows it before it happens. These companion doctrines are called "omniscience" and "foreknowledge." To apply these propositions to the text in Jeremiah, not only did God know His plan for Jeremiah while he was in the womb, He knew it before Jeremiah was conceived. After all, God predestined Christians to be His "before the foundation of the world" (Eph. 1:4). However, if Simmons's interpretation is applied consistently, one would conclude that God simply does not know His plan for us until some later point—certainly late enough to be after our birth. Such a doctrine of God is fraught with difficulties. When carried to its logical conclusion it is ludicrous. God is made to know only that which our social agenda will allow Him to know—such as His plan for Jeremiah's life but no one else's.

An objection based on God's foreknowledge could be raised here: because of God's foreknowledge He knew that abortion would be legalized and He knew which babies would be aborted, so He has no plan for those babies who will be aborted. To the contrary, God relates to abortion the same way He relates to murder. God has a plan for the person who is murdered. The murderer, however, makes a sinful choice independent of the will of God and cuts off God's perfect plan for the life of the one killed and for the murderer. The same is true in the case of abortion.

Exodus 21:22–25 is another important text when considering the nature and value of pre-born human life:

> If men struggle with each other and strike a woman with child so that she gives birth prematurely, yet there is not injury, he shall surely be fined as the woman's husband may demand of him; and he shall pay as the judges decide. But if there is any further injury, then you shall appoint as a penalty life for life, eye for eye, tooth for tooth, hand for hand, foot for foot, burn for burn, wound for wound, bruise for bruise.

This passage has been interpreted by some to suggest that the mother's life was deemed more valuable than the baby's life. This has been called the "miscarriage interpretation." According to this view, these verses describe a miscarriage in which the fetus dies. A fine was assessed on the one who caused the death of the baby in the womb. The fine was determined by the husband and ratified by the court. However, if the mother was injured (v. 23), a greater penalty would be invoked. Specifically, the principle of *lex talionis* (law of retaliation) was to be applied—if she died, the assailant was to die; if she was injured, the assailant would be equally injured; "eye for eye, tooth for tooth," and so forth (vv. 24–25). This interpretation, by implication, teaches that the infant's life is not as valuable as the mother's, because the penalty for the infant's life is not as great.

There are problems with this interpretation. First, the text does not state that the baby dies. Literally, the text says, "Her children come out." This could refer to a live birth as well as a miscarriage. In fact, the Hebrew verb used here is the word used ordinarily for normal births, not for the death of a child. It would have been easy enough for the Hebrew writer to state that "the child dies," but he does not. Since he does state that the "children come out," and does not state that the

224 | Thinking Against the Grain

baby dies, is it not reasonable to conclude that the "children" survived? The most likely interpretation is that the assailant pays a fine for causing the premature birth.

A second problem with the miscarriage interpretation is that the identity of the one who has "any further injury" is not clear. Note the sentence, "and strike a woman with child so that her children come out, yet there is no further injury, he shall surely be fined" (Exod. 21:22). The injury could have been to the mother or to the "children" who "come out," or to both. Since this is not specified, the penalties assessed for injuries may have applied to injury to the child, the mother, or both. The Hebrew writer doesn't distinguish between penalties for injuring the mother and for injuring the child. Far from devaluing the life of the unborn child, this passage places the life of the child on the same level as the life of the mother. This does not surprise students of the Bible, for they are aware of passages such as those already cited that refer to fetuses as people for whom God has a plan.

Third, the miscarriage interpretation usually compares Exodus 21:22–25 to abortion, but this cannot be done reasonably, for the injury foreseen in the Mosaic statute is not intentional. Trauma to the body of a pregnant woman sometimes causes premature delivery. Here men are struggling with each other, and a pregnant woman is accidentally struck. The situation of a doctor, or anyone else, intentionally killing a child without harming the mother is a different matter altogether.

Based on the facts I have mentioned, however, we may conclude that even if the fetus was harmed accidentally, a fine was to be imposed. And if the child, or mother, died, the assailant was also to die, "life for life." Even though the death of the child was unintentional, the men were intentionally fighting near a pregnant woman. Therefore, the one who caused the death would be held responsible.

The important point here is that the death of the fetus was regarded as the death of a human being, whose life was just as valuable as the life of the mother. John and Paul Feinberg conclude their extended discussion of this passage by writing,

This is the only place in Scripture where the death penalty is required for *accidental* homicide! The obvious condition of the woman should have been a signal for caution on the part of the men, and when they were negligent, the most severe penalty was required. This passage is a special case, but not one that downgrades or devalues developing babies or pregnant women. On the contrary, it shows the extreme importance God places on both.[14]

During the ministry of Jesus, "they were bringing even their babies to Him, so that He would touch them" (Luke 18:15). The Greek word translated "babies" is *brephos*. Luke also writes about John the Baptist when he was still in the womb of his mother Elizabeth: "When Elizabeth heard Mary's greeting, the baby leaped in her womb" (Luke 1:41a). Elizabeth had been pregnant for six months at this point. The word translated "baby," referring to a fetus, is the same term used of the babies who were brought to Jesus. Luke, then, does not distinguish between babies brought to Jesus and babies still in the womb; both were babies. Further, Luke 1:15b states that "he will be filled with the Holy Spirit while yet in his mother's womb." Whatever this refers to specifically, it is most certainly another indication that this was a human being.

"What is the significance of the biblical truth that a fetus is a human child?" It is significant because if it is true, and it is, then everything the Bible teaches about how to treat people applies to the way we treat pre-born people. Some people say that they support *choice*, not *abortion*. This position is impossible to justify if one accepts the Bible's high regard for pre-born human life, because this position would support the choice to kill a human being. From whence does one derive such a right? Certainly it is not in the Bible. Do people derive the right to kill from the United States Supreme Court? The Supreme Court has made such killing legal, but the fact that something is legal does not mean it is right. In the 1857 Dred Scott decision (Scott v. Emerson), the United States Supreme Court ruled that black people were not legal persons according to the United States Constitution, and that slaves were the property of owners and could be bought, sold, or killed at the owners' discretion. The members of the Supreme Court were wrong then, and they are wrong now.

What is almost inconceivable is that in the court decision that legalized abortion, Roe v. Wade, the Supreme Court appealed to privacy rights and did not even bother to decide whether a fetus is a person. Justice Harry Blackmun wrote, "We need not resolve the difficult question of when life begins." If the court could not decide when human life begins, by what twisted logic did the court affirm that the unborn fetus can be killed? Theologian Harold O. J. Brown has posed an appropriate analogy. What would we think of a hunter who saw something move in the bushes, was unable to resolve the difficult question of whether he saw a human or other animal, but decided to shoot to kill anyway?[15]

Assuredly, the Bible does not leave the question unresolved, but even for those who do not believe the Bible, if the question is unresolved, shouldn't we protect life until we are sure it is not human?

Before leaving this question, I would like to suggest a similar question for those who support abortion. If a fetus is not a human being, what is it? Certainly no one can deny that the fetus is alive. Since it is alive, what kind of life is it if it is not human? Is it a bird, a fish, a tulip? To argue that it is anything other than human life is nonsensical. Is it really possible to refute the following argument?

> Since species-specific DNA strands, identifying the fertilized egg as human, are present at conception, a human person with rights is present at conception. There is substantial identity between the fertilized egg, the viable fetus, the infant, the child, the adult and the elderly person.[16]

Consider the fact that society officially regards an eagle fetus as an eagle. A fine is assessed for destroying an eagle egg because it is illegal to kill an eagle. If everyone recognizes that an eagle egg is an eagle, why is there a debate over whether a human fetus is a human? Furthermore, why does society charge a fine for killing an eagle egg but allows doctors to be paid for killing human fetuses? Something is wrong with our culture's system of values.

God's View of Taking Pre-born Life

What does God think about the killing of a child in the womb? This question may sound presumptuous. How can we know what God thinks about anything? Nothing, of course, unless He chooses to tell us, and He has done just that. In Amos 1:13, the Lord says, "For three transgressions of the sons of Ammon and for four I will not revoke its punishment, because they ripped open the pregnant women of Gilead in order to enlarge their borders." In the first two chapters of the book of Amos, God announces His punishment on the Near East nations of the eighth century B. C. He also specifies the sins committed by each nation that justify His punishment.

In the case of Ammon, their crime was an attack on Gilead during which they "ripped open the pregnant women." In other words, they violently terminated the pregnancies of the women of Gilead. Probably their purpose in so doing was to prevent an increase in the population of their enemies so that there would be fewer people to revolt against their rule. What is the reason given for this violence? It was "to enlarge their borders." The Ammonites wanted more land and power, and they killed the innocent unborn in order to reach that objective. Therefore, the judgment of God was falling on that nation.

What are the reasons given for today's killing of the innocent unborn? Based on the statistics cited above, we can state with confidence that circumstances such as rape, incest, or the threat of the mother's death account for only about 1 percent to 3 percent of abortions. Some 75 percent of women having abortions say that having the child would "interfere with their lives," so at least that percentage of abortions takes place because the babies would be too inconvenient, too embarrassing, or too expensive. Frederica Mathewes-Green researched the reasons women have abortions. She read all the survey results, like those cited above. Then, in numerous cities around the country she personally interviewed in group settings many women who had made the choice to abort. Her research did not contradict the surveys already made, but it added a new dimension. Women indeed have abortions for the sake of convenience, but the reasons a baby would be inconvenient for women often involve pressure from others. Many women are pressured by their parents to have an abortion. For example, one mother told her daughter, "If you continue this pregnancy, you can't live in my house." Another mother, embarrassed by an out-of-wedlock pregnancy, said, "You have a choice: the baby or the family." Mathewes-Green commented, "This is not the 'choice' that pro-choice partisans imagine. 'Freedom of choice' brings to mind the image of a stylish, confident woman considering an array of possibilities. . . . 'Lose your child or lose your home' is a very different sort of choice, and hardly an empowering one."[17]

Mathewes-Green also found that the fathers of the aborted children were a strong influence on the women's choice of abortion. In her research, she found that most women did not really want to abort, but they also did not want to be rejected by the important people in their lives—family members, church members, coworkers, or a boyfriend. She comments,

> Abortion is a convenience for sexually exploitative men who find it easier to pay for an abortion than to be responsible for the life they helped to begin. In fact, abortion makes it easier for everyone—the woman's boss, her school, her landlord, her family, her church—to ignore her plight and the impositions it might cause them.[18]

Mathewes-Green's research does not exonerate women who have abortions; they are guilty of taking a human life. However, this research does help to complete the picture of culpability. The woman is joined in her guilt by those around her who contribute to the pressure and inconvenience of bringing a human life into the world. These people could have chosen to support the woman and the baby—emotionally and financially. Instead, they chose the opposite. They are also guilty of choosing death because of inconvenience, embarrassment, or expense.

This research demonstrates that the killing of pre-born babies at the turn of the twenty-first century is not unlike the killing of pre-born babies by the Ammonites in the eighth century B. C. The responsibilities of raising a child make it difficult to "enlarge our borders," whether that means protecting a preferred lifestyle, saving money, or maintaining a reputation. Like the Ammonites of old, our own selfish agendas are more important than the lives of unborn children, so we kill them. Therefore, the judgment of God will fall on us. We, like the Ammonites, will be judged for our execution of the innocent unborn. Cultures reap what they sow. The law of the harvest is part of God's design for human life. Cultures and individuals that sow murder and disrespect for human life will reap anguish and inhumanity.

Another biblical phenomenon that is analogous to modern abortion is described in several passages in the Old Testament:

> "You shall not give any of your offspring to offer them to Molech."
>
> —Leviticus 18:21a

> "They have filled this place with the blood of the innocent and have built the high places of Baal to burn their sons in the fire as burnt offerings to Baal, a thing which I never commanded or spoke of, nor did it ever enter My mind."
>
> —Jeremiah 19:4c–5

> "They built the high places of Baal that are in the valley of Ben-hinnom to cause their sons and their daughters to pass through the fire to Molech."
>
> —Jeremiah 32:35

> "You slaughtered My children and offered them up to idols by causing them to pass through the fire."
>
> —Ezekiel 16:21

These verses describe God's reaction to the practice of child sacrifice. Certainly the comparison of modern abortion to ancient child sacrifice is unpalatable to those who consider themselves enlightened, pro-choice moderns. Regrettably, however, the analogy fits.

The command against child sacrifice in Leviticus was given to God's people as they prepared to enter Canaan. The most likely reason God gave them this command is that some of the people who lived in Canaan were practicing child sacrifice. Indeed, archaeology has shown that some ancient Near East cultures, including Canaanite culture, practiced child sacrifice as a routine religious rite. God wanted His people to know that this practice was against His will, so He commanded them to refrain from it. The passages in Jeremiah and Ezekiel show that God's people did not refrain from sacrificing children at certain points in their history. God's prophets were compelled to speak against it.

The ancient practice of child sacrifice can be compared to modern abortion for at least two reasons. The first is obvious. They both have to do with the intentional killing of children.

The second reason is not as apparent, but it is just as real. Child sacrifice was practiced as part of fertility religions. In fertility religions, the objective was to secure fertility from the gods. In order to do this, devotees often used sympathetic magic to influence the gods. That is, if they wanted the gods to bless them with an abundant harvest, they would offer to the gods a gift from the harvest. In order to entice the gods to cause their flocks to reproduce abundantly, they offered an animal from the flock. To secure a blessing of many children, they offered a child to the gods. In order to see the philosophical connection with abortion, we must remember the purpose of child sacrifice—material blessing. Fertility religion was not about obedience to the gods; it's objective was to control them. The gods had to be coerced to give the worshipers what they wanted. Fertility worship was really self-worship; they worshiped the god of "more for me." Archeologists who excavated the ancient city of Carthage have theorized that child sacrifice had religious trappings but was really a matter of economics and population control. The wealthy disposed of their children more commonly than the poor in order to protect their standard of living.

> The institution of child sacrifice may have assisted in the consolidation and maintenance of family wealth. One hardly needed several children parceling up the patrimony into smaller and smaller pieces. Even where primogeniture was the rule, family claims of one sort or another might easily disperse the wealth too widely.[19]

The situation is hardly different today. I will never forget pleading with a family not to abort a child, only to hear the mother of the pregnant girl say, "But we don't have insurance for childbirth." It still brings me pain to recall that a child died because an upper-middle-class family did not want to pay the bill for the delivery. In the statistics as to why abortions are performed today, there is no disputing that "more for me" is a prime motive for abortion today—more income after expenses, more convenience, more relational harmony, more autonomy, more leisure time. The liturgy has been updated, but it's still the same god of "more for me." Only now the priests wear surgical masks and we have learned to dispose of the children before birth while the mother is anesthetized. But the result is the same—dead children.

God has made it clear that He is displeased with the killing of children. He judged it thousands of years ago. How is it possible to suppose that He is more pleased with the practice today? To the contrary, God's disposition toward child sacrifice has not changed. Of the things God hates, one of them is still "hands that shed innocent blood" (Prov. 6:17b).

Mother and Doctor as Gods

"But what about the rights of the mother?" An ethical tension exists between the rights of the fetus and the rights of the mother. Stated another way, it is the right to life versus the right to control one's body. The right to control one's body is guaranteed by Western governments, but it is not an unqualified right. Civil societies all decide that the right to control one's body is limited by concerns that are deemed of higher value, like the protection of persons and society from driving while intoxicated, use of narcotics, or involving the body in criminal acts.

Once we accept the biblical perspective that a pre-born child is a human life with the same value that is given to other human citizens, the inevitable conclusion is that taking that life is murder. And no person, including a mother, has the right to murder. Until recently, no civilized society has given people the right to murder as an alternative to suffering economic hardship and physical discomfort. Now this fundamental axiom of civil societies is being challenged by the assertion that some people have the right to decide whether another should live or die without any due process of law. The basis for this assertion is that some lives are not worthy to be lived or cause undue hardship on those who are already part of society. In the past, this decision was always recognized as God's alone.

In rehearsing the factors that mothers must consider in deciding whether to abort their babies, pro-choice ethicist Paul Simmons described a pregnant woman as "a complex, many-sided creature with god-like abilities." He went on to call the decision about abortion "a god-like decision." He explained, "Like the Creator, she reflects upon what is good for the creation of which she is agent. As steward of those powers, she uses them for good and not ill—both for herself, the fetus, and the future of humankind itself."

Two questions cry out for an answer from this remarkable statement. First, by what stretch of the imagination can abortion ever be called good for the fetus? Perhaps Dr. Simmons believes that in some cases abortion would be preferable to living with some illness or as an "unwanted" child. But preferable for whom? Few people would choose for themselves to be murdered rather than live a difficult life. But Dr. Simmons believes mothers can make that choice for their children, and that it will be "good" for the baby.

That leads to a second question: Do humans really have "god-like" status so that we may decide whether someone else has the right to live? Schaeffer and Koop argued that abortion is a natural result of a low view of human life. That is, "If the modern humanistic view of man is correct and man is only a product of chance in a universe that has no ultimate values, why should an individual refrain from being cruel to another person?"[20] Schaeffer and Koop are correct, but the sad irony is that the opposite is also true. When human life is valued more highly than it should be, we begin to imagine that we are individually sovereign and have the wisdom and authority to make "god-like decisions." And make no mistake, the decision to end another human life is a god-like decision.

Some people have the heady feeling of divinity because of humanity's technological advances. To return to the McCaughey septuplets, Dr. Nancy Snyderman, medical correspondent for *Good Morning America,* argued that some of the fetuses should have been aborted to increase the possibility that the others would survive. When reminded by host Charles Gibson, on the air, that the McCaugheys wanted to leave survivability in the hands of God, Snyderman responded by saying, "But it's already out of the hands of God, Charlie. This is modern technology created by man." Do not miss Dr. Snyderman's point: The decision of whether an innocent person should live or die is "out of the hands of God" because modern technology has invested the divine prerogatives in humans. R. Albert Mohler wrote this about Snyderman's words: "Her comments reveal the unbridgeable gulf between the Christian worldview and modern secularism. A culture shaped by naturalistic humanism will define life on its own terms and to its own convenience. Such a culture will kill at will."[21] Mohler is right.

This chapter has been about your choice on the issue of abortion, but the larger issue is your choice on the issue of worldview. Are you willing to believe that the biblical perspective concerning pre-born human life is true, or will you adopt a perspective that is in contradiction with the Bible and more closely associated with another belief system? Are you willing to embrace a Christian worldview even when it contradicts commonly held societal beliefs? Some Christians have adopted a biblical perspective on virtually every issue of life, but on abortion they capitulate to the culture. This may be because of peer pressure, the distress of extreme personal circumstances, or merely convenience.

The theme of this book is loving God with our minds. Our love for God will be tested most at the very point at which Christian thinking makes us most unlike the world, and therefore makes us most susceptible to persecution. During the 1992 presidential campaign, vice-presidential candidates Al Gore and Dan Quayle debated one another. Al Gore cornered Dan Quayle with a question about the rights of a pregnant woman. He said several times, "Do you believe in the right of a woman to choose?" and "I want to hear you say, 'I believe in the right of a woman to choose.'" Quayle sought to avoid the challenge, as many Christians are trying to avoid it today. Though Quayle didn't say it, the correct answer would have been, "I do not believe that anyone has the right to take the life of another human being." It may not make good politics these days, but it's the truth.

Truth is needed in the debate about abortion. The abortion industry shields pregnant women from the fact that the abortionist will dismember, painfully poison, or suck the brains from the child within them, lest this information cause stress to the mother.[22] Abortion providers hide the fact that women still experience "post-abortion syndrome," long-term depression and guilt because of what they have allowed the abortionist to do.[23] Abortion supporters are silent about the guilt that abortionists themselves have experienced.[24] They have lied about abortion protestors and about pro-life pregnancy centers.[25] Even the woman behind the pseudonym "Jane Roe" in the original Roe v. Wade case has confessed that she lied to the court when she claimed that her pregnancy was the result of rape.[26] Truth has been in short supply in the pro-choice movement.

It is sad when the culture is gullible to such lies. It is sadder still when Christians accept them. They must set aside the truth of the Bible in order to do so. In the days to come, will the church believe the truth of the Bible, and will the church have the courage to speak that truth, even when it is not politically correct to do so?

Recently a newborn baby was found in a trash can at Disney World.

Apparently, the mother had left the child there to die. That story was followed on the evening news by the ups and downs of the stock market and the day's political posturing in Washington. A baby left to die. No expression of grief, no moral outrage. Just, "A baby was left to die. In other news. . . ." What kind of moral indifference produces only blank-faced objectivity in the face of such villainy? Shame on him. Shame on all of us. Then there was the Associated Press story about a young mother who gave birth in her bathroom, threw the naked newborn infant out the second-floor window into an alley in three-degree weather, then went to school. A neighbor heard the baby cry and rescued her, though she suffered skull fractures and hypothermia.[27]

The mother who threw her baby out the window was charged with aggravated battery, and authorities sought to bring charges against the mother who left her child in the Disney World trash container. Such criminal charges represent what must be the greatest ethical irony in history. Only moments before these mothers harmed their children, a doctor could have killed the babies legally by partial-birth abortion. Not only would the doctors have been immune from prosecution; they would have been paid. God help us.

CHAPTER 11

Think Biblically, Act Locally: The Christian and the Environment

Men do what they think. Whatever their worldview is, this is the thing which will spill over into the external world. This is true in every area, in sociology, in psychology, in science and technology, as well as in the area of ecology.[1]

—*Francis Schaeffer*

Then the Lord God took the man and put him into the garden of Eden to cultivate it and keep it.

—*Genesis 2:15*

The messages on two billboards express the direction of popular thinking about the environment. Both billboards display pictures of the earth from space. The text on one of the billboards reads, "Love Your Mother." The other is emblazoned with the words "Think Globally, Act Locally." The obvious message of the first billboard is that the earth is our mother, so we should care for her. The idea of the earth mother draws on some of the most ancient pagan nature religions. The use of this image by the environmental movement is not merely a clever advertising gimmick to promote environmental awareness and action. Many leaders and philosophers in the ecological movement really practice nature religion. Their theological agenda indicates the ideological struggle in Western Europe, Australia, the U.K., and North America at the outset of the twenty-first century.

Mother Earth has surfaced in assorted religions and philosophies. The concept is closely aligned with animism which reveres spiritual forces that inhabit nature. Animists, in the most basic form of their beliefs, try to placate the spirits that animate buildings, rocks, trees, and other parts of their world. It is not quite accurate to say that animists look to these spirits as "gods" in any ultimate power sense, but pantheism does propose that everything is part of the ultimate god. Such ideas are closely connected to Eastern religions such as Hinduism and Buddhism, but they are antithetical to Christianity. These religions, or philosophies, share the idea that the earth is living or empowered by a divine energy. Some ancient pagan religions took the further step of claiming that humans arose from the earth; hence "she" is our mother.

The exhortation to "Think globally, act locally," also is an environmental message. It is a call for grass-roots activism that encourages us to think of the global implications of our local actions. In other words, if everyone in the world acted the way we do, what would be the global effect on the environment and the environmentalist political agenda? While it's a good idea to think globally, for Christians there is a better alternative. I suggest we think biblically.

The Conflict

Again we find ourselves in the midst of a cultural battle over how to think about the environment. The conflict shows up in the oddest places—Disney movies and Broadway musicals, for example. In *The Lion King*, when the bad lion gains control, the environment immediately becomes a wasteland. The message is clear—only bad people don't take care of the environment. *The Lion King* also exalts Eastern religious philosophy in its view of the "circle of life," complete with a high priest who takes his spiritual cues from listening to nature. *Pocahontas* also has talking trees and evil men who want to cut them down. Disney, however, is not unique in this emphasis. A survey by the Center for Media and Public Affairs discovered that 90 percent of Saturday morning cartoons depict frightening scenarios of imminent environmental disaster. The villains are usually evil capitalists or mad scientists.[2]

If the entertainment media producers don't convince their viewers to become pantheists while they are children, not to worry. Hollywood produces plenty of animist entertainment for adults, too. According to these films, the earth itself is alive. In *Twister*, a climatologist is convinced that tornadoes are deliberately trying to kill her. *Outbreak* suggests that if humans fumble around with the rain forests, the earth will send a nasty virus to kill us all. That movie is based on the best-selling book *The Hot Zone*, in which author Richard Preston writes, "The earth is mounting an immune response against the human species. It is beginning to react to the human parasite." Similarly, in the book *Jurassic Park*, on which the movie by the same name was based, one character says, "This planet lives and breathes. If we are gone tomorrow, the earth will not miss us."[3]

The entertainment industry is not the only place where this ideological battle is being waged. Politics is another front in the debate. Environmental policy is usually a major part of the platforms of political candidates. In 1992, world leaders gathered in Rio de Janeiro for an Earth Summit. In 1997, a similar meeting was held in Kyoto, Japan. Inevitably, such discussions hinge on the relative importance of economic development versus slowing the depletion of natural resources. It's people versus the planet. A good example of this debate took place in 1988 when James Lovelock, an atmospheric scientist, got into an argument with Mother Teresa at Oxford University's Global Forum for Survival. Mother Teresa said that if we take care of the people on the planet, the earth will survive. Lovelock countered that if we take care of the earth, the problems of humankind will be solved. One gave priority to humans, and the other to nature.[4]

The cultural conflict over the environment inextricably mixes philosophy, religion, and political policy. In the philosophical debate, Christianity is often accused of being the primary cause of wrong thinking regarding the environment, and is therefore singled out as the primary cause of our ecological crisis. A seminal article with this view, which appeared in *Science* magazine in 1967, is still cited today. The article was written by medieval historian Lynn White and was originally an address delivered to the American Association for the Advancement of Science. In his address, White called Christianity "the most anthropocentric religion the world has ever seen" and claimed that Christianity bore "a huge burden of guilt" for encouraging humankind's abuse of the earth. White went on to say,

> More science and more technology are not going to get us out of the present ecologic crisis until we find a new religion, or rethink our old one. . . . Both our present science and our present technology are so tinctured with orthodox Christian arrogance toward nature that no solution for our ecologic crisis can be expected from them alone. Since the roots of our trouble are so largely religious, the remedy must also be essentially religious. [5]

White's case against Christendom has become conventional wisdom in the environmental movement, and environmentalism has become a powerful cultural force. A large number of diverse organizations fit under this umbrella, among them Windstar Foundation, Sierra Club, Friends of the Earth, Earth Island Institute, Gaia, Earth First!, the Findhorn Community, the Green Party, and the Ausable Institute for Environmental Studies. With evangelistic fervor, such groups seek to raise public awareness by education and such events as Earth Day. Some groups enlist the help of high-profile entertainer spokespersons such as Tom Cruise and Robert Redford. The more activistic groups, like Greenpeace and Earth First! stage demonstrations or put metal spikes into trees to thwart logging efforts.

For Christians, however, becoming environmentally aware and active is not a matter of political pressure; it is a matter of discipleship. To be a disciple of Jesus means to live by His Word. So the question for Christians is: What does God's Word says about the environment? As we answer that question, we can have guidance to respond properly to

such environmental issues as air pollution, toxic waste, tropical defor-
estation, depletion of the ozone layer, and local disputes over landfills
and water quality.

Not only is a Christian view of ecology a matter of discipleship. It is
also a matter of evangelism. Surveys' results differ somewhat, but as
much as 60 percent of the U.S. population consider themselves
environmentalistic in outlook. If Christians are to influence a society
increasingly concerned about ecological issues, and if we are to lead
individuals in that society to commitment to Christ, we will need to
show how that commitment contributes to the well-being of the earth.

A Christian Perspective on the Environment

While I disagree with Lynn White's contention that Christianity is
to blame for our environmental woes, there is a hint of truth in this
complaint. Over the centuries, Christians have been slow to develop a
Christian worldview regarding the stewardship of the earth, and this
has contributed to the decline of the environment. Wrong thinking
has led to wrong living. For example, preoccupation with the second
coming of Christ has caused some to be unconcerned about long-
term environmental issues. Some Christians also emphasize the spiritual life to the extent that they neglect the physical world, treating it as
a necessary evil, not as God's good creation. Other Christians have
interpreted God's charge in Genesis 1:28 to have dominion over the
earth as a divine license for plundering land and resources. Environmental critics of Christianity overlook the fact that such ideas do not
represent orthodox Christianity but are distortions of truth.

Christianity and the Bible support care for the earth. However, cari-
catures of Christian teaching abound, and some of these have led to
faulty environmental thinking. What we need is a thoroughly biblical
view of the environment that can be carefully distinguished from re-
vivals of paganism, as well as from misguided promotion of rampant
development. In the following pages we will consider some biblical
principles.

God Created Everything

The Bible begins with the words, "In the beginning God created the heavens and the earth." God is the sovereign Creator who spoke the world into existence. He said, "Let there be light," and there was light. Before He began to create, nothing on earth or in the heavens existed. When He spoke, He created something out of nothing. This fundamental biblical truth sets Christianity apart from other religions and philosophies. Paul used this theme in his address to philosophers in Athens. He looked at their numerous idols and temples, fully aware that the Greek gods were merely projections of human attributes, and he proclaimed, "The God who made the world and all things in it, since He is Lord of heaven and earth, does not dwell in temples made with hands; nor is He served by human hands, as though He needed anything, since He Himself gives to all people life and breath and all things" (Acts 17:24–25).

The fact that God created everything teaches us several important truths about Him. First of all, His word is powerful. He merely spoke, and what was not, came into existence. The potency of God's Word is a great encouragement to believe and follow what He says in the Bible. It is true, and its effects are powerful. Second, the fact that God created something out of nothing shows us that God is both like and unlike humans. Humans create. We like to make things and to combine different kinds of matter creatively. In that way we are like God. On the other hand, no human has ever created something out of nothing. We cannot merely speak something into existence. In that way God is unlike us.

A third truth we learn from the fact that God spoke and the universe existed is that He is other than creation. He is not part of the created order; He stands over it to call it into existence and to sustain its life. He is not merely some kind of life force at work in nature, as the *Star Wars* movies would have us believe. He is a personal God who relates to the creation as the One who spoke it into existence.

The reason this biblical truth is so important for Christians to affirm today is that many in the environmental movement are teaching something entirely different. Some claim that all things are one. By that they mean that the cosmos and everything that exists is of one and the same essence. To describe this cosmology, they use such terms as *life force, consciousness, mind, chi energy,* or *being.* Not only do some New Age environmentalists teach that all things are one, but they also believe that all is God. For example, Jane Roberts, who claimed to channel for an entity called Seth, referred to God as "All That Is." The philosophical term for that idea is *pantheism*—everything is God. For a pantheist, there is no ultimate difference between God, a person, a tree, the wind, a sea urchin, or crabgrass. All is god.

No wonder then, that these people are concerned about the environment—it is god. When they speak of "reverence for nature," they don't mean *respect.* They mean *reverence.* Nature is divine.

One expression of this idea is the Gaia movement. *Gaia* was the name given by the ancient Greeks to their goddess of the earth. Modern followers of Gaia claim that the earth is alive. It is not merely that things on the earth are alive; the earth itself is alive and has divine power. A Gaian scientist named Rowena Pattee Kryder says that Gaia, or the earth, "talks to herself" and to us, her children. When things go well on earth, Gaia is happy, but when we humans goof up, "Gaia reacts with earthquakes, tornadoes, floods, and extreme weather changes that force us to reassess our values, work together, and create a way of life anew."[6]

This animistic philosophy stands in utter conflict with the teaching of the Bible. However, this philosophy pervades contemporary culture, and many Christians do not recognize it as paganism. Even Christians speak in a metaphorical sense of "Mother Nature." We must recognize the danger of doing this in the current climate, for it has become more than verbal shorthand for the created order. It can be interpreted as capitulation to paganism. If we desire to develop and express a worldview that is consistently Christian, we must excise such pagan ideas from our thinking and speaking and begin to speak of God as the Creator.

244 | Thinking Against the Grain

God Sustains His Created Order

Two parts of this statement should be highlighted. First, everything is God's because He created it and will one day consummate it. The Bible says, "The earth is the Lord's, and all it contains" (Ps. 24:1a). Second, God sustains what He created. Paul wrote to the Colossians that "all things were created through Him and for Him," but also "in Him all things hold together" (Col. 1:16b, 17b). We saw that the Bible attributes the creation to the power of God's Word. The writer of Hebrews affirms that God "upholds all things by the word of His power" (Heb. 1:3b). The perpetuation of the created order is due solely to the watchcare of Almighty God through the sustaining power of His Word. Jesus emphasized God's loving care of His world by saying that not even a sparrow falls to the ground "apart from your Father" (Matt. 10:29b). Jesus emphasized God's personal involvement in the maintenance of the created order when He said that the heavenly Father feeds the birds of the air and clothes the grass of the field (6:26, 30).

God Values Each Part of the Environment

According to the biblical account, after each stage of creation God looked at what He had created and "saw that it was good." God takes delight in what He has created, and so should we. Second, God sent Jonah to preach to Ninevah because of His compassion for the people of Ninevah. In the verse in which God affirms His compassion for the people, He adds "as well as many animals" (Jonah 4:11). Why would God include the animals in a statement about His compassion? Evidently He included them because He cared about the animals of Ninevah also.

God Wants Us to Enjoy His Creation

God intends for humans to enjoy the created order. Genesis 2:9 states, "The Lord God caused to grow every tree that is pleasing to the sight and good for food." *Pleasing* to the sight and *good* for food. God intentionally created the world for the enjoyment of His children. After the flood, God extended His provision of food to include not only the plant kingdom but also the animal kingdom. "Every moving thing that is alive shall be food for you; I give all to you, as I gave the green plant" (9:3).

The Hebrew text of Genesis 2:9a is straightforward: "Every tree, pleasing to the sight, good for food." God built beauty into His world. Before He placed man in the garden, He created plants that were intended to be regarded as beautiful.

I'm glad He did. I enjoy the beauty of nature. I love watching the birds, looking in wonder at the sunset, gazing at the autumn woods when God takes gold, orange, brown, red, yellow, and green, and paints them together into a resplendently colorful scene. I think of the beauty and grandeur of sites such as the Grand Canyon, Niagara Falls, the contrasting topography of Palestine, the tree-covered Appalachians, the snow-capped peaks of the Alps, the glacier-fed streams of Alaska, and the breathtaking underwater scenes on the Bahama shelf. It is all so beautiful! And to think that one of God's purposes in creating it was for our enjoyment makes it all the more beautiful to those who know Him.

Francis of Assisi is remembered for his love of nature. One writer said that Francis was the least worldly and yet the most worldly of individuals. He was not of this world in that he separated himself from its sin, yet his profound love for the natural world made him "worldly." We should follow his example and have nothing to do with the sin of this world, but everything to do with loving and caring for the created order. The very idea of beauty carries with it a responsibility—we are to *keep* the world beautiful.

God Cares for Every Species

God chose to create species of plants and animals in their various forms. The Bible records that God created each kind of plant and animal "after its kind"—with genetic consistency and species specificity. And after He created each species, God said that it was good. When

God destroyed life on the earth with a flood, He instructed Noah to salvage animals from every species, "clean" and "unclean." The purpose for this animal rescue operation was "to keep offspring alive on the face of all the earth" (Gen. 7:2–3). After the flood, God made a covenant with Noah in which He promised never to destroy the earth by flood again. God included not only mankind in His covenant but also established this covenant "with every living creature" (9:10). Perhaps modern environmentalists would be impressed to know that God used Noah to rescue endangered species. If it is important to God to preserve each species, it should also be important to us.

People Have a Unique Role in Creation

Humanity is both part of the created order and separate from it. The biblical account of creation shows several points of contact between humans and the other animals. For example, the Hebrew phrase that describes the nature of the animals is also used of humankind (compare Gen. 2:7, 19). Animals and Adam were all created from the ground. Humans were not even given a separate day of creation; we were created on the same day as the animals (1:24–27). Humans are linked with the rest of creation. Millard Erickson expressed it this way:

> In some sense we are kin with the rest of the creation. One does not have to hold that we are evolved from them to believe this. It merely means that, like them, we also are creatures and the same Creator has created us. Thus, like them, we are finite and depend on God for our existence. . . . If we fully realize this, we know that the empathy we feel or should feel for the other human beings also will, to a lesser extent, extend to the rest of the creation as well.[7]

Erickson also identified an error he called "anthropological docetism." He defined it as "a situation in which humans are not thought of as participating fully in the realm of nature, as not really part of it." The danger of this wrong thinking, Erickson writes, is that "we might tend to forget the limitations of our created nature and similarly neglect the interdependence of the human and the rest of the creation."[8]

While it is important to remember our connection with the rest of creation, we also should remember the companion biblical truth that we are separate from the rest of creation. Although there are similarities between God's creation of humans and His creation of the other animals, there are also dissimilarities. We are created in the image of God. That statement is not made of any other part of God's creation. In the creation of the first man, God "breathed into his nostrils the breath of life" (Gen. 2:7b). God actually breathed life into the man, and that is said of no other part of creation. The creation account describes God communicating with the first man and woman, devoting more attention to them than to any other part of creation. Like all life on the earth, we are created beings, not divine. Yet we were created in a way that sets us apart from the rest of creation.

Many in the environmental movement disagree with these ideas about relative worth. The idea that humans are more valuable than trees or bugs is regarded as a form of bigotry. Some call the idea "speciesism"—the egocentric valuing of one's own species more highly than one ought. In fact, some would not only claim that we are not a special creation of God, but we are *less* valuable than other species. Some environmentalist writers compare humans to a cancer spreading across the globe, implying that the earth would really be better off without us.

This is the necessary conclusion of pantheism. If all is god, then no meaningful value distinction can be made between humans and the tropical fish in their aquariums. In India, where beliefs in reincarnation and pantheism are foundational to the culture, cows and rats are allowed to eat food needed by humans. Animals prosper while humans starve on the streets because no spiritual discontinuity between humans and animals is recognized.

The Bible says that God created humans in a way that sets us apart from the rest of creation. To be sure, we may walk outside one evening, look up at all the stars in the night sky, and say with the psalmist,

248 | Thinking Against the Grain

"When I consider Your heavens, the work of Your fingers, the moon and the stars, which You have ordained; what is man that You take thought of him, and the son of man that You care for him?" (Ps. 8:3–4). In humility, we may feel insignificant in comparison with the vastness of the universe. Nevertheless, if our worldview is biblical we will reach the same conclusion as the psalmist, who wrote, "Yet You have made him a little lower than God, and You crown Him with glory and majesty! You make him to rule over the works of Your hands; You have put all things under his feet" (vv. 5–6).

God Provided Management to Care for the Earth

God gave humanity the task of managing the environment. The earth does not belong to us; it belongs to God. Yet God has put us in charge of it. We are managers or stewards, according to God's design from the beginning. Genesis 2:15 states, "Then the Lord God took the man and put him into the garden of Eden to cultivate it and keep it." We are the ones God intended to care for the earth. When God was about to create the first man and woman, He said, "Let them rule over the fish of the sea and over the birds of the sky and over the cattle and over all the earth, and over every creeping thing that creeps on the earth" (1:26b). After God created them, He repeated, perhaps for emphasis, the same idea: "Be fruitful and multiply, and fill the earth, and subdue it; and rule over the fish of the sea and over the birds of the sky and over every living thing that moves on the earth" (v. 28). As evidence that the first man accepted his God-given role of management, in 2:19–20 he named all the animals God had created. That was a function of ruling and responsibility.

Man's role of ruling, or subduing, the earth is complemented by the fact that God also put people in the garden of Eden "to cultivate it and keep it" (Gen. 2:15b). We are not merely to utilize the earth, or exploit it. We are to *care* for it. People should be a blessing, not a blight, to the created order. If we are intended to be responsible managers of the earth, we should take responsibility for actions that affect the environment. Person by person, we can make a difference in the way creation is treated.

Sin Hurts Creation

The environment has been affected negatively by human sin. Romans 8:19–22 is a difficult section of Scripture to interpret. However, what is clear is that the creation is suffering because of human sin.

> For the anxious longing of the creation waits eagerly for the revealing of the sons of God. For the creation was subjected to futility, not willingly, but because of Him who subjected it, in hope that the creation itself also will be set free from its slavery to corruption into the freedom of the glory of the children of God. For we know that the whole creation groans and suffers the pains of childbirth together until now.

Erickson proposes two general interpretations, both of which are helpful in our attempt to understand our relationship to the environment. The first interpretation hearkens back to the curse that came upon man because of his sin. "In that curse, God affected the creation in certain ways which keep it from witnessing to God's glory and greatness as God originally intended." The creation, then, is something less than God intended. It has been affected negatively by sin.

The second possible meaning of this passage of Scripture is that "humans, through their sinful activity, bring the creation into bondage."[9] Of course, we see this happen all the time. We are to rule the environment, but we are not to abuse it. People, however, cross the fine line between those two all the time. People are often motivated by greed, not the good of the environment. Greed causes them to disregard the effects of their actions on God's creation. The point of Romans 8 is that by our sinful decisions the environment is subjected to futility, slavery, and pain.

What Affects the Environment Also Affects Us

What is good for the environment is good for mankind. After God created humans, He gave to them plants for food (Gen. 1:30).

Therefore, if plant life on the earth is harmed in any way, our food source is harmed. Later, after the flood, God also gave humans the animals to eat. According to the Bible, we may eat plants and animals. However, the food source of most of the animals we eat is also plants. Therefore, if plant life on the earth is mishandled and damaged, humans have neither plants nor animals to eat. Though our environmental interest is not to be motivated by selfishness, certainly it is in our best interest to care for the environment.

Creation Glorifies God

The environment bears witness to the glory of God. Psalm 19:1 states, "The heavens are telling of the glory of God; and their expanse is declaring the work of His hands." This poetic language points to the reality that the created order has a revelatory function; it reveals something of the nature of God. The created universe is constantly expressing a message. It declares that God is glorious. He has made the vast expanse of the heavens.

Theologians have traditionally divided revelation into two kinds, special and general. Special revelation is found in the Bible, which reveals propositional truth, and the person of Jesus the Messiah, who is the Truth and reveals truth about what God is like. General revelation is what the created order reveals. We may learn something about God from creation.

Certainly we may learn of the *existence* of God by looking at nature. This is the very point Paul made when he wrote to the Christians in Rome. He wrote that those who do not turn to God will experience His wrath (Rom. 1:18). "They are without excuse" because "that which is known about God is evident within them; for God made it evident to them." How did God make information about Himself evident to them? "Since the creation of the world His invisible attributes, His eternal power and divine nature, have been clearly seen, being understood through what has been made" (vv. 19–20). Part of the nature of God may be learned through looking at the nature God created. If people do not submit to that truth about the existence and nature of God, they will be held responsible.

Perhaps it is appropriate that this book should end on such an ominous note. In the clash of worldviews in our culture, the stakes are high. Those who do not believe God and turn to Him will experience His wrath and will be separated from Him forever. Christians are compelled to develop a biblical worldview, not just for the privilege of saying that we are right. We are battling for the souls of men and women, boys and girls. The consequences are eternal. If I read the newspaper correctly, a lot of people in our society are uneasy, even in despair, about the future of planet Earth. We who know the God who holds the future can offer His hope and truth to an increasingly apprehensive humanity. For those without Christ, this world is the best they will ever experience. Christians can offer eternal life in heaven that comes from being a disciple of Jesus.

But life after death is not all He offers. He can make us into new people right now through His presence in us. He can change the way we think as we allow Him to shine the light of His Word into our minds. He can change us into the kind of people who relate in the most healthy way possible to Him, to others, and to ourselves, our possessions, and the earth. Let Him make *you* into what He intends you to be. He can do it. He *is* the Creator.

Notes

Introduction

1. Carl F. H. Henry, *Twilight of a Great Civilization* (Westchester, Ill.: Crossway, 1988), 27.
2. I borrowed this phrase, "the repeal of reticence," from Rochelle Gurstein's book on the loss of modesty in Western culture, *The Repeal of Reticence: America's Cultural and Legal Struggles over Free Speech, Obscenity, Sexual Liberation, and Modern Art* (New York: Hill and Wang, 1996).
3. James W. Sire, *Discipleship of the Mind: Learning to Love God in the Ways We Think* (Downers Grove, Ill.: InterVarsity, 1990), 97.
4. Reported in *World*, 20 December 1997, 17.
5. Quoted in *Christianity Today*, 8 July 2002, 9.
6. Allan Moseley, *What's Life All About? Foundations for a Biblical Worldview from Genesis 1–12* (Nashville: Lifeway Christian Resources, 2001), 5.
7. James W. Sire, *The Universe Next Door: A Basic Worldview Catalog*, 2d ed. (Downers Grove, Ill.: InterVarsity, 1988), 16–17.
8. R. C. Sproul, *Lifeviews: Make a Christian Impact on Culture and Society* (Old Tappan, N.J.: Revell, 1986), 25–26.
9. Ronald Nash, *Worldviews in Conflict: Choosing Christianity in a World of Ideas* (Grand Rapids: Zondervan, 1992), 16.
10. James Davison Hunter, *Culture Wars: The Struggle to Define America* (New York: Basic Books, 1991), 44–45. Emphasis Hunter's.

11. Ibid., 45.
12. Quoted in James W. Sire, *Habits of the Mind: Intellectual Life as a Christian Calling* (Downers Grove, Ill.: InterVarsity, 2000), 37.

Chapter 1

1. J. Gresham Machen, "Christianity and Culture," *Princeton Theological Review* 11 (1913): 13.
2. Harry Blamires, *The Christian Mind: How Should a Christian Think?* (London: SK, 1963), 4, 7.
3. Mark Noll, *The Scandal of the Evangelical Mind* (Grand Rapids: Eerdmans, 1994), 1.
4. Alister McGrath, *A Passion for Truth: The Intellectual Coherence of Evangelicalism* (Downers Grove, Ill.: InterVarsity, 1996), 9.
5. William Lane Craig, *Reasonable Faith: Christian Truth and Apologetics*, rev. ed. (Wheaton, Ill.: Crossway, 1994), 14–15.
6. George M. Marsden, *The Outrageous Idea of Christian Scholarship* (New York: Oxford University Press, 1997), preface. Cf., George M. Marsden, *The Soul of the American University: From Protestant Establishment to Established Nonbelief* (New York: Oxford University Press, 1994).
7. Marsden, *Outrageous Idea*, preface.
8. These statistics were gathered from "Barna Research Online," at www.barna.org. Specifically, the research archives were consulted, as well as the article "Americans Are Most Likely to Base Truth on Feelings," 12 February 2002. Accessed 23 September 2002.
9. Os Guinness, *Fit Bodies, Fat Minds: Why Evangelicals Don't Think and What to Do About It* (Grand Rapids: Baker, 1994).
10. David F. Wells, *No Place for Truth: Or Whatever Happened to Evangelical Theology?* (Grand Rapids: Eerdmans, 1993), 222–57.
11 J. P. Moreland, *Love Your God with All Your Mind: The Role of Reason in the Life of the Soul* (Colorado Springs: NavPress, 1997), 188–89.
12. John Seel, *The Evangelical Forfeit: Can We Recover?* (Grand Rapids: Baker, 1993), 83.

13. Quoted in James W. Sire, *Discipleship of the Mind: Learning to Love God in the Ways We Think* (Downers Grove, Ill.: InterVarsity, 1990), 38.

14. Donald S. Whitney, *Spiritual Disciplines for the Christian Life* (Colorado Springs: NavPress, 1991), 227.

15. Guinness, *Fit Bodies, Fat Minds,* 19.

16. Allan Bloom, *The Closing of the American Mind: How Higher Education Has Failed Democracy and Impoverished the Souls of Today's Students* (New York: Simon and Schuster, 1987), 59–60.

17. Stephen B. Douglass and Lee Roddy, *Making the Most of Your Mind* (San Bernardino, Calif.: Here's Life, 1983), 72–83.

18. Terry Mattingly, "Wake Up Before the Credits Roll," in *Christianity Today,* 16 September 1991, 15.

Chapter 2

1. Gilbert Highet, *Man's Unconquerable Mind* (New York: Columbia University Press, 1954), 28.

2. Francis A. Schaeffer, *Escape from Reason* (Downers Grove, Ill.: InterVarsity, 1968), 7.

3. Ibid., 16ff.

4. For an introduction to Kierkegaard as one of the nineteenth-century inspirations for postmodernism, see Millard J. Erickson, *Truth or Consequences: The Promise and Perils of Postmodernism* (Downers Grove, Ill.: InterVarsity, 2001), 75–84. For a somewhat sympathetic review of "the disturbing Dane" and his thought, see Roger L. Shinn, *The Existentialist Posture: A Christian Look at Its Meaning, Impact, Values, Dangers* (New York: Association Press, 1959).

5. S. D. Gaede, *Where Gods May Dwell* (Grand Rapids: Eerdmans, 1985), 35.

6. Phillip E. Johnson, *Reason in the Balance: The Case Against Naturalism in Science, Law, and Education* (Downers Grove, Ill.: InterVarsity, 1995), 37–38.

7. Stephen W. Hawking, *A Brief History of Time* (Toronto: Bantam, 1988), 12.

8. Carl Sagan, *Cosmos* (New York: Random House, 1980), 4.

9. Francis Crick, *The Astonishing Hypothesis: The Scientific Search for the Soul* (New York: Scribner's, 1994), 258.

10. Johnson, *Reason in the Balance*, 7.

11. Ronald H. Nash, *Worldviews in Conflict: Choosing Christianity in a World of Ideas* (Grand Rapids: Zondervan, 1992), 116.

12. Benjamin Wiker, *Moral Darwinism: How We Became Hedonists* (Downers Grove, Ill.: InterVarsity, 2002), 40.

13. David F. Wells, *No Place for Truth: Or Whatever Happened to Evangelical Theology?* (Grand Rapids: Eerdmans, 1993), 126.

14. Two excellent sources that raise serious (and thus far unanswered) questions about the evidence for evolution are Michael J. Behe, *Darwin's Black Box: The Biochemical Challenge to Evolution* (New York: Free Press, 1996); and Phillip E. Johnson, *Darwin on Trial*, rev. ed. (Downers Grove, Ill.: InterVarsity, 1993).

15. Johnson, *Reason in the Balance*, 12.

16. Crick, *The Astonishing Hypothesis*, 3.

17. Ibid., 258.

18. R. C. Sproul, *Lifeviews: Make a Christian Impact on Culture and Society* (Old Tappan, N.J.: Revell, 1986), 31.

19. Samuel Enoch Stumpf, *Socrates to Sartre: A History of Philosophy*, 2d ed. (New York: McGraw-Hill, 1975), 116.

20. Brad Inwood and L. P. Gerson, *Hellenistic Philosophy: Introductory Readings* (Indianapolis: Hackett, 1988), 5.

21. This argument is well-developed in Wiker, *Moral Darwinism*, 31–58.

22. John Stuart Mill, *Utilitarianism*, quoted in Alburey Castell, *An Introduction to Modern Philosophy in Seven Philosophical Problems*, 2d ed. (New York: Macmillan, 1963), 289–90.

23. Ibid., 292.

24. Sproul, *Lifeviews*, 131.

25. David Harvey, *The Condition of Postmodernity: An Enquiry into*

the Origins of Cultural Change (Cambridge, Mass.: Blackwell, 1990), viii, 39.
26. Ibid., 38.
27. Alister McGrath, *A Passion for Truth: The Intellectual Coherence of Evangelicalism* (Downers Grove, Ill.: InterVarsity, 1996), 163–64.
28. Terry Eagleton, "Awakening from Modernity," *Times Literary Supplement*, 20 February 1987, 194.
29. Ihab Hassan, "The Culture of Postmodernism," *Theory, Culture and Society* 2 (1985): 123–24; cited in Gene Edward Veith Jr., *Postmodern Times: A Christian Guide to Contemporary Thought and Culture* (Wheaton, Ill.: Crossway, 1994), 43–44.
30. This expression is borrowed from Veith, as is "advocacy scholarship" (see Veith, *Postmodern Times*, 51).
31. Cited in Harvey, *The Condition of Postmodernity*, 39; from Charles Jencks, *The Language of Postmodern Architecture* (London: Academy Editions, 1984), 9.
32. Stanley J. Grenz, *A Primer on Postmodernism* (Grand Rapids: Eerdmans, 1996), 6.
33. Millard J. Erickson, *Postmodernizing the Faith: Evangelical Responses to the Challenge of Postmodernism* (Grand Rapids: Baker, 1998), 86.
34. Ibid., 56.
35. Gene Edward Veith Jr. and Andrew Kern, *Classical Education: Towards the Revival of American Schooling* (Washington, D. C.: Capital Research Center, 1997), 56. Veith and Kern also demonstrate the deleterious effects of postmodernism on each level of public education (ibid., 4–7, 54–59).
36. Patricia Waugh, ed., *Postmodernism: A Reader* (London: Edward Arnold, 1992), 5.
37. McGrath, *A Passion for Truth*, 185.
38. Grenz, *A Primer on Postmodernism*, 7.
39. Veith, *Postmodern Times*, 58.
40. Barna Research Group, "Americans Are Most Likely to Base Truth on Feelings," www.barna.org. Accessed 23 September 2002.

41. Neil Postman, *Amusing Ourselves to Death: Public Discourse in the Age of Show Business* (New York: Penguin, 1985), 108–9.

42. Grenz, *A Primer on Postmodernism*, 34–35.

43. Francis Schaeffer, *How Should We Then Live?* (Old Tappan, N.J.: Revell, 1976), 218ff.

44. Allan Bloom, *The Closing of the American Mind* (New York: Simon and Schuster, 1987).

45. D. A. Carson, *The Gagging of God: Christianity Confronts Pluralism* (Grand Rapids: Zondervan, 1996), 13–22, 97–98.

46. Os Guinness, *Fit Bodies, Fat Minds: Why Evangelicals Don't Think and What to Do About It* (Grand Rapids: Baker, 1994), 105.

47. Grenz, *A Primer on Postmodernism*, 19–20.

48. Quoted by Charles Colson, "Why Tolerance Turns to Intolerance: Christians Living a Biblical Worldview," *BreakPoint with Charles Colson*, commentary #020507 (Prison Fellowship Ministries, 7 May 2002), www.breakpoint.org.

49. Kevin J. Vanhoozer, *Is There a Meaning in This Text? The Bible, the Reader, and the Morality of Literary Knowledge* (Grand Rapids: Zondervan, 1998), 25.

50. For brief overviews of various ways of understanding the relationship of text and reader, see John Barton, *Reading the Old Testament: Method in Biblical Study*, rev. ed. (Louisville: Westminster/John Knox, 1996), 209–17; or Grant R. Osborne, *The Hermeneutical Spiral: A Comprehensive Introduction of Biblical Interpretation* (Downers Grove, Ill.: InterVarsity, 1991), 377–80.

51. George Aichele, Fred W. Burnett, et al., *The Postmodern Bible: The Bible and the Culture Collective* (New Haven, Conn.: Yale University Press, 1995), 25. For another source that provides a definition, see Edgar V. McKnight, "Reader-Response Criticism," in *To Each Its Own Meaning: An Introduction to Biblical Criticisms and Their Application*, ed. Steven L. McKenzie and Stephen R. Haynes (Louisville: Westminster/John Knox, 1993), 197–219.

52. Aichele, Burnett, et al., *The Postmodern Bible*, 278.
53. Fernando F. Segovia, "'And They Began to Speak in Other Tongues': Competing Modes of Discourse in Contemporary Biblical Criticism," in *Reading from This Place: Social Location and Biblical Interpretation in the United States*, ed. Fernando F. Segovia and Mary Ann Tolbert (Minneapolis: Fortress, 1995), 1:32.
54. Vanhoozer, *Is There a Meaning in This Text?* 9.
55. Harvey, *The Condition of Postmodernity*, 51.
56. Mieke Bal, *Lethal Love: Feminist Literary Readings of Biblical Love Stories* (Bloomington, Ind.: Indiana University Press, 1987), 37–67.

Chapter 3

1. Gene Edward Veith Jr., *Postmodern Times: A Christian Guide to Contemporary Thought and Culture* (Wheaton, Ill.: Crossway, 1994), xii.
2. A few recommended resources in the "intelligent design movement" are William Dembski, ed., *Mere Creation* (Downers Grove, Ill.: InterVarsity, 1998); idem, *Intelligent Design* (Downers Grove, Ill.: InterVarsity, 1999); and J. P. Moreland, ed., *The Creation Hypothesis: Scientific Evidence for an Intelligent Designer* (Downers Grove, Ill.: InterVarsity, 1994).
3. Quoted in an editorial by Joel Belz, "Uncurbed Dogma," *World*, 31 January 1998, 5.
4. Richard J. Bernstein, *Beyond Objectivism and Relativism* (Philadelphia: University of Pennsylvania Press, 1985), 1.
5. Walter Truett Anderson, *Reality Isn't What It Used to Be: Theatrical Politics, Ready-to-Wear Religion, Global Myths, Primitive Chic, and Other Wonders of the Postmodern World* (San Francisco: Harper and Row, 1990), 10–12.
6. Dan McCartney and Charles Clayton, *Let the Reader Understand: A Guide to Interpreting and Applying the Bible*, 2d ed. (Phillipsburg, N.J.: Presbyterian and Reformed, 2002), 117.

7. D. A. Carson, *The Gagging of God: Christianity Confronts Pluralism* (Grand Rapids: Zondervan, 1996), 102–3.
8. Alister McGrath, *A Passion for Truth: The Intellectual Coherence of Evangelicalism* (Downers Grove, Ill.: InterVarsity, 1996), 191.
9. David Harvey, *The Condition of Postmodernity: An Enquiry into the Origins of Cultural Change* (Cambridge, Mass.: Blackwell, 1990), 52.
10. Ibid.
11. Francis Schaeffer, *The God Who Is There* (Downers Grove, Ill.: InterVarsity, 1998), 56, 124.
12. I borrowed this phrase from McGrath, *A Passion for Truth*, 225–26; it has also been used by the noted philosopher of religious pluralism, John Hick.
13. P. D. James, *Original Sin* (New York: Warner, 1994), 303. Cited by Jessie Wise and Susan Wise Bauer, *The Well-Trained Mind: A Guide to Classical Education at Home* (New York: Norton, 1999), 415.
14. Quoted by Steve DeVane, in "'Post-modern Christians Need to Feel Jesus, Campolo Says,'" *Biblical Recorder* 164, no. 5 (7 February 1998): 9.
15. McGrath, *A Passion for Truth*, 215.
16. R. Alan Culpepper, "The Relationship Between the University and the Church: Why Does It Matter?" *The Southern Baptist Educator* 62, no. 2 (winter 1997–98): 5.
17. Ibid.
18. *Christianity Today*, 16 December 1983, 40.
19. Julia Duin, "Episcopal Adversaries Grudgingly Earn Respect," *Christianity Today*, 14 December 1992, 60.

Chapter 4

1. Eric S. Cohen, "Professor Fired for Teaching Shakespeare! Announcing the 1998 Campus Outrage Awards," *Campus*, spring 1998, 10–11.

2. As quoted by J. Stanley Oakes Jr., "Adam and Eve Go to College," *Tabletalk,* March 1992, 10.
3. Quoted by Glenn M. Ricketts, "Multiculturalism Mobilizes," in *Academic Questions.* Cited by J. Stanley Oakes, Jr., in "Adam and Eve Go to College," *Tabletalk,* March 1992, 10.
4. Ted Olsen, "Separation of God and Gridiron," *Christianity Today,* 10 June 2002, 13.
5. Sarah Trafford, "Confessions of a Women's Studies Spy," www.cultureandfamily.org. Accessed 13 August 2002.
6. Erin Curry, "Three Students Go to Court for Right to Distribute Religious Literature," *Baptist Press News,* 3 June 2002, www.bpnews.net.
7. Mark A. Kellner, "Muslim Class Prayer," *Christianity Today,* 7 October 2002, 17.
8. Jeff McKay, "Another Exhibit Draws Fire at Brooklyn Museum of Art," *Baptist Press News,* 19 February 2001, www.bpnews.net.
9. Victoria Barnett, *For the Soul of the People: Protestant Protest Against Hitler* (New York: Oxford University Press, 1992).
10. "Hate Crimes Against Gay, Lesbian, Bisexual, and Transgender Americans," on the National Gay and Lesbian Task Force Web site, www.ngltf.org. Accessed 3 October 2002.
11. Joe Loconte, "The Battle to Define America Turns Violent," *Christianity Today,* 25 October 1993, 74–76.
12. Tim Stafford, "Move over ACLU," *Christianity Today,* 25 October 1993, 24.

Chapter 5

1. Charles W. Colson, "Kingdoms in Conflict," *First Things,* November 1996, 34–38.
2. One recent place where Kuyper's statement appears is David K. Naugle, *Worldview: The History of a Concept* (Grand Rapids: Eerdmans, 2002), 16.
3. The report can be found at www.uscifr.gov. The mainstream media response to the 2002 report consisted of one article in

The Washington Times and an editorial in the *Kansas City Star.* Charles Colson, "God and Caesar: Monitoring the Balance," *BreakPoint with Charles Colson,* commentary #020613, 13 June 2002.

4. *George* magazine, December 1996.

5. David P. Gushee, "From Despair to Mission: Toward a Christian Public Theology for the New Millennium," in *Christians and Politics Beyond the Culture Wars: An Agenda for Engagement,* ed. David P. Gushee (Grand Rapids: Baker, 2000), 41.

6. Some helpful resources in this regard are: Charles Colson, *Kingdoms in Conflict* (Grand Rapids: Zondervan, 1987); Don E. Eberly, *Restoring the Good Society: A New Vision for Politics and Culture* (Grand Rapids: Baker, 1994); and George Grant, *The Changing of the Guard: The Vital Role Christians Must Play in America's Unfolding Political and Cultural Drama* (Nashville: Broadman and Holman, 1995).

7. Michael L. Cromartie, "The Evangelical Kaleidoscope: A Survey of Recent Evangelical Political Engagement," in *Christians and Politics Beyond the Culture Wars: An Agenda for Engagement* (Grand Rapids: Baker, 2000), 25–26.

8. Jim Burgin, "The Christian Reconstruction Movement," *Search,* Winter 1992, 13.

9. Stephen L. Carter, *The Culture of Disbelief: How American Law and Politics Trivialize Religious Devotion* (New York: Basic Books, 1993).

10. Quoted by George W. Bush in a speech to the 2002 Southern Baptist Convention, at www.bpnews.net. Transcript accessed 14 June 2002.

11. Philip Yancey, "The Folly of Good Intentions," *Christianity Today,* 23 October 1995, 96.

12. Carl F. H. Henry, *Has Democracy Had Its Day?* (Nashville: Christian Life Commission, 1996).

Chapter 6

1. Gary Almy and Carol Tharp Almy, *Addicted to Recovery: Exposing the False Gospel of Psychotherapy: Escaping the Trap of Victim Mentality* (Eugene, Ore.: Harvest House, 1994), 159.
2. Tom Wolfe, "The 'Me' Decade and the Third Great Awakening," *New York,* 23 August 1976, 26–40.
3. See, for example, Robyn M. Dawes, *House of Cards: Psychology and Psychotherapy Built on Myth* (New York: Free Press, 1994), 234–51; Paul C. Vitz, *Psychology as Religion: The Cult of Self-Worship,* 2d ed. (Grand Rapids: Eerdmans; Carlisle, UK: Paternoster, 1994); and Michael A. Wallach and Lise Wallach, *Psychology's Sanction for Selfishness: The Error of Egoism in Theory and Therapy* (San Francisco: Freeman, 1983).
4. An example of a minister/counselor/writer who wholly adopted self-love as the proper goal of counseling is Cecil G. Osborne, *The Art of Learning to Love Yourself* (Grand Rapids: Zondervan, 1976).
5. Richard Lee Colvin, "Losing Faith in the Self-Esteem Movement," *Los Angeles Times,* 25 January 1999, 1.
6. See ibid. and Vitz, *Psychology as Religion,* 15–23.
7. Christopher Lasch, *The Culture of Narcissism: American Life in an Age of Diminishing Expectations* (New York: Norton, 1979), 25. Though dated, Lasch's cultural critique and nuanced discussion of the nature, causes, and effects of narcissism remains helpful.
8. John Piper, "Is Self-Love Biblical?" *Christianity Today,* 12 August 1977, 6.
9. Robert H. Schuller, *Self-Esteem: The New Reformation* (Waco, Tex.: Word, 1982), 47–48, 68–69.
10. Paul Brownback, *The Danger of Self Love: Re-Examining a Popular Myth* (Chicago: Moody, 1982), 9.
11. Dave Hunt and T. A. McMahon, *The Seduction of Christianity* (Eugene, Ore.: Harvest House, 1985); and Dave Hunt, *Beyond Seduction* (Eugene, Ore.: Harvest House, 1987).

---

12. For a full development of the worldview implications of this basic conception of creation, sin, and redemption, see Charles Colson and Nancy Pearcey, *How Now Shall We Live?* (Wheaton, Ill.: Tyndale, 1999).

13. John Calvin, *Institutes of the Christian Religion,* trans. Henry Beveridge, 2 vols. (Grand Rapids: Eerdmans, 1966), 2:10.

14. Carl Rogers, *A Way of Being* (New York: Houghton Mifflin, 1980), 81.

15. Thomas à Kempis, *The Imitation of Christ* (New York: Grosset and Dunlap, 1978), 4, 12, 124–25, 133.

16. Corrie ten Boom with John and Elizabeth Sherrill, *The Hiding Place* (New York: Bantam, 1974), 194–95.

17. William Byron Forbush, ed., *Foxe's Book of Martyrs* (Philadelphia: John C. Winston, 1926), 9.

18. Augustine, *The City of God,* trans. Marcus Dods (New York: Random House, 1950), 477.

Chapter 7

1. Wendell Berry, *The Hidden Wound* (San Francisco: North Point, 1989), 65–66. Quoted in James W. Sire, *Habits of the Mind: Intellectual Life as a Christian Calling* (Downers Grove, Ill.: InterVarsity, 2000), 112.

2. Plato, *The Republic,* trans. B. Jowett, ed. Louise Ropes Loomis (Princeton, N.J.: D. Van Nostrand, 1942), bk. 9, 461, 476.

3. Richard J. Foster, *Money, Sex, and Power: The Challenge of the Disciplined Life* (San Francisco: Harper and Row, 1985), 5.

4. Robert Wuthnow, *God and Mammon in America* (New York: Free Press, 1994), 18.

5. Herbert Welch, ed., *Selections from the Writings of John Wesley* (Nashville: Abingdon, 1942), 208.

6. Rodney Clapp, "Why the Devil Takes Visa," in *Christianity Today,* 7 October 1996, 24.

7. Ibid., 24–25.

8. Quoted by J. De V. Graaf, in *Theoretical Welfare Economics* (Cambridge: Cambridge University Press, 1957), 44.

9. George N. Monsma Jr., "The Socio-Economic-Political Order and Our Lifestyles," in *Living More Simply: Biblical Principles and Practical Models*, ed. Ronald J. Sider (Downers Grove, Ill.: InterVarsity, 1980), 182–84.

10. Clapp, "Why the Devil Takes Visa," 21.

11. Wuthnow, *God and Mammon in America*, 126.

12. John and Sylvia Ronsvalle, *Behind the Stained Glass Windows: Money Dynamics in the Church* (Grand Rapids: Baker, 1996), 34–37.

13. Keith Hinson, "Inheritance Windfall May Bypass Churches," *Christianity Today*, 7 April 1997, 58.

14. John C. Haughey, *The Holy Use of Money: Personal Finance in Light of Christian Faith* (New York: Doubleday, 1986), 10.

15. Quoted in *The Baptist Program*, April 1992, 10.

16. John White, *The Golden Cow: Materialism in the Twentieth-Century Church* (Downers Grove, Ill.: InterVarsity, 1979), 12, 38.

17. Peter H. Davids, "New Testament Foundations for Living More Simply," in *Living More Simply: Biblical Principles and Practical Models*, ed. Ronald J. Sider (Downers Grove, Ill.: InterVarsity, 1980), 53.

18. Foster, *Money, Sex, and Power*, 56.

19. Ibid., 11–12.

20. Mike Bellah, *Baby Boom Believers* (Wheaton, Ill.: Tyndale, 1988), 65.

Chapter 8

1. "Trends in Sexual Risk Behaviors Among High School Students—United States, 1991–2001," 27 September 2002, in the *Morbidity and Mortality Weekly Report*, www.cdc.gov/mmwr. Accessed 9 October 2002.

2. Stephanie J. Ventura, William D. Mosher, Sally C. Curtin, Joyce C. Abma, Stanley Henshaw, "Trends in Pregnancy Rates for the United States, 1976–97: An Update," *National Vital Statistics Reports* 49, no. 4 (6 June 2001).

3. Centers for Disease Control, www.cdc.gov/nchs/fastats/stds.htm. Accessed 9 October 2002.

4. Centers for Disease Control, www.cdc.gov/nchs/products/pubs/pubd/hus/listables.pdf#53. Accessed 9 October 2002.

5. R. Albert Mohler, "Full Circle: Telling the Truth in a Sex-Crazed Society," *The Christian Index*, 13 August 1992, 2.

6. David Roach, "Talk of Adult-Child Sex Follows Path of Premarital, Homosexual Sex," *Baptist Press News*, 1 August 2002, www.bpnews.net.

7. Jodi Wilgoren, "Scholar's Pedophilia Essay Stirs Outrage and Revenge," *The New York Times on the Web*, 30 April 2002, www.nytimes.com.

8. Ken Walker, "Internet Pornography Frequented by 20 Percent of U. S. Adults, Studies Show," *Pastors.com*, 24 April 2002, www.pastors.com.

9. Eric Schlosser, "The Business of Pornography," *U. S. News and World Report*, 10 February 1997, 42–50.

10. For an insightful response to the irresponsibilities of the feminist movement, including sexual lifestyles, see Danielle Crittenden, *What Our Mothers Didn't Tell Us: Why Happiness Eludes the Modern Woman* (New York: Simon and Schuster, 1999).

11. Randy C. Alcorn, *Christians in the Wake of the Sexual Revolution: Recovering Our Sexual Sanity* (Portland, Ore.: Multnomah, 1985), 31.

12. Reported by Adelle M. Banks, "Speaker Tells Teens to Just Say No to Sex," *The Orlando Sentinel Tribune*, 14 July 1993, D8.

13. "How Common Is Pastoral Indiscretion?" *Leadership*, winter 1988, 12.

14. Reported by Anastasia Toufexis, "What to Do When Priests Stray," *Time*, 24 September 1990, 79.

15. Mission statement of the ISTI [Interfaith Sexual Trauma Institute].
16. "OK to Be Gay Christian, According to Survey in Episcopal Church," *Durham Herald-Sun,* 23 October 1993.
17. Reported by Randy Frame, "Sexuality Report Draws Fire," *Christianity Today,* 29 April 1991, 37–38.
18. Alcorn, *Christians in the Wake of the Sexual Revolution,* 9.
19. William Frey, "Really Good Sex," *Christianity Today,* 19 August 1991, 12.
20. Cited in *National and International Religion Report* 8, no. 9 (18 April 1994): 6.
21. Gerhard Friedrich, ed., *Theological Dictionary of the New Testament,* trans. Geoffrey W. Bromiley (Grand Rapids: Eerdmans, 1972), 8:169–80.
22. Don Feder, "CDC Opts to Wage Its Own Trojan War," *The Boston Herald,* 19 August 1993, 29.
23. Robert C. Noble, "There Is No Safe Sex," *Newsweek,* 1 April 1991, 8.

Chapter 9

1. Thomas E. Schmidt, *Straight and Narrow? Compassion and Clarity in the Homosexuality Debate* (Downers Grove, Ill.: InterVarsity, 1995), 11.
2. Quoted in John R. W. Stott, *Involvement,* vol. 2, *Social and Sexual Relationships in the Modern World* (Old Tappan, N.J.: Revell, 1985), 216.
3. Schmidt, *Straight and Narrow?* 89.
4. For a more thorough discussion of this issue of interpretation, see William W. Klein, Craig Blomberg, and Robert L. Hubbard Jr., *Introduction to Biblical Interpretation* (Dallas: Word, 1993), 278–83.
5. Peter J. Gomes, *The Good Book: Reading the Bible with Mind and Heart* (New York: William Morrow, 1996), 154.
6. Marion L. Soards, *Scripture and Homosexuality: Biblical*

Authority and the Church Today (Louisville: Westminster/John Knox, 1995), 22–24.

7. Richard B. Hays, "Awaiting the Redemption of Our Bodies," *Sojourners* 20 (July 1991): 19. For a more complete treatment of this passage see Richard B. Hays, "Relations Natural and Unnatural: A Response to John Boswell's Exegesis of Romans 1," *The Journal of Religious Ethics* 1, no. 1 (spring 1986): 185.

8. Gomes, *The Good Book,* 158.

9. Ibid., 155, 159.

10. Examples of this sort of approach are John Boswell, *Christianity, Social Tolerance and Homosexuality* (New Haven, Conn.: Yale University Press, 1980), 106–7, 338–53; L. William Countryman, *Dirt, Greed and Sex* (Philadelphia: Fortress, 1988), 119, 128; and R. Scroggs, *The New Testament and Homosexuality* (Philadelphia: Fortress, 1983), 62–65, 101–9, 127.

11. David F. Wright, "Homosexuals or Prostitutes? The Meaning of *Arsenokoitai* (1 Corinthians 6:9, 1 Timothy 1:10)," *Vigiliae Christianae* 38 (1984): 125–53. For an excellent summary of Wright's work see Schmidt, *Straight and Narrow?* 95–96.

12. Soards, *Scripture and Homosexuality,* 70–71.

13. Marilyn Bennett Alexander and James Preston, *We Were Baptized Too* (Louisville: Westminster/John Knox, 1996), xviii.

14. Mahan Siler, "The Blessing of a Gay Union; Reflections of a Pastoral Journey," *Baptists Today,* 19 March 1992, 11.

15. Keith Hartman, "Christianity Should Not Be Excuse for Personal Bigotry," *The Chronicle* (student newspaper at Duke University), 10 October 1991, 7.

16. Simon LeVay, quoted by R. Albert Mohler in "Thoughts and Adventures: Commentary on the Times," 15 November 1999, 1.

17. Christine, E. Gudorf, "The Bible and Science on Sexuality," in *Homosexuality, Science, and the "Plain Sense" of Scripture,* ed. David L. Balch (Grand Rapids: Eerdmans, 2000), 121.

18. Phyllis A. Bird, "The Bible in Christian Ethical Deliberation Concerning Homosexuality: Old Testament Contributions," in *Homosexuality, Science, and the "Plain Sense" of Scripture,* ed.

David L. Balch (Grand Rapids: Eerdmans, 2000), 144–45.

19. Martin Luther, "Lectures on Genesis," vol. 1 of *Luther's Works*, ed. Jaroslav Pelikan (St. Louis: Concordia, 1958), 122.

20. Martin Luther, "Lectures on Galatians," vol. 26 of *Luther's Works*, ed. Jaroslav Pelikan (St. Louis: Concordia, 1963), 58.

21. John Boswell's revisionist attempts to prove the church did not oppose homosexuality until the Middle Ages *(Christianity, Social Tolerance, and Homosexuality)* and even regularly performed gay marriage ceremonies *(Same-Sex Unions in Premodern Europe* [New York: Villard, 1994]) have been thoroughly dismantled by scholarly scrutiny. See Richard John Neuhaus, "The Public Square: In the Case of John Boswell," *First Things* 41 (March 1994): 56–59; and Robin Darling Young, "Gay Marriage: Reimagining Church History," *First Things* 47 (November 1994): 43–48.

22. Yonat Shimron, "Pullen Memorial Breaks New Ground," *The News and Observer*, 29 April 2002, www.newsobserver.com.

23. For example, see the article on the Protestant Episcopal Seminary in Virginia by Diane Amussen, "Virginia Seminary Adopts New Sex Policy," *In Trust*, spring 1997, 4.

24. Douglas L. LeBlanc, "Homosexual Ordinations Cause Parish to Leave," *Christianity Today*, 10 January 1994, 44.

25. Janet Chismar, "Homosexual Ordination Vote Widens Gap Between Presbyterian Factions," *Baptist Press*, www.bpnews.com. 20 June 2001.

26. Todd Hertz, "Gay United Methodist Keeps Job," *Christianity Today*, 5 August 2002, 20.

27. "Methodists Revoke Pastor's Credentials," *Religious News Service*, cited in *Christianity Today*, 10 January 2000, 21.

28. Peter T. Chattaway, "Canadian Anglican Diocese Endorses Same-Sex Unions," *Christianity Today*, 5 August 2002, 18.

29. Randy Frame, "Seeking a Right to the Rite," *Christianity Today*, 4 March 1996, 66.

30. Andres Tapia, "Homosexuality Debate Strains Campus Harmony," *Christianity Today*, 22 November 1993, 38.

31. This line of thinking was expressed well by Mark T. Coppenger, "Coppenger: Bible has Final Word on Homosexuality," *Light,* September–October 1992, 9.

32. Hays, "Awaiting the Redemption of Our Bodies," 21.

33. Don Schmierer, *An Ounce of Prevention: Preventing the Homosexual Condition in Today's Youth* (Nashville: Word, 1998).

34. For further information about such studies see Richard G. Howe, "Homosexuality in America: Exposing the Myths" (Tupelo, Miss.: The American Family Association, 1994), 10–11; Stanton L. Jones and Mark A. Yarhouse, *Homosexuality: The Use of Scientific Research in the Church's Moral Debate* (Downers Grove, Ill.: InterVarsity, 2000); and Schmidt, *Straight and Narrow?* 131–59.

35. Hays, "Awaiting the Redemption of Our Bodies," 21.

36. Schmidt, *Straight and Narrow?* 110–14.

37. Jane Gross, "Second Wave of AIDS Feared by Officials in San Francisco," *The New York Times National,* 11 December 1993, 1, 8.

38. Cal Thomas, "Pro-Choice on Change?" *World,* 13 September 1997.

Chapter 10

1. Stan Guthrie, "RU-486 Deaths Prompt Outcry," *Christianity Today,* 10 June 2002, 16.

2. Francis A. Schaeffer and C. Everett Koop, *Whatever Happened to the Human Race?* (Old Tappan, N.J.: Revell, 1979), 31, 34.

3. John S. Feinberg and Paul D. Feinberg, *Ethics for a Brave New World* (Wheaton, Ill.: Crossway, 1993), 47. The 1997 figures supplied by the Centers for Disease Control differ a little, with 21 percent of all pregnancies ending in abortion. Among unmarried women, 41 percent of pregnancies ended in abortion. "Teen Pregnancy Rate Reaches a Record Low in 1997," 12 June 2001; www.cdc.gov/nchs/releases/01news/trendpreg.htm. Accessed 9 October 2002.

4. Stanley K. Henshaw and Kathryn Kost, "Abortion Patients in 1994–1995: Characteristics and Contraceptive Use," Family Planning Perspectives, http://www.guttmacher.org. Accessed 10 June 2003.
5. *National Right to Life News,* 20 October 1988.
6. Jack Willke and Barbara Willke, *Abortion: Questions and Answers* (Cincinnati: Hayes, 1985).
7. Cited in Mike Yorkey and Glenn Stanton, "Are Americans Pro-Life or Pro-Choice?" *Focus on the Family* magazine, November 1994, 4.
8. Cited as "Abortion and Religious Beliefs," *Christianity Today,* 28 April 1997, 84.
9. This estimate was made by Congressman Tom Coburn, who was cited in *Family News from Dr. James Dobson,* May 1997, 1.
10. "Doctrinal Erosion Led to Soft SBC Abortion Stance," *The Christian Index,* 11 March 1993, 6–7.
11. Steve Kloehn, "Septuplets Raise Troubling Issues for Faithful," *Chicago Tribune,* 24 November 1997, sec. 1, 1, 11.
12. Paul D. Simmons, *Personhood, the Bible and the Abortion Debate* (Washington, D. C.: The Religious Coalition for Abortion Rights Educational Fund, 1987), 11.
13. Ibid.
14. Feinberg and Feinberg, *Ethics for a Brave New World,* 65.
15. Cited by Erwin W. Lutzer, *Exploding the Myths That Could Destroy America* (Chicago: Moody, 1986), 115.
16. Feinberg and Feinberg, *Ethics for a Brave New World,* 60.
17. Frederica Mathewes-Green, "Why Women Choose Abortion," *Christianity Today,* 9 January 1995, 22.
18. Frederica Mathewes-Green, "Why I'm Feminist and Prolife," *Christianity Today,* 25 October 1993, 13.
19. Lawrence E. Stager and Samuel R. Wolff, "Child Sacrifice at Carthage: Religious Rite or Population Control?" in *Biblical Archaeology Review,* January–February 1984, 31–51.
20. Schaeffer and Koop, *Whatever Happened to the Human Race?* 26.

21. R. Albert Mohler, "No Room in the Womb?" in *World,* 15 November 1997, 21.

22. Cal Thomas, "Choice Enhancer," *World,* 8 June 2002, 20.

23. Gary Bauer, "Victims of 'Choice,'" *Focus on the Family Citizen,* April 1989, 6–7.

24. David L. Schiedermayer, *Biblical Perspectives in Clinical Ethics: Abortion, Euthanasia, and AIDS* (Richardson, Tex.: Christian Medical and Dental Society, 1989), 13.

25. Tim Stafford, "Inside Crisis Pregnancy Centers," *Christianity Today,* 17 August 1992, 20–24; Lynn Vincent, "False Witnesses?" *World,* 5 October 2002, 19–28.

26. Mark A. Kellner, "'Jane Roe' Plaintiff Joins Pro-Life Movement," *Christianity Today,* 11 September 1995, 70.

27. "Teen Tosses Newborn into Bitter Cold, Goes to School," in *The Herald-Sun,* 6 January 1995, A3.

Chapter 11

1. Francis Schaeffer, *The Complete Works of Francis Schaeffer* (Westchester, Ill.: Crossway, 1982), 5:6.

2. Cited in Charles Colson, *Burden of Truth: Defending Truth in an Age of Unbelief* (Wheaton, Ill: Tyndale, 1997), 7.

3. Ibid., 103–4.

4. Tod Connor, "Is the Earth Alive?" *Christianity Today,* 11 January 1993, 25.

5. Lynn White is cited by several evangelical writers. One is Richard D. Land, "Overview: Beliefs and Behaviors," in *The Earth Is the Lord's: Christians and the Environment,* ed. Richard D. Land and Louis A. Moore (Nashville: Broadman and Holman, 1992), 18.

6. Cited in Connor, "Is the Earth Alive?" 25.

7. Millard J. Erickson, "Biblical Theology of Ecology," in Land and Moore, eds., *The Earth Is the Lord's,* 45.

8. Ibid., 46.

9. Ibid., 40.

Index